Public Policy and Politics

Series Editors: Colin Fudge and Robin Hambleton

Public policy-making in western democracies is confronted by new pressures. Central values relating to the role of the state, the role of markets and the role of citizenship are now all contested and the consensus built up around the Keynesian welfare state is under challenge. New social movements are entering the political arena: electronic technologies are transforming the nature of employment; changes in demographic structure are creating heightened demands for public services; unforeseen social and health problems are emerging; and, most disturbing, social and economic inequalities are increasing in many countries.

How governments – at international, national and local levels – respond to this developing agenda is the central focus of the Public Policy and Politics series. Aimed at a student, professional, practitioner and academic readership, it aims to provide up-to-date, comprehensive and authoritative analyses of public policy-making in practice.

The series is international and interdisciplinary in scope, and bridges theory and practice by relating the substance of policy to the politics of the policy-making process.

Public Policy and Politics

Series Editors: Colin Fudge and Robin Hambleton

PUBLISHED

Danny Burns, Robin Hambleton and Paul Hoggett, *The Politics of Decentralisation: Revitalising Local Democracy*

Stephen Glaister, June Burnham, Handley Stevens and Tony Travers, *Transport Policy in Britain* (second edition)

Christopher Ham, *Health Policy in Britain: The Politics and Organisation of the National Health Service* (fifth edition)

Ian Henry, *The Politics of Leisure Policy* (second edition)

Christopher C. Hood and Helen Z. Margetts, *The Tools of Government in the Digital Age*

Peter Malpass and Alan Murie, *Housing Policy and Practice* (fifth edition)

Robin Means, Sally Richards and Randall Smith, *Community Care: Policy and Practice* (third edition)

David Mullins and Alan Murie, *Housing Policy in the UK*

Gerry Stoker, *The Politics of Local Government* (second edition)

Marilyn Taylor, *Public Policy in the Community*

Kieron Walsh, *Public Services and Market Mechanisms: Competition, Contracting and the New Public Management*

FORTHCOMING

Rob Atkinson and Simin Davoudi with Graham Moon, *Urban Politics in Britain: The City, the State and the Market* (second edition)

Robin Hambleton, *Reinventing Local Governance*

Public Policy and Politics
Series Standing Order
ISBN 0–333–71705–8 hardback
ISBN 0–333–69349–3 paperback
(outside North America only)

You can receive future titles in this series as they are published. To place a standing order please contact your bookseller or, in the case of difficulty, write to us at the address below with your name and address, the title of the series and an ISBN quoted above.

Customer Services Department, Macmillan Distribution Ltd
Houndmills, Basingstoke, Hampshire RG21 6XS, England

The Tools of Government in the Digital Age

Christopher C. Hood
and
Helen Z. Margetts

palgrave
macmillan

First published 2007 by
PALGRAVE MACMILLAN
Houndmills, Basingstoke, Hampshire RG21 6XS and
175 Fifth Avenue, New York, N.Y. 10010
Companies and representatives throughout the world

PALGRAVE MACMILLAN is the global academic imprint of the Palgrave Macmillan division of St. Martin's Press, LLC and of Palgrave Macmillan Ltd. Macmillan® is a registered trademark in the United States, United Kingdom and other countries. Palgrave is a registered trademark in the European Union and other countries.

Some material included in this work was previously published in *The Tools of Government* by Christopher C. Hood (1983).

ISBN-13: 978-0-230-00143-5 hardback
ISBN-10: 0-230-00143-2 hardback
ISBN-13: 978-0-230-00144-2 paperback
ISBN-10: 0-230-00144-0 paperback

This book is printed on paper suitable for recycling and made from fully managed and sustained forest sources. Logging, pulping and manufacturing processes are expected to conform to the environmental regulations of the country of origin.

A catalogue record for this book is available from the British Library.

A catalog record for this book is available from the Library of Congress.

10 9 8 7 6 5 4 3 2 1
16 15 14 13 12 11 10 09 08 07

Printed in China

To the memory of our parents: Margaret Cropper, Jill Scott Taylor, David Hood and David Margetts

Contents

List of Tables and Figures x

Acknowledgements xi

Introduction xiii

1 Exploring Government's Toolshed 1

Government as a toolkit 2
Pay-offs of the 'toolkit perspective' 11
The focus and limits of the book 14
Where do we go from here? 19

2 Nodality 21

Detecting with nodality: nodal receivers 21
Effecting with nodality 28
The toolset in context 34
Conclusion 48

3 Authority 50

Detecting tools based on authority: requisitions 51
Effecting with authority: tokens of authority 56
The toolset in context 68
Conclusion 77

4 Treasure 78

Detecting with treasure: rewards 80
Effecting with treasure: from customized to open payments 85
The toolset in context 93

5 Organization 102

Detecting with organization: ergonomic detectors 103
Effecting with organization: direct action or treatment 106
The toolset in context 116

6 Comparing the Tools of Government 126

Government tools or tools of government? 126
Tools of which government? 128
Inside government: comparing government agencies 130
Retooling: change over time 134
The measurability of the toolkit approach 138
Conclusion 143

7 Evaluating Government's Toolkit 144

Appraising government's use of tools: intelligent policy design 144
Reviewing alternatives: a rational choice? 146
Matching the tool to the job 149
Economizing on bureaucracy 152
A moral dimension? 161
Conclusion 165

8 Alternative Approaches to the Tools of Government 167

The institutions-as-tools approach: the tools of government as forms of organization 168
The politics-of-instrument-choice approach 169
Generic institution-free typologies of tools 171
The three approaches compared: a phoney war? 173
How the tools analysis of this book relates to other generic institution-free analyses of public policy instruments 174
The challenge of digital-age technology for the analysis of public policy instruments 177
Conclusion 183

9 **Looking Ahead: The Tools of Government in the Digital Age** 184

The future as an extrapolation of the past: a new world of cyber-detection, group-targeting and variable nodality 184

Same tools, different governments 192

Sharpening government's tools? 196

References 204

Index 215

List of Tables and Figures

Tables

1.1 Government effectors 9
1.2 Government detectors 10
1.3 Amnesia's government and some of the individuals with whom it deals 19
6.1 Applying government's tools: three (fictional) government agencies and some of their tools 132
6.2 Visibility and accessibility of three foreign office sites 142
6.3 Dimensions of nodality compared across three foreign offices 143
7.1 Implementing a government drive for vegetarianism: eight possible measures 162
9.1 Digital government and digital society: four types 194

Figures

1.1 Government detectors and effectors 3
1.2 Eight basic types of government tool 4
7.1 Constraint and 'depletability' 156

Acknowledgements

We have presented elements of this work at a number of forums and we are very grateful to the audiences and participants who provided valuable comments and criticisms. Christopher Hood presented some of the earliest ideas for the book at the James Martin Institute in Oxford in 2004. Helen Margetts presented ideas from the book relating to digital technologies at the Annual Conference of the American Political Science Association in August 2006, the Information Communication and Society conference in York in September 2006, a session of an ESRC seminar series on Administrative Justice, also in York in September 2006, and to Oxford Internet Institute staff research seminars during 2005–6. We are particularly grateful to Josep Colomer, Patrick Dunleavy, Tobias Escher, Klaus Goetz, Charles Raab, Limor Shifman and Ralph Schroeder for discussions and ideas which have fed into the text. We would like to thank Gillian Hood very much for compiling the index. We are deeply indebted to Steven Kennedy for his robust encouragement to complete the project.

CHRISTOPHER C. HOOD
HELEN Z. MARGETTS

Introduction

Why Read This Book, Why Care About the Tools of Government?

You may be a conservative looking for a way to resist all governments' various attempts to interfere with your world. You may be a radical committed to using the resources of the state for ambitious social engineering projects to get closer to your ideal society. Or you may be politically agnostic, seeking to understand the various options for government to shape society. Whoever you are, this book is central to your concerns. That is because it aims to offer you a clinical and dispassionate account of the range of instruments that are available to governments to gather information about you and to shape your behaviour in pursuit of its policies. Unlike most books on public policy, it is not sector-specific, but looks across the whole range of government's activities. Unlike most books on public administration, it pays little or no attention to what goes on inside government's organizational machinery. The plotting and power plays, convoluted decision processes and elaborate rearrangements of the bureaucratic furniture are not covered here. Instead, it focuses on the point where government meets individuals. They may be citizens or (increasingly in the digital age) other governments' citizens. Government could hardly be said to be a neglected subject today – indeed, we started to draft this introduction at a conference attended by about 8,000 political scientists – but, surprisingly perhaps, no other book offers such a broad-ranging analysis of the tools of government.

Whether you're a spectator in public policy, watching the moves, or a player looking for angles to develop your game, this book offers you an analytic ABC. There is no shortage of books telling you how complex, intertwined and indeterminate everything is in government and public policy. It is no doubt salutary for everyone to be reminded of that inescapable fact from time to time. But analysis in its literal sense has to begin with breaking complex entities down into basic components, naming the parts and limiting the number of things that are allowed to vary at once. And books that do that for government are not in nearly such plentiful supply. This book sets out to give you a way of breaking down otherwise intractable complexity into a limited number of basic elements. So if you're a spectator, you will be armed with a better way of identifying what you're looking at. And if you're a player, you will have a more comprehensive way of identifying what could be available to you – or your opponents – as tools for change.

Finally, whether you're interested in the past or the future, in your own society or other places, this book offers an analytic approach that you can use. It can be applied to different times and places, as we show by giving examples that range over historical periods, regimes and policy domains. Indeed, the approach may be as useful for historical and 'diachronic' (cross-time) analysis as for contemporary analysis. It may be most useful when you want to use it for comparison or to 'distance' yourself from an apparently familiar domain, in the way that anthropologists have to do when they turn from studying remote tribes in far-flung places to looking at their own societies. As we show in the book, the analytic approach is particularly useful when we use it to explore what if any difference the technologies of the digital age make to the instruments of government. Digital technologies have been hyped by some as fundamentally reshaping all human relationships, dismissed and ignored by others as irrelevant to the fundamentals of law and government. To get any grip on that slippery but important question, we need a method of analysis that is technology-free. So the approach used in this book, drawn from the basic components of control theory in cybernetics, can help us to track down more precisely what is different about the tools of government in the digital age as compared to those of earlier technological eras. And while, again, no one could claim that the technology of the digital age was a neglected subject today – attracting as it does millions of research dollars and producing millions of words of greater or lesser profundity – no other available book does *that* either.

If you don't fit into any of those categories, of course, this book is probably not for you!

Chapter 1

Exploring Government's Toolshed

> To ask 'What does government do?' is to state a plain man's question in plain man's language. The answer is by no means simple.
>
> (Rose, 1976, p. 247; Rose and Peters, 1978, p. 67)

Well, what *does* government do, exactly?

If a young child asked you this question, what would you say? Responding to that sort of naive query isn't simple, because there are so many possible ways in which it could be answered. Consider only three, out of a myriad of possibilities.

One possible reply would be to try to describe what happens 'inside' government – how decisions are made, how orders are passed down the line, how information moves about. If we chose to answer the question in this way, we would be telling a story about government's decision processes. It is the kind of story that has become familiar through political diaries and memoirs. The story would be punctuated by telephone calls, emails and documents, interminable meetings, lights burning into the night, petty squabbles and jealousies, sex scandals, sleaze allegations, panics, heart attacks and nervous breakdowns, and actors of varying importance, competence and ambition. We would soon become immersed in all those interesting but elusive questions about power, influence, who-said-what-to-whom and when. Not a child's territory, exactly.

But that is only one way of looking at what government does. A second type of answer might focus on the *subjects* in which governments today are interested, rather than on the arcane plottings in the chancelleries. That would take us on to an entirely different tack. We would find ourselves trying to list everything that government nowadays concerns itself with, for one reason or another. Very quickly that list would become bewilderingly long and heterogeneous. From government's birth-control pills for cats in Denmark to its seals on domestic gas meters in Britain: government's spoor (its cloven hoof, some would say) appears everywhere. We would soon have to simplify, reducing the mass of specific interests down to a few major and general purposes that governments have, or say they have.

Either of these approaches would make sense as a way of describing 'what government does'. A third possibility – different again – is to describe the *tools* that government uses, rather than what it uses those tools for or how it reaches its decisions. We can imagine government as a set of administrative tools – such as tools for carpentry or gardening, or any other activity. Government administration is about social control, not carpentry or gardening. But there is a toolkit for that, just like anything else. What government does to us – its subjects or citizens – is to try to shape our lives by applying a set of administrative tools, in many different combinations and contexts, to suit a variety of purposes.

These three approaches to 'what government does' are rather like the famous Indian legend of the six blind men describing an elephant. On first encountering such an animal, each gets part of the whole picture. This book, however, is about 'what government does' only in the third sense. It is about the tools or instruments that government uses at the point where it comes into contact with 'us', the world outside. It focuses on the mechanics rather than on the ends of government, and on what government does to society rather than on what happens inside government.

This chapter briefly sets the scene, in four sections. The first section lays out some of the different kinds of basic tools which government has available to it. The aim is to provide the reader with an outline plan of government's toolkit which will be explored further in later chapters. The second section, developing the brief introduction at the outset of the book, is an explanation of what can be got out of looking at government from a 'toolkit perspective': in other words, why it is worth reading the book. The third section is an explanation of the focus and limitations of the approach being taken here, in the hope of avoiding confusion as to what the book is about. The fourth is a 'road map' – a brief explanation of the structure of the book.

Government as a toolkit

If we were looking at a physical collection of tools, we could 'take in' that collection more easily if we could separate its contents into a few broad types at the outset, distinguishing (say) hammering tools from digging tools, measuring tools and cutting tools. When it comes to government's collection of tools – which are not physically assembled in a single place – it is all the more important to be able to identify broad classes if we are to avoid being swamped by detail and unable to distinguish theme from variations. By making two sets of simple distinctions, we can begin to make sense of the apparent complexity of the instruments which government uses on us.

Detectors and effectors

First, we can distinguish between government's tools for 'detection' and its tools for 'effecting'. This distinction is summarized in Figure 1.1. *Detectors* are all the instruments government uses for taking in information. *Effectors* are all the tools government can use to try to make an impact on the world outside.

The terms 'detector' and 'effector' will be strange to some readers. They come from cybernetics, the science of general control systems (see Ashby, 1956; Beer, 1972; Klaus, 1973; Kramer and de Smit, 1977; Dunsire, 1978, pp. 59–60). They are the two essential capabilities that any system of control must possess at the point where it comes into contact with the world outside. This applies

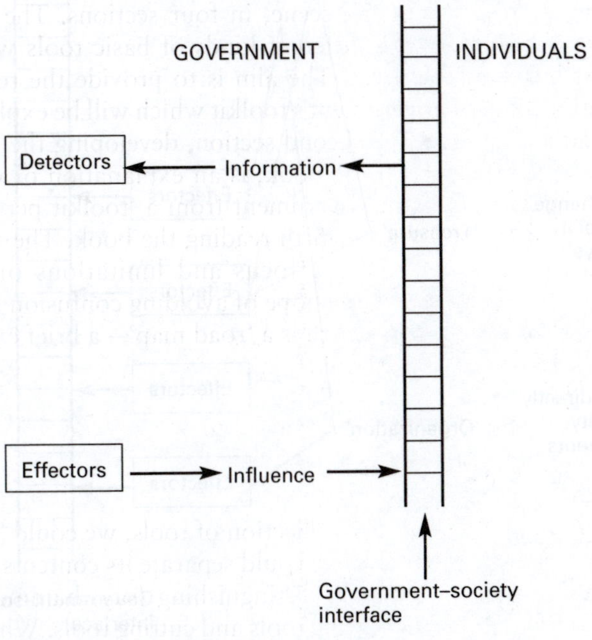

FIGURE 1.1 ***Government detectors and effectors***

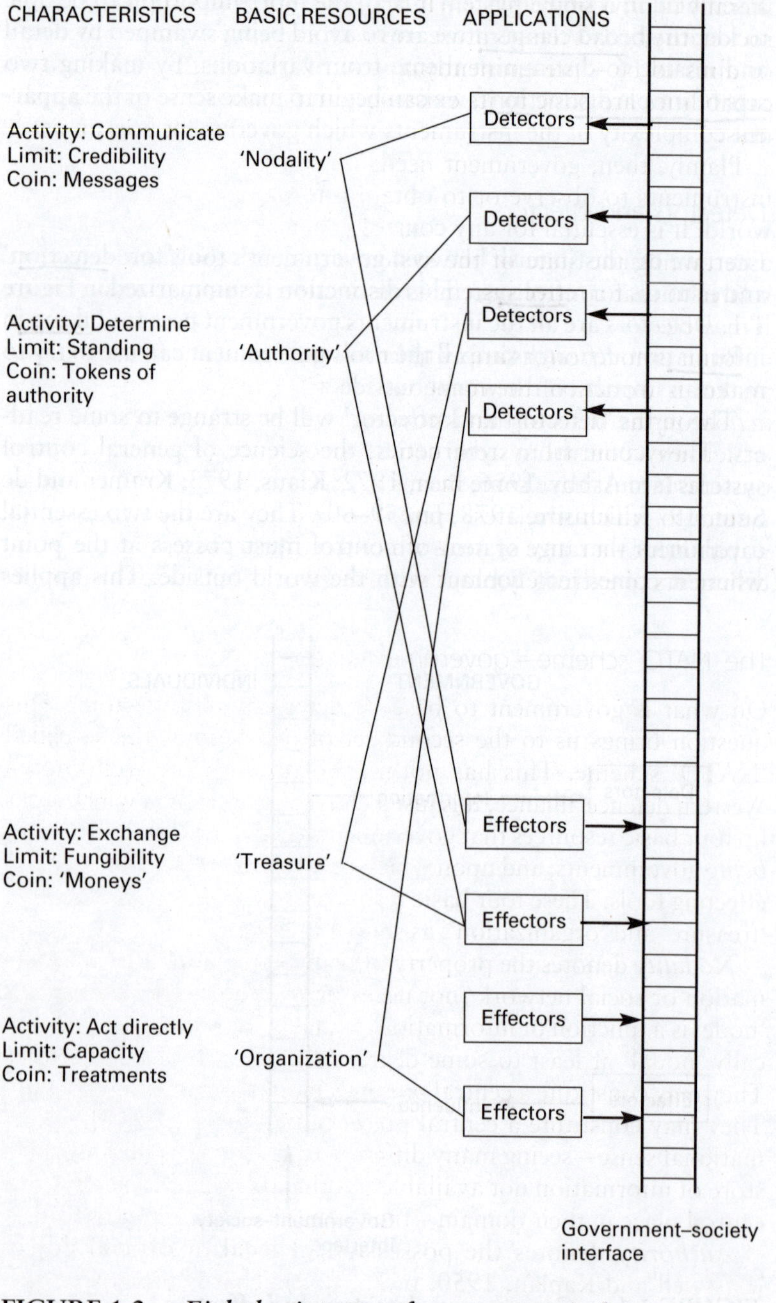

FIGURE 1.2 *Eight basic types of government tool*

literally to *any* control system in art or nature (a mousetrap, a moon rocket, the body's temperature control). For government, which is – or aims to be – pre-eminently a way of controlling society, these capabilities are basic to its existence, and certainly to its effectiveness.

Plainly, then, government needs to employ a host of detecting instruments to observe or to obtain information from the outside world. It is essential for any control system to have some means of ascertaining the state of the system or of the world outside as it relates to that control system – temperature, pressure, or whatever it may be.

But it is not enough simply to know what is going on. No control system is worthy of the name unless it is capable of taking some *action* on the basis of that knowledge. This is the second point at which any control system comes into contact with the world outside. It must have some means of trying to adjust the state of the system to which it relates. Here we come to the 'business end' of government – a range of tools which vary from the gentlest of blandishments to extremely blunt instruments.

The 'NATO' scheme – government's basic resources

On what is government to base its detectors and effectors? This question brings us to the second set of distinctions, the so-called 'NATO' scheme. This has nothing to do with the well-known Western defence alliance. It is just a convenient acronym which sums up four basic resources that governments tend to possess by virtue of *being* governments, and upon which they can draw for detecting and effecting tools. These four basic resources are 'nodality', 'authority', 'treasure' and 'organization', as shown in Figure 1.2.

Nodality denotes the property of being in the middle of an information or social network (not necessarily 'dead centre'). Strictly, a 'node' is a junction of information channels. Governments are typically 'nodal' at least to some degree in one or all of three senses. They may constitute a central presence in the form of a 'figurehead'. They may constitute a central presence in a more narrowly informational sense – seeing many different cases and thus building up a store of information not available to others. Often, they sit in some central place in their domain – the Rome to which all roads lead.

Authority denotes the possession of legal or official power (Lasswell and Kaplan, 1950, p. 76, n. 2). That is the power officially to demand, forbid, guarantee, adjudicate. 'Authority' in this sense is traditionally seen as one of the defining properties of government, though its source, base and level may vary widely.

Treasure denotes the possession of a stock of moneys or 'fungible chattels'. That means not only (or necessarily) money in the common, everyday sense of banknotes or coins, but anything which has the money-like property of 'fungibility' (Rose and Peters, 1978, p. 25) – that is, the capacity to be freely exchanged. Governments in most cases possess at least some stock of 'treasure' in this sense.

Organization denotes the possession of a stock of people with whatever skills they may have (soldiers, workers, bureaucrats), land, buildings, materials, computers and equipment, somehow arranged. In many circumstances 'organization' will be linked with the other three basic resources, but it is not a simple derivative of them, in that it is logically possible to possess organization in this sense without (say) treasure or authority – as when a plundering army lives by pillaging the countryside. Governments in most cases possess at least a minimum of 'organization'.

Each of these four basic resources gives government a different capability, can be 'spent' in a different way, and is subject to a different limit. Thus:

1 *Nodality* gives government the ability to traffic in information on the basis of 'figureheadedness' or of having the 'whole picture' (Simon *et al.*, 1950, p. 191). Nodality equips government with a strategic position from which to dispense information, and likewise enables government to draw in information for no other reason than that it is a centre or clearing-house. The limiting factor is *credibility*, and the 'coin' – how government spends this resource – is messages sent and received.
2 *Authority* gives government the ability to 'determine' in a legal or official sense, using tokens of official authority as the coin, and subject to a limit of legal *standing*.
3 *Treasure* gives government the ability to exchange, using the coin of 'moneys' and subject to a limit of 'fungibility'. Government may use its treasure as a means of trying to influence outsiders or as a way of buying 'mercenaries' of various kinds, or buying information, subject to a limit of *solvency*.
4 *Organization* gives government the physical ability to act directly, using its own forces rather than mercenaries. The coin is 'treatments' or physical processing, and the limiting factor is *capacity*.

As can be seen from Figure 1.2, each of these four properties can be used as the basis for tools of both detecting and effecting. Thus government can obtain information simply on account of its nodality (or by making itself nodal), by buying it, by officially demanding it, or by extracting it by means of some physical device. Similarly it can try to influence the world outside by sending out messages on the basis of its nodality, by authority, by treasure and by organization.

These four resources are different in several ways, as we will show in later chapters. For example, some may be 'self-renewing', while others cannot be. And some may introduce more constraint into the environment of government's subjects than others. Very roughly, that level of constraint could be said to rise as government moves from nodality-based tools to those based on treasure, and then to authority-based and in turn to organization-based tools. In simple terms it could be said that 'nodality' works on your knowledge and attitudes, 'authority' on your rights, status and duties, 'treasure' on your bank balance, and 'organization' on your physical environment or even on your person.

By combining the two control mechanisms and the four types of resources – as in Figure 1.2 – we get eight basic kinds of tool that government can use at the point where it comes into contact with the world outside. Each of these eight types will be discussed and explored further in subsequent chapters. We use different ways to categorize effectors and detectors, as follows.

For effectors, in each chapter we investigate how the four basic kinds of effecting tool can each be used by government in a *particular* or *general* way. This is a thread that will run through the entire discussion. *Particular* applications are those that are directed at specific and named individuals, organizations or items: for example, when government issues permits to individuals whom it has 'vetted' for some purpose. *General* applications are those that are beamed at the world at large and thus apply to whomever it may concern: for example, when government issues some prohibition or order that applies to everyone or anyone. In between the particular and the general come a variety of 'group' applications.

This is only a rough distinction, and even the four basic 'NATO' types are by no means totally independent of one another, overlapping somewhat at the margin. But it gives us a workable basis from which to begin. For effectors, for example, by crossing the 'particular–group–general' distinction with the four elements of the NATO scheme, we find twelve basic kinds of effectors – three for each

NATO resource. These are shown in Table 1.1 on page 9. The chapters in this part of the book explain and discuss the twelve elements in Table 1.1 and unpack this simple toolkit further into subtypes.

Turning to detectors, here we are concerned with the other side of the picture: that is, how government obtains information about the world outside. As noted above, each of government's four basic resources can be used for 'detecting' as well as for 'effecting', shown in Table 1.2.

Thus nodality may cause government to receive information in the same way as it may give government a reason to be listened to. People may give government information simply because of its social centrality and visibility – 'because it's there'. Information of this kind is in a certain sense free for government, and the detectors that pick it up are here called *nodal receivers.*

Second, government can use its legal authority and demand information. This kind of detector is termed *requisitions,* to mean information that is collected in the form of an official demand (characteristically accompanied by threatened sanctions for non-compliance).

Third, government's resource of treasure can be used to buy information. This kind of detector is here termed *rewards*, but it goes a little beyond treasure in a narrow sense, denoting information which government gets in return for any kind of tangible quid pro quo.

Fourth, government can use its organization to get information, in the form of physical or mechanical contrivances for scrutiny which largely bypass human motivation. These are here called *ergonomic detectors.*

In fact, the parallel between these four types of detector and the four types of effector discussed above is by no means exact, as will be seen. But it is close enough to serve as a starting point, so that the reader can place the discussion of detectors in relation to that of effectors.

However, when it comes to government detection, it makes less sense to distinguish between particular and general applications. Instead, the emphasis here is laid on the distinction between 'active' and 'passive' modes of government information-gathering. The difference between the two lies in the degree of initiative or mobility that government requires to obtain the information in question. Thus when government observes us from a fixed watchtower, it is passive. When it knocks on our door or stops our car in the street to pursue its inquiries, government is active. Clearly, there are many

TABLE 1.1 *Government effectors*

Basic resource	*Nodality (Chapter 2)*	*Authority (Chapter 3)*	*Treasure (Chapter 4)*	*Organization (Chapter 5)*
Coin (how government spends or uses the resource)	Messages	Official tokens	Moneys	Treatments
Level of application				
Particular	Bespoke messages	Directed tokens	Customized payments	Individual treatments
Group	← Group targeted and conduited applications →			
General	Broadcast messages	Blanketed tokens	Open payments	At-large treatments

TABLE 1.2 *Government detectors*

	Nodal receivers	*Rewards*	*Requisitions*	*Ergonomic detectors*
Passive (government at a fixed point or not taking initiative)	Unsolicited tenders (unconditional)	Unsolicited propositions	Obligations to display	Turnstiles
	Ear trumpet	Advertised rewards	Obligations to notify	Fixed scanners
		Applications (information as a by-product)	Returns	
	Scrutiny of free media (active search within government offices)	Information exchange (informants pool information with government for mutual benefit	Interrogation (active search, but informant required to attend on government)	Mobile scanners
Active (government operating away from home or taking initiative)	Direct inquiry (government waits on informant)	Active propositions (made by government to prospective informant)	Inspections	Hidden scanners

intermediate points between these two extremes. For simplicity, activity and passivity will here be taken as a combination of initiative and mobility, though it would be possible to take the two separately.

It should perhaps be stressed once more at this point that, just as applied to effectors, the interest here is exclusively on the instruments that government uses at its interface with the world outside. When it comes to detection, that means we are interested only in the tools by which government extracts information from its subjects. We do not consider how that information is used or processed (or not, as the case may be) within government's machine. There are many fascinating things to be said about that process, but they will not be said here. We are concerned with ingestion, not digestion.

Pay-offs of the 'toolkit perspective'

This book is by no means the first or only attempt to explore the tools used by government. The approach taken here was first developed over 20 years ago, in the pre-digital age, by one of us in an earlier version of this book, simply called *The Tools of Government* (Hood, 1983). In Chapter 8 we show how the approach taken here compares with that taken by other analysts of government instruments. Of course there are any number of alternative ways of laying out government's tools, no one of which is necessarily 'correct'. We could refine or subdivide *ad infinitum,* depending on whether we want a scale that is large or small, general or area-specific.

But we will not compare minor differences of classification between one author and another, at least not until Chapter 8 and not much then. This is not that kind of book. A question that *does* need to be pursued, however, relates to the 'pay-offs' derivable from the 'toolkit' approach to government. What advantage could there be in looking at government in this way, as opposed to our other two possible ways of describing what government does – a 'decision-making' or 'field of activity' perspective? Three main kinds of pay-off are briefly discussed below.

Making sense of complexity

First, having a sense of the basic tools available to government helps us to make sense of what seems at first sight to be the bewildering complexity of modern government's operations. Look at government activities in terms of government's many purposes or interests, as we saw earlier, and the list is endless. Look at those activities as the application of a relatively small set of basic tools, endlessly repeated in varying mixes, emphases and contexts, and the picture immediately becomes far easier to understand.

In fact (to take an analogy to which we will return later) it is like approaching each object that we encounter as some combination of a relatively small number of chemical elements rather than as a completely new physical substance. The same principle applies to the understanding of each unique piece of music as a combination of a limited number of notes or understanding each particular dance as a combination of basic physical routines as in labanotation. By looking at things this way, we can easily understand something that we have not seen before and even invent hypothetical new combinations for ourselves.

Similarly, comparisons become much easier to handle; indeed, much of the fascination of exploring government's tools is to compare the instruments brought to bear on a certain problem by different governments or by the same government at different times. The same instrument may be used for many different purposes.

This is just as well, for if government really had to design a completely new tool for each new subject in which it became interested, it would require far greater powers of innovativeness and imagination than governments can in practice be expected to possess. As it is, the same basic set of tools appears again and again as governments face up to 'new' problems, such as computer privacy or the regulation of reproductive technology. Only the mixture varies. This means that if we can grasp the basics of government's toolkit, we can have a better sense of what 'they' – government, officialdom, authority – can do in any given case and what problems they may face.

Picking the tool for the job

Thus – and this is the second main pay-off – a knowledge of government's toolset may be useful, not merely as a way of understanding government, but also for diagnostic purposes.

Government, like human beings themselves, is a tool-using animal. If it desires (say) defence, education, health – even birth control for cats – it must find and employ instruments that will actually produce such things. Otherwise its 'policies' or purposes will be no more than fantasies. It is by applying its tools that government makes the link between wish and fulfilment.

It hardly needs to be said that this link is frequently problematic and highly politicized. Selecting the right tool for the job often turns out to be a matter of faith and politics rather than of certainty. Indeed, it is not uncommon to find that the choice of 'instruments' attracts much hotter political debate than the ends being sought. For example, aims like preventing suicide or anti-social drinking may seem unexceptionable, but how can they actually be attained? Will an extension of suicide-prevention counselling discourage suicide attempts or positively encourage people to flirt with death? Will an extension of the permitted opening hours for bars reduce or increase the incidence of anti-social drinking?

If the operation of government's tools were unproblematic, it could be left to 'technocrats', and the rest of us could concentrate on the purposes that government should pursue. Things are not like that in reality. Knowing something about what is in government's toolkit can at least help us to think about ways of doing better when – as so often happens – things go wrong. Such knowledge enables us to survey the main kinds of implements that might be used to address any given subject with which government may find itself dealing. If one tool fails to answer the purpose in any particular case, we can look systematically for others which might do the job. Thinking in these terms can provide some antidote to the all-too-common assumption in government affairs that things could not possibly be handled in any other way than they are at present.

Picking the 'tools for the times': the digital age

The two pay-offs discussed so far could apply at any time. But it could be argued that it is especially useful to revisit government's toolkit *now.* Since this approach was first developed (Hood, 1983) there has been a dramatic change in societal use of digital technologies. Of course, in one sense such technologies have been around in many governments for a long time, even back to the 1980s and earlier. But in contrast to earlier technologies, from the 1990s the internet and related technologies have greatly changed the way that many individuals behave in society at large (for working, shopping and recreation, for instance), and changed the way governments do or could interact with individuals and firms. Looking at these changes now, while the digital age is still developing and the pre-digital era still fresh in the mind of anyone over thirty, offers a particularly good vantage point for observing the implications for government's use of its toolkit.

Such a change does not mean that new policy problems have appeared or old ones disappeared. Rather, they present themselves in new ways. Take, for example, gambling addiction and school bullying, two social problems with which governments have long grappled. Both these activities have now moved online, with some research suggesting that internet gambling is more addictive and 'cyber-bullying' via text message more damaging to children than their offline equivalents. Cyber-crime is a new phenomenon that makes increasingly heavy demands on the resources and ingenuity of government as well as business. Moreover, at the time of writing, addiction to the internet itself is recognized as a new form of addiction, with compensation claims being raised by individuals said to have been damaged by compulsion to use the internet, raising questions for government action to deal with the consequences. Looking at how government employs its tools to deal with such problems gives us an important angle of vision on change in the digital age, as government searches for 'new' instruments – many of which can be understood as old instruments in a new technological context.

Of course, such effects will vary between countries, as we shall show later, since internet penetration varies from virtually nothing to around 90 per cent and different types of regime face different challenges in using the technologies themselves. But even in those countries where internet penetration is low the impact of the digital age is still felt. For example, variations in internet use can widen inequalities within and across countries, and internet-mediated transnational networks (for instance, for crime, terrorism or social movements) can challenge governmental authority.

We are not, of course, suggesting that other possible ways of looking at 'what government does' do not have pay-offs too. But they do not have *these* pay-offs.

The focus and limits of the book

To focus on government's toolkit, we need lenses which necessarily distort other aspects of government. This is unavoidable in any kind of inquiry; and it is important to be clear about it to prevent confusion or false expectations. Four points especially need to be stressed.

Focusing on the government–society interface

First, the book explores the tools used by government *only* at the interface between government and society, as was shown in Figure 1.1. That is the point at which 'they' (governments) meet 'us' (individuals). The book says nothing about the tools used *within* government to control and coordinate its own far-flung activities and agencies.

Exactly where the government–society interface is, of course, depends on how you choose to define the boundaries of government, and here that is deliberately left somewhat imprecise. In reality, of course, that interface is often extremely fuzzy. Much has been written in recent years about 'governance' in the sense of institutional arrangements that span levels of government and straddle the divisions between public bureaucracy, private firms and not-for-profit 'third sector' organizations. There is also a longer-standing literature about the way that government can be 'colonized' by the non-government sector and vice versa, so that the boundaries become deliberately blurred. The same thing can happen at a much more down-to-earth administrative level, too, producing well-known puzzles as to whether one locates organizations such as defence-contracting firms or 'parastatal' bodies as part of 'government' or not.

Such disputes are far from trivial, but they belong to a different kind of discussion. For the purpose of exploring government's toolkit, it does not matter much what the answers to these questions are, because where exactly you decide to draw the boundary between government and the world outside affects only the overall proportions in which government tools are used, not the basic elements themselves. For us, it is sufficient to adopt the naive perspective of the person in the street who believes that there is a clear distinction between governments and the rest of humanity, and that government is what 'they' do to 'us'.

Treating government as a totality

Second, the book looks at government in general and as a totality. This too is a simplification of something that is very complicated in reality. The approach is general in the sense that it does not necessarily refer to any particular government or level of government. The tools that are discussed are generic to government. They are used in every country; most of them are common not only in the present day, but go back far into the past.

Treating government as a totality – to begin with, at least – obviously involves a radical analytic simplification. Everyone knows that 'in reality' government consists of a host of different 'cells' or agencies, often squabbling and at cross purposes with one another. And the 'governance' perspective referred to earlier reminds us that public authorities often work in concert with other organizations as well as with each other, in ways that may involve complex patterns of conflict and cooperation. But once again it is sufficient for us to adopt as a starting point the perspective of the man in the street who does not divide government into its many component parts or agencies, but rather sees 'officialdom' as a whole – a monolith. We shall come to 'disaggregation' later on.

'Unlearning' conventional descriptions of government activity

Thinking of government as a totality and ignoring all the 'office politics' and other processes which go on inside it may well involve some degree of mental readjustment or 'unlearning' of what we already know. A third kind of 'unlearning' that is required – difficult, but equally necessary if we are to concentrate on government's toolkit – is to forget everything we know about how government *itself* describes its activities.

The reason for this is that governments tend to describe their activities officially in terms of purposes or fields of concern, not instruments, and it is very important not to confuse the two. When governments draw up budgets, the headings tend to be descriptions of their purposes, especially in modern budgeting systems. When they divide their tasks into agencies, the boundaries tend – at least at the topmost level – to reflect the purposes being pursued. It is for this reason that we can easily come to think of purposes or fields of activity (defence, health, education and so on) as the 'natural' way of describing what government does.

But if we want to think in terms of tools or instruments, we must deviate from the conventional way of thinking both negatively and positively. First, negatively, we must unlearn preconceived categories based on the purposes of government. Identifying a set of tools is quite different from listing government's interests or purposes – our second possible way of answering the conversation-stopping child's question that we started with. The same tool can often be used for many different purposes or applications. Think of the axe in the hands of the firefighter, the forester, the executioner; or the mallet in the hands of the Boy Scout, the shoemaker, the judge. Indeed, it has already been pointed out that a tool can often be taken right out of context and used for some purpose quite other than that for which it is ostensibly designed: that is something that happens quite often in government.

Second, positively, if there is no satisfactory, ready-made official language for describing government's toolkit, we must invent our own. It goes without saying that most government officials going about their daily tasks no more 'see' those tasks in terms of detectors and effectors or of the components of the 'NATO' scheme than Molière's M. Vautrin (in Molière's famous play *Le Bourgeois Gentilhomme*) conceived of himself as speaking prose. And when the eight kinds of basic government tool that have already been outlined are further subdivided later in the book, other terms will have to be contrived to denote the devices involved. Some of these names may seem infelicitous, but they are only labels: the reader is welcome to substitute his or her own terms. What *does* need to be stressed is that the labels that are used to describe government's tools do not spring from a mere love of neologism, but from the absence of any existing coherent official usage which would serve the purpose. Since government's tools do not come with labels on them, we must work out our own language.

Finally, this book says nothing about whether government's tools *ought* to be used extensively or modestly – whether government should be interventionist or laissez-faire. An agnostic stance is deliberately taken on such matters. The book is addressed to readers of both persuasions.

Citizens, partial citizens, non-citizens, would-be citizens

In exploring the government–society interface, we also start by treating 'society' as a totality, in the sense of all individuals and organizations with whom government might interact, whoever and wherever they might be. Just as with the divisions within 'government', there are many ways of breaking down that totality. One very traditional one is to distinguish between government's dealings with individuals and organizations within its own jurisdiction or territory, and its dealings with those located elsewhere (for example, foreign aid, disaster relief, military intervention, decisions on who to admit as asylum-seekers or immigrants). That can get complicated if, for instance, the entire population of a territory is evacuated because of some disaster; and, as we shall see later, the digital age has produced new ways in which we as individuals can interact with governments other than our own, notably in the way that we can obtain information from them.

Another very traditional distinction between the classes of individual with whom government deals involves the distinction between citizens and non-citizens. Conventionally, the former have rights (such as voting or the ability to run for public office) and responsibilities (such as military service or jury service obligations) that do not apply to the latter. But that simple dichotomy too can be further elaborated almost *ad infinitum*. After all, some individuals with full civic entitlements and duties by right of birth can be temporarily or permanently deprived of full citizenship (for instance, during their childhood, when they are in prison, living abroad or are categorized as mentally unfit). They might not have effective citizenship, for instance if they are not able to speak the language of the country. And those who are not full citizens can also be divided into those who are recognized by the state as on the path to such entitlements and duties (for example, by rights to reside or to reside and work) and those who are residing or working within government's territory or jurisdiction without formal entitlements to do so (such as illegal immigrants or criminals).

Table 1.3 summarizes some of these distinctions for the imaginary (and no doubt instantly forgettable) state of Amnesia. Much of the Amnesian government's dealings will be with the individuals in the top left-hand cell of the table (unless most of its citizens live outside its territory for some reason, the whole country has been evacuated, or Amnesia has a government-in-exile). But Amnesia will be a very unusual country if its government's dealings do not include significant numbers of interactions with individuals in the other three cells of the table. Moreover, digital-age and related developments may well mean that Amnesia's government finds itself dealing with an increasing proportion of individuals outside the top left-hand cell of the table – for example, migrants, students and guest workers without full citizenship rights (and in some cases consciously rejecting any 'citizenship' path and seeking to be invisible to the state), cyber-criminals and others located elsewhere but with virtual interactions with the Amnesian government. That is why in this book we do not use the conventional American usage of 'citizens' to refer to the individuals with whom government deals, but use the term 'individuals' to cover all the categories in Figure 1.1. But of course, as we shall argue later, some of those categories of individuals are likely to prove much easier for government to reach with its toolkit than others.

TABLE 1.3 ***Amnesia's government and some of the individuals with whom it deals***

	Resident	*Non-resident*
Full citizens	Amnesians living in Amnesia with full citizenship rights and duties as a result of birth or naturalization	Amnesians with full citizenship rights living, working or holidaying abroad (at least on a short-term basis)
Partial citizens	Amnesians with full citizenship by birth who are children, prisoners or mentally unfit; citizens of other states with rights of residence or employment in Amnesia (and who may be recognized as on the path to full citizenship)	Amnesians who live and/or work abroad and thereby forfeit or avoid full citizenship (for example, obligations to pay Amnesian tax, do Amnesian military service or serve on Amnesian juries)
Non-citizens	Criminals and illegal immigrants temporarily or permanently living or working in Amnesia	Citizens, partial citizens and 'non-citizens' of other states with whom Amnesia has dealings abroad, those seeking rights of residence or employment in Amnesia

Where do we go from here?

So much for the whys and wherefores. You now need a quick sketch of the course that the book takes from here.

Chapters 2 to 5 lay out the toolkit for each of the four NATO tools, building on the basic components that have already been described and summarized in Figures 1.1 and 1.2. In each chapter we discuss first government's detectors and then go on to discuss its effecting tools.

Chapters 6 and 7 look at the toolbox as a whole, and in a more analytic way. Chapter 6 shows how a comparatively simple conception of government's tools can be used as an analytic device, as a means for reducing the apparent complexity of government operations to a comprehensible level. As we have already noted, government's tools or instruments – in one sense extremely diverse and 'all around us' – can be made comparatively simple by 'reading' them as permutations, refinements and variations on a listed number of basic types like musical notes or dance steps. The toolkit approach can be used to compare governmental activity across countries, over time and within governments. There is also potential, we suggest, for quantifying these comparisons, in terms of how the use of the four NATO tools changes over time or varies across organizations.

Chapter 7 takes a more normative approach, considering some of the ways we might judge government's choice and application of its tools and how the toolkit approach might aid 'intelligent' policy design. Government's tools are, of course, potentially dangerous. Like most tools, they are benign or malign according to the purpose of the user. Many tools can be used as weapons. All of government's tools, even the most innocent-seeming of them, can be and often are used as instruments of repression. Their application therefore raises hot moral issues as well as what at first sight may seem to be more neutral questions of economy and effectiveness. The chapter considers what use of tools might contribute to a government's aim to 'use bureaucracy sparingly', both in terms of economizing on bureaucracy and minimizing the extent to which a government's interventions bring 'trouble, vexation and oppression' upon its citizens.

Chapter 8 looks at other toolkit approaches to the study of government, noting that most of them more or less disregard the implications of the digital age and considering what some of those implications might be. Chapter 9 concludes in the same vein, drawing together from the rest of the book those digital changes that are in some way generalizable. We apply a broad-brush categorization of countries in terms of the effects of digital technologies on governmental interactions, to capture the variations we have observed throughout the analysis. And finally, we consider the extent to which digital technologies could lead to a 'sharpening' of government's tools in the future.

Chapter 2

Nodality

> 'But . . .', I attempted to explain, '. . . that's just phony. It's dishonest, it's juggling with figures, it's pulling the wool over people's eyes.' 'A government press release, in fact', said Humphrey.
>
> (Lynn and Jay, 1981, p. 74)

One of the four basic resources of government discussed in the last chapter was 'nodality', that is, the property of being in the middle of a social network. This central position provides government with one of the ways it can 'detect' and build information or a panoramic picture. And this probably gives it a reason to be listened to, quite apart from any of its other government-like properties, unless it forfeits all credibility.

This chapter is about tools based on nodality. It is in three parts. The first section examines how government uses its nodal position as the basis of detection or information-gathering tools. Then the chapter turns to the use of nodality as an effecting tool. The second section concentrates on the information government puts out *itself* – giving a broad outline of devices available to government for giving out information. The discussion begins with the most particular devices – those cases where government tailors its message to each individual informee – and ends with the most general, where the message is directed to the world at large or to whomever it may concern. The third section of the chapter discusses the contexts in which different kinds of nodality tools are used. It explores the potential combinations and permutations of nodal detectors and information-dispensers; the ways in which nodal tools have changed in the digital age; and the conditions affecting the types of tools which are used in practice.

Detecting with nodality: nodal receivers

Much of 'what government does' consists of obtaining information in one way or another and one of the ways of doing so is through nodality. There's no such thing as a 'free lunch', it is commonly said, but some lunches are certainly cheaper than others, and it is the same with information. Some information can be obtained free, or at relatively low cost, by doing no more than inserting oneself as a 'node' in an information network, for instance by being on many people's email address lists or signing up for email alerts. This is the kind of information that is picked up by what are here called 'nodal receivers'. As the name implies, government is here relying mainly on its resource of 'nodality' – centrality, visibility, interconnectedness – with its other resources only in the background, though they may play some part.

The most passive kind of nodal receiver picks up information that is volunteered spontaneously. We can label this kind of detection *unsolicited tenders*. This is information that government obtains, not by diligent search, but simply by maintaining a passive presence. Government does not have to pump or prime and certainly does not pay for such information in any direct sense, except perhaps in terms of the amount of listening time involved, and the effort involved in separating wheat from chaff, or signal from noise.

Even as individuals, we receive a lot of information in this way, from the bore, the gossip, the advertiser, the junk-mail distributor, and so on; and the more 'nodal' we are, the more we are likely to receive. To government this effect will typically apply all the more: its nodality means that it will obtain information of some kind even if it does nothing but drink in what is offered in the form of unsolicited tenders.

Information obtained in this way will naturally come in varying forms. It may consist of warnings, threats or criticisms from other governments or bodies such as business lobbies or labour unions. It may be information about specific wrongdoing, offered by busybodies, maleficiaries or rivals of the individual or organization concerned. Jeremy Bentham (1931, p. 411) thought that in such matters 'the worst principles have their use as well as the best; envy, hatred, malice, perform the task of public spirit'. Information of this type may consist of tasters or free samples of information, sent to government in the hope of tempting it to pay for more. It may even be information prompted by patriotism or public-spiritedness, as in the case of individuals who tell government about the flying saucers that they have seen or of inventors (such as Henry Bell, the builder of the first steamship) who spontaneously send details of their work to government in the belief that it may be of interest. (Needless to say, the British government treated Bell's information with 'cold neglect', as plainly irrelevant to naval warfare: Mitchell, 1971, p. 131.) It may take the form of anonymous warnings to government agencies of imminent terrorist attack, such as an anonymous phone call to a US embassy on 16 May 2001 (preceding the al-Qaida suicide attacks on New York and Washington on 11 September 2001) warning that 'Bin Laden supporters were planning an attack in the United States using "high explosives"' (National Commission on Terrorist Attacks, 2004, p. 256).

Perhaps we might say that in a certain sense information of this type is offered for a reward. But the informer's reward in these cases lies in heaven, in the propagation of a cause, in the hope of seeing another's discomfiture, in the hope of making a sale later, or in other forms too complicated to probe here. The point is that government does not have to pay directly for information of this type, and this may be important, especially when public feelings are running high.

Similarly, to describe information of this type as 'free' to government is to ignore what economists call opportunity costs: that is, what might otherwise have been done with the time involved. Indeed the cost to government of this kind of information lies precisely in the screening process that it must undertake to separate the gold from the dross. Reverting to our previous example, the sheer frequency of warnings to US intelligence agencies of possible terrorist attack in the summer of 2001 made the significance of each individual warning hard to assess. And it often happens that multiple groups compete to claim responsibility for bomb attacks just as mentally troubled individuals may confess to crimes they have not committed, making it more difficult for government to identify the real culprit who may remain silent.

Information as by-product

Other types of information may come to government as a 'free' by-product of what it does in its interaction with individuals. For example, electronic ticketing systems for public transport such as Hong Kong's 'Octopus' card and London's equivalent 'Oyster' card, plus road tolls and congestion charge systems amass a vast range of information about passengers' journeys in those transport areas. Government can use such information in an aggregated way, for instance in planning future transport developments, and it can also use it in an individual way to track particular users, such as suspected criminals.

Much of the information that government obtains as a by-product is connected to its use of other tools, such as information required to support tax returns (linked to authority); information collected to verify social security benefit claims (linked to treasure); or population health data obtained from government-provided health care in those countries where government provides such services directly (linked to organization).

It is true that democratic governments typically choose to limit their use of such 'by-product' information by convention or legal safeguards such as data protection or freedom of information legislation. But such information is nevertheless available to be used in circumstances in which such safeguards do not apply or are laid aside (as in 'war on terror' or other emergency conditions).

As with unsolicited tenders, the use of such by-product information is far from 'costless', except in the sense that government does not buy the information directly. It is often technically difficult or impossibly laborious to interrogate huge tax-processing systems without complex, high-risk and expensive modifications to the system. And the sheer quantity and specificity of data collected in transport systems may make it difficult for government to obtain meaningful information about specific policy options. A tollgate at the entrance to a motorway, for example, generally includes a camera which will photograph all registration plates so that violations can be followed up. But to process the registration number data of all vehicles for other purposes, for instance to analyse repeat journeys, often turns out to be costly, laborious and technically difficult. Only in conditions when the stakes are very high is government likely to pay the high costs of harvesting such information by-products.

'Ear trumpet'

Certainly, when information has to be actively sought, it ceases to be 'free' in an even more obvious sense. But government can still obtain information on the basis of its nodality alone (that is, without needing to reward, demand or physically constrain), even when it is active. The lowest rung of this ladder comes when government starts to prompt its citizens to come to it with information.

By such prompting, government can remain passive in the sense of being an immobile observer (no bureaucrats need leave their offices) while making itself highly receptive to incoming information and encouraging the public to act as informers. As well as local offices and advice centres, devices such as free telephone hotlines and call centre services, reply-paid postcards and envelopes, easily recognizable (or easily found via search engines) email and website addresses are commonly used by government to make itself accessible to incoming information. Government is not, of course, alone in using such devices: they are ubiquitous, from the radio phone-in programme to the hotlines for troubled individuals that are maintained by voluntary organizations. This tactic is here termed *ear trumpet* – an old-fashioned kind of hearing aid consisting of a large trumpet held against the ear and directed at whoever was speaking. 'Ear trumpet' is the 'prompted query response' of the section above turned inside out, and it is widely used by government bureaucracies in practice.

There are at least two types of ear trumpet in this sense. One consists of channels by which people can give information anonymously (or with a minimum of personal information conveyed) without the problems and perhaps dangers from hostile sources that a face-to-face encounter with government bureaucracy may involve. Governments have long maintained such channels, from the official letter boxes that were placed around St Mark's Square in the days of the Venetian Republic for the receipt of anonymous information to be examined by state inquisitors (Bentham, 1931, p. 458) to modern systems for individuals to inform government officials or the police about neighbours whom they suspect to be dealing in drugs, fraudulently claiming benefit payments or otherwise breaking the law. This device is commonly used in the operation of price control schemes and consumerist legislation. Similarly, the US General Accounting Office (GAO) has long used a 'freefone' system for members of the public to volunteer information about waste and misappropriation within the agencies monitored by the GAO, and in the 1980s the state government of New South Wales in Australia even operated a so-called 'dob-a-job' scheme that encouraged individuals anonymously to nominate individual members of the state public service for dismissal, on the grounds that their jobs were unnecessary.

The second type of ear trumpet cannot in general ensure anonymity, because it involves collecting information about government's interactions with particular citizens. The commonest form consists of channels for citizens to complain about some aspect of their dealings with a government agency, for instance with a complaints division or to an Ombudsman's office. When using this type of ear trumpet, the detection process may be able to start anonymously but will soon involve the collection of more detailed information in order to be able to deal with the complaint. Once the information is obtained, however, it may be used in an anonymous way to improve operations for the future, for example through reports by Ombudsman's offices on specific areas of government service which are receiving high levels of complaints, geared at improvement of that service.

Scrutiny of free media

Of course, government can insert itself as a 'node' into an information system by means more direct than the 'ear trumpet' device. *Scrutiny of free media* is one such means. This device does not depart from the passive mode in the sense that it need not involve anyone working outside government's offices. Government officials commonly devote considerable care to scrutinizing media sources, both of the general kind and of specialist types such as trade journals or special interest magazines. Thus a local newspaper story of an individual losing a large sum of cash through housebreaking may be read with interest by the local tax inspector to see if it tallies with that individual's tax records (*Taxation*, 1964), advertisements for credibility-straining 'miracle' products may be closely studied by consumer protection officials and personal advertisements in general or specialist papers or on websites may be looked at carefully by police checking on stolen goods or paedophilia. Sometimes governments get lucky, as in June 2006 when Italian tax officials watching a charitable football game noticed the former Argentinian football star Diego Maradona sitting in the audience sporting two Rolex watches. The watches were then seized (which Italian tax police are authorized to do if something is 'within plain sight') and sold to go some way to paying Maradona's $39 million tax bill built up during his time as a player for Naples in the 1980s (*BBC News Online*, 7 June 2006).

Electronic media have drastically increased the range of sources available and the modes of search in the scrutiny of free media. Indeed it is now commonplace for government policy-makers (as well as school and university students) to gather information for their activities by using internet search engines of a kind that did not exist even a decade ago. But the problem facing governments in the scrutiny of such free media is again that of separating the gold from the dross and avoiding injudicious use of information of this type, as was discovered by the British government in 2003 when it published a document outlining the threat posed by Iraq's supposed weapons of mass destruction, based on information freely available on the internet, notably a PhD thesis written years before. The document was widely derided as a 'dodgy dossier' and deemed to contain no new or convincing evidence of a threat; meanwhile the author of the PhD thesis complained of plagiarism (www.channel4.com, 6 February 2003, 8 June 2003).

Direct inquiry

The most active kind of nodal receiver is *direct inquiry.* Here government officials go out 'into the streets', as it were, to gain information from people directly, though still without employing any overt reward or threat. A cloak-and-dagger example is the 'sting' operation mounted by law-enforcement agencies to catch offenders, as in the case of fake websites or press advertisements designed to catch paedophiles by obtaining their credit card details (www.news.bbc.co.uk, 18 December 2003). A less controversial example is that of government public opinion surveys. For example, during the Second World War the British government became worried that psychological warfare and enemy bombing would erode public morale, causing confidence in the government to collapse and fostering a mutinous or revolutionary spirit. As a result, an agency originally known as 'Cooper's Snoopers' (Ogilvy-Webb, 1965, pp. 61–2) was set up to conduct questionnaire surveys among the general public to discover their attitudes, and this organization was the origin of the present-day plethora of polling, surveys and focus groups used by British governments. Such surveys range from general attitude surveys to more specific surveys of family expenditure but the type that belong in the nodality category are not authority-based in the sense that citizens are not compelled to answer the questions (in contrast to, say, government censuses or tax returns). Of course, now that the carrying out of such surveys has grown into a substantial (and worldwide) industry, government pays polling companies to carry out such research, so this is no longer a purely 'nodal' receiver, but relies on government's treasure-wielding capability as well, often involving sums and levels of activity that would have been unimaginable sixty years ago. For example, in 2004, the consultancy Accenture, which produces a global ranking of e-government services, found that the government of Canada commissioned some 200 focus groups in a single year (*Financial Times*, 23 June 2004).

Effecting with nodality

So far we have looked at the uses of nodality for detection – obtaining information – but nodality can also be used as a basis for effecting tools that are designed to shape individuals' behaviour. Governments have used information – or disinformation – as an effecting tool since ancient times and continue to place heavy reliance on this instrument. Indeed nodal 'effecting' tools are used so extensively by modern government that in the course of a lifetime almost everyone will find that they need to obtain and understand a great deal of information from government in one form or another. And whether or not they deliberately seek out information from government, they will find themselves exposed to a barrage of government propaganda issuing from almost every conceivable communications medium, including, for instance, recruiting posters that urge youths to fight for king and country, official lavatory paper bearing the message 'NOW WASH YOUR HANDS', TV advertisements and junk-mail leaflets. They may find themselves accessing government websites, attending government exhibitions, consulting government registers, seeking government's advice. On occasion, without any solicitation on their part, they may receive personal messages from government: for example, if public authorities want to demolish their house or if they have won a prize in a government lottery.

Even outside what are conventionally thought of as media of communication, we can be exposed to messages from government, sometimes 'subliminal' messages that come across without our being aware of it. For instance, government frequently seeks to emphasize its own dignity or majesty by the appurtenances of 'awesome magnificence' (Sennett, 1977; Lasswell and Fox, 1979, p. 40), as in the stage management of pomp, ceremonies, regalia, architectural massiveness, ornateness and formality and paraded displays of military might. Traditionally its law courts have borrowed much of the apparatus of costume drama, employing clothes, buildings and other stage props designed to overawe the uninitiated: courtroom formalities, the presence of legal dignitaries in elaborate wigs and robes, or of military officers in full dress uniform, as in the case of a court martial.

Suppression of information

Of course, all too frequently it is what government *does not* tell us that really counts. Secrecy is as important as dissemination in government's use of information, and there are almost as many ways of keeping a piece of information secret as there are of broadcasting it.

The most obvious way is merely to keep silent. For example, when there was a bad grain harvest in 1981, the government of the former Soviet Union chose simply to leave the relevant figures out of its economic statistics. The government of the People's Republic of China was slow and reluctant to give details of the incidence of SARS (Severe Acute Respiratory Syndrome) in China during the epidemic of 2003. Some governments do not publish potentially embarrassing data on the incidence of suicide and few outside some US states publicly reveal data about the identity or whereabouts of sex offenders released from custody. Indeed, the French government destroyed its own electoral register for Ploërmel in 1873 to postpone a difficult election (Machin, 1977, p. 23).

Another time-honoured way of suppressing one type of information is by propagating another. Governments frequently 'edit' the facts, presenting information with a selective emphasis that is designed to mislead. Much was written about government 'spin' in the USA and UK in the 1990s and early 2000s (for instance, Kurtz, 1998; Jones, 1999), but the general phenomenon was less new than the terminology or the particular forms that presentational strategy took at that time. As long ago as 1948 George Orwell in his classic novel *Nineteen Eighty-Four* drew attention to the way that governments tended to use words that denote the opposite of what they are really doing. For instance, government may choose to endow its own offices, agencies or policies with names that serve to conceal their real purpose or activity. A notorious case was the so-called State Research Bureau which operated in Uganda during the Idi Amin dictatorship of the 1970s. In reality, this organization's 'research' consisted of tracking down and murdering people who were opposed to that government. And government offices and programmes often change their names quite frequently to confuse their enemies or to give an appearance of rejuvenation or of a change in direction.

A third way for government to suppress information is by blatant 'disinformation', as commonly happens in wartime. To take only one well-known example, the British government in the Second World War repeatedly claimed that only military targets were being bombed in Germany, at a time when it was in fact Cabinet policy to bomb civilian targets (Knightley, 1975).

Governments often make such claims and, indeed, it commonly happens that the more information that government wishes to suppress, the more carefully it will have to try to structure what is available. Camouflage – both in its military and looser colloquial sense – often entails a laborious task of putting out misleading information.

A more roundabout use of nodality is the unofficial 'leakage' of information from the government's bureaucracy by 'moles' or press briefings from unacknowledged sources. Indeed, if a pig may (so it is said) sometimes be made to go forward by pulling it backwards by the tail, so government may give its information greater drama and currency by apparently trying to keep it secret. In this way, government disseminates information by appearing to suppress it, in line with the well-known maxim that nothing should ever be believed until it has been denied by at least three government departments. Suppression and propagation of information can often be opposite sides of the same coin.

Direct information propagation

Of course, there are many ways in which governments may propagate information other than reliance on nodality. Government can do the job by using the tools that will be discussed in the next few chapters. It can pay others to promote some cause or to give out information, using its credit card or cheque book as the chosen instrument. Or it can *require* others to propagate certain types of information, as happens with the regulations which it lays down for food labelling, bankrupt and limited liability companies, or health warnings on cigarette packs.

Similarly, when government wants to suppress information, there are other ways of doing the job than creating diversions with its own messages. Government may use its legal authority to permit and forbid, for example in censoring the news media or forbidding citizens to propagate or even access information which the authorities choose to label as seditious, pornographic, heretical or blasphemous (many Arab states including Saudi Arabia, Bahrain and the United Arab Emirates at the time of writing seek to prevent individuals from accessing certain parts of the internet). Similarly, governments may use 'organization' for the purpose, as in the case of China's internet-filtering regime, said to be the most sophisticated effort of its kind in the world (Zittrain and Edelman, 2004a), which blocks content transmitted through web pages, weblogs, online discussion forums, university bulletin board systems and email messages. Internet users in China will frequently find themselves blocked if they seek access to websites containing content related to Taiwanese and Tibetan independence, Falun Gong, the Dalai Lama, the 1989 Tiananmen Square incident, opposition political parties, or anti-communist movements. Sometimes government may use organization for such purposes even more directly, such as physically seizing or destroying dangerous information by exposing film, wiping computer hard disks and burning or shredding books or papers.

We will come to applications such as these later. For now we shall concentrate on government uses of information as an effector that rely mainly on its nodality.

Bespoke messages

The most 'particular' form of information that government dispenses can be called *bespoke messages*, borrowing a term from tailoring, because the information is individually tailored to each informee. There are at least three main ways in which government can convey a 'bespoke message'. The first and strongest form, where the information is most bespoke (the equivalent of a tailored suit), we term *direct notification*. Here the government conveys a message by making an approach itself, not even pretending to 'wait to be asked'. When government uses direct notification, citizens do not need to seek information or to maintain a look-out.

Applications of direct notification range from relatively mundane messages to more fundamental ones. An example of the first is the reminder sent to us by government to inform us that our driving licence, dog licence, work permit or some other entitlement is about to expire. Such promptings can be generated automatically by officials scanning databases for key dates. They are likely to be more widespread in the few countries where state population registers are reliable and effectively linked with electronic service delivery, such that reminders can be generated without any intervention when key dates are passed, for example when someone reaches pensionable age and becomes eligible for certain benefits and allowances (a process known as 'zero touch' in the e-business world). More fundamental kinds of direct notification include the letter, visit or telephone call by government to inform the next of kin of a soldier's death, or the direct visit by government officials, as when police knock on individual house doors to warn of a gas leak or a dangerous animal or criminal on the loose. In such cases, notification is less likely to be conducted digitally rather than physically, face to face.

The advantage of direct notification is obvious. It is the most certain way for government to get a message across to the very individuals it wishes to reach. Government has little alternative but to use this instrument when it is trying to communicate with people who are illiterate, apathetic, distracted, generally incompetent or socially isolated or who do not speak the language of the country.

Modern database technology linked to digital communication technology has certainly reduced the cost of conveying routine individualized information to large numbers of people, in business and government and the like, once the original programming costs have been met. But that sort of programmed information tends to depend on the informees being alert to such messages and as soon as we go outside the conveyance of routine information to a more highly charged kind of message – such as serving a summons for individuals to appear in court – the use of this instrument can take a heavy toll of any government's limited resources if a large number of people have to be approached separately with a message tailor-made for each individual case.

Direct notification involves government actively providing information to individual citizens. The next two kinds of 'bespoke message' are both *responses,* where the information-dispenser has to be 'triggered' from outside by the informee seeking access in some way.

The first of these is to provide replies tailored to unsolicited questions. We could call this an *unprompted query response.* Government gives information out in this way when it cannot predict accurately what may be demanded. Most government organizations have general purpose enquiry points of some kind (often located at the very end of a long chain of other messages on websites or phone menus) to handle – or head off – awkward questions that may come out of the blue. Alternatively government may use this device when it has information which for one reason or another it does not wish to propagate, without invoking formal secrecy. By 'waiting to be asked', thereby throwing all the onus on to the would-be informee and by acting with computer-like literalness, thus volunteering information only when exactly the right question is asked, government may make the acquisition of official information by outsiders all but impossible without a high degree of pertinacity, expertise or luck, even in a formal 'freedom of information' environment.

The third method of conveying a bespoke message is similar, in that it involves a reply tailored to each individual enquiry. The difference is that in this case the question does not quite come out of the blue. Government actually *invites* individuals to seek enlightenment, by advertising the information that it has available.

We could call this a *prompted query response*. The 'response' may on occasion be access to raw information rather than the provision of processed information: for example, when government allows us to search for entries in one of its many registers or repositories in physical or virtual form to research our family tree or check out the details of a company or a development proposal. The message here is 'particular' only in the fairly weak sense that each customer selects items from the store in accordance with his or her particular requirements – rather like 'pick your own' stores or market gardens which invite us to select and collect the individual items that we want to buy instead of having them ready packaged.

A somewhat more 'particular' form of the prompted query response is individual counselling and advice. Governments in many countries have operated advice services for farmers as a part of their efforts to develop or modernize agriculture, and similar services are often also offered to small businesses as well by government development agencies seeking to encourage budding entrepreneurs. Other applications include individualized advice to consumers on their legal rights, rehabilitation advice to ex-convicts who wish to 'go straight', advice on contraception or domestic conflict, and 'dial-a-counsellor' services.

Government's 'nodality' may equip it well for giving out information in this way, on the basis of the many different cases which it sees. It may thus be able to act as a broker in information even if it has no ideas of its own at all and developing internet technology offers new possibilities for extending such brokerage. Moreover, such brokerage may offer a convenient way of interspersing technical information, for which there is a real demand – to the extent that outsiders are prepared to come to government for counselling – with persuasion of a rather less neutral type.

Group-targeted messages

The opposite of a bespoke message is a standard message which is beamed at the world at large, and this type is considered in the next section. But there is also an important in-between type that has also developed in new ways with modern database technology, since almost every organization now has at least one mailing list or 'customer database': that is, the message which government directs to a particular group rather than to somebody or to anybody. This type can be termed the *group-targeted message*.

Like bespoke messages, 'group-targeted' messages can come in several forms. Sometimes, government may use a 'reply' as the outlet for its information, like the bespoke 'query responses' discussed earlier. An example might be a government-staged press conference, when a specified group – sometimes a carefully invited group that has been vetted and summoned to a meeting at short notice – is invited to seek enlightenment (if that is what it is) from government.

Sometimes, on the other hand, government may direct its message at groups on the 'direct notification' principle. For example, most governments send official publicity material, which depicts their regime in a favourable light or publicizes what the country produces or investment opportunities for foreign firms, to selected individuals and organizations who are supposedly influential in other countries. Government frequently uses similar techniques on its home ground, when it seeks to harness opinion-leaders as part of an information campaign. Or it may use voluntary organizations with a 'street-level' presence to convey information about government services or benefits. In the UK, such intermediaries account for 45 per cent of all contacts with the Disability and Carers Service (which administers benefits to those with who need assistance with care or mobility) and 23 per cent of all contacts with the Pensions Service (NAO, 2007).

These examples are cases of groups being used as intermediaries for the wider transmission of a government message. But on occasions the group in question may be the final target. Take the problem – encountered in most health-care systems – of how to limit the costs of drug-prescribing by doctors, given that the brands of medicine that are most heavily advertised or promoted by drug companies tend to be far more expensive than generic alternatives. In principle, the problem can be addressed by various instruments, including treasure (monetary incentives to doctors to choose cheaper generic drugs) or authority (limited lists of drugs that doctors are allowed to prescribe). But in the 1970s the UK government sought to tackle the problem by simply sending information packs to doctors involved in the government health service. The information was not originally 'personalized' to each doctor, as it would be if government were using 'direct notification' (a version of personalized information came later). Rather, it was directed to doctors as a group on the assumption that the information packs would help doctors identify and prescribe those types of medicine that represented the best value for money. Since government paid the bulk of the cost of the drugs that were prescribed by doctors, it had a clear interest in laying such information before them, but as it turned out more than a group-targeted message was needed to deal with the problem (see Stirton, 2005).

Targeting information to, and through, groups is a basic standby for any publicist, not only for government, but the device is widespread in modern government, given the importance of news media and of powerful pressure groups seeking to act as opinion-leaders. Using groups for diffusing a message has the advantage of relative economy; it is perhaps the social equivalent of the spreading of plant seeds through the medium of birds, by the production of attractive, edible berries.

'Broadcast' messages

The opposite of a 'bespoke message' to an individual is a general message to the world at large or to whomever it may concern. The latter can be termed *broadcast messages,* but broadcasting must here be understood in a wide sense, and does not necessarily refer to transmission by electronic media.

At least three main types of 'broadcast messages' can be distinguished: the privished message, the packaged self-serve message and propaganda.

Privished messages 'Privishing' is a word sometimes used in publishing, meaning to publish something in such a way that it remains relatively 'private', that is, confined to a small circle. The term is used here, for want of a better word, to denote the kind of message which government gives to the world at large in such a way that anyone who takes the trouble or knows the code may gain access to the information. But the message is propagated in such a way that it requires some considerable degree of effort on the part of the informee to 'tune in'. It needs active decoding or is transmitted in a form that is not designed to reach the uninformed or uninitiated.

There are a number of ways that a message can be privished

while ostensibly being made freely available. For example, a publication can be put on general sale, but at such a high price that very few people will buy it. An obscure medium may be used, such as a small ad in a specialist journal or official gazette rather than an attention-grabbing advertisement on a popular website or on TV at peak viewing time, or a full-page spread in a mass-circulation daily newspaper or magazine. Or the message may be made so cryptic that even when transmitted through a general information medium, only a few people will know the code necessary to read it – as in the case of those cryptic messages unintelligible to outsiders that lovers put in the newspapers on St Valentine's Day in some countries.

Many of government's messages are privished, for good or bad reasons. An example of the former is government's seamarks and lighthouses, which send out messages to whomever it may concern. To actually read the message, however, requires some degree of training and application on the part of the informee. Government weather reporting is another case in point: in the United Kingdom, weather forecasts for shipping are transmitted through a general purpose radio station, but to understand them you need to know where the government's weather stations are and what the numbers being reported refer to. Government's 'published' details of patent applications – compressed technical jargon in an official gazette – are a further example. Where there is a clearly defined specialist audience, privishing may be quite sufficient to reach government's intended informees. It all depends on how attentive and informed the audience is.

Packaged self-serve messages Somewhat less 'exclusive' than the 'privished message' is what we can call the *packaged self-serve message*. As the name implies, government is here using the methods of the self-service store or restaurant to convey a package of information to whomever it may concern. In contrast to the 'privished message', much less is required of the informee, but this mode still requires outsiders to take some initiative to obtain the proffered package. It is the approach of the kind of dating agency that invites you to pick your mate from 5,000 photographs rather than the one which offers candidates suitable to you personally after some screening process (which is a 'bespoke message'). The information is not personalized in any way. It is standard, packaged, preselected and available to anyone who chooses to take the trouble to pick it up. Of course, for such information presented via websites, only people with internet access will be able to see it, so a significant subsection of the population will be excluded (10 per cent in some Scandinavian countries and 30 per cent of North America, but 85 per cent of South America, 97 per cent of Africa as a whole and virtually 100 per cent of several African countries (Burundi, Rawanda, Tanzania, for example) at the time of writing).

Government, like every large organization, goes to great lengths to pre-package standard information, the availability of which may well be heavily advertised to attract customers. Such packaging takes many forms, from the ubiquitous 'frequently asked questions' pages on websites to computer-controlled telephone enquiry systems (press 1 for *x*, 2 for *y*, 3 for *z*, etc.) and travelling exhibitions. The advantage of this 'FAQ' approach is that it can reduce the need for bespoke messages, which tend to require considerable effort and expense to convey once they go beyond standardized routine information. But, like privished messages, self-serve information will only be effective if the prospective informees are sufficiently interested to want to help themselves to the packages on offer. Widespread use of the internet and search engines makes a great difference here, but even this approach presupposes levels of trust, motivation and competency that will often not exist in practice.

Propaganda Much, if not all, of government's information output can be seen as 'propaganda' in the sense that it is designed to persuade or to structure the informee's perception rather than to convey purely neutral or technical information. Propaganda in *that* sense has a very long history, going back at least as far as Pope Gregory XV's *Congregatio de Propaganda Fidei* of 1622 (Zijderveld, 1979, p. 68). But the term 'propaganda' is used here more narrowly and neutrally to denote the kind of general information for which government does not wait to be asked, but rather seeks to press upon the world at large. When it uses propaganda, government speaks to its subjects in such a way that the large-print, voluble message is forced down the public's throat willy-nilly. The message is standard and aimed at a mass audience. No investment of effort or knowledge is required before the message can be read or obtained, in contrast to privished or self-serve messages.

Government propaganda in this sense is common enough. Even under relatively liberal regimes, the public at large may be bombarded with general government exhortations and warnings –

to save fuel or water, join the armed forces, beware the ill effects of tobacco, avoid dropping litter, give blood, drive safely, lock up valuables, watch out for unattended bags that could be terrorist bombs, avoid using electric lawnmowers when the grass is wet, and so on. We, the public, do not seek this kind of government information deliberately. It seeks us.

Governments have always used propaganda, although its style keeps changing as media develop. Perhaps the first mass-propaganda campaign in the modern style by the British government came in the 1870s, when handbills addressed to the public at large, advertising a new government savings bank, were dropped through every letter box in the country (Clark, 1971, p. 23). Since then, of course, mass-propaganda techniques have changed enormously, especially with the development of psychological warfare (Brown, 1963, p. 87).

Government propaganda can vary widely in the directness of the message being conveyed. Sometimes that message is immediately recognizable and self-consciously conveyed through a conventional communications medium in the traditional 'agit-prop' style. The set-piece government broadcast, the poster or leaflet campaign, the large-scale newspaper advertisement are all standard propaganda routines, employed by every government from time to time.

On the other hand, there are also less straightforward, more subtle ways for government to press a message on the public at large. It may intersperse persuasion with an ostensibly neutral or technical message, as traditionally applied to the radio stations of the competing world powers in the Cold War period. Government may sugar the pill by slipping its message into an apparently quite untainted source. This is the reason why Lenin believed cinema films to be the ideal vehicle for political persuasion (Jarvie, 1970, p. 57). Even in Britain, government used a radio soap opera as a medium for trying to influence the farming community in the 1950s and 1960s (Ogilvy-Webb, 1965, p. 113) and during the Second World War its Special Operations Executive mounted a sizeable 'black propaganda' effort (that is, propaganda that does not acknowledge its source) to try to shift US public opinion in favour of participation in the war (see Mackenzie, 2002). Indeed, there is perhaps a tendency in Western countries for government to move away from the traditional mass-propaganda techniques of a more palpable kind towards more subtle kinds of spin.

The tool-set in context

Having picked out a handful of ways in which government can use its nodality to 'detect' and use information as an 'effecting' tool, the third part of this chapter considers how these tools may be combined and how they have changed in the digital age, and concludes by looking at the circumstances that are likely to govern the use of the different kinds of messages considered here.

Combinations and permutations

It would be easy to expand the number of types of nodality-based tools for detecting and effecting tools well beyond the dozen or so that have been considered here. But even a fairly small number of basic elements, if they can be combined freely, can produce a wealth of 'hybrids'. For the seven kinds of information-dispensing tools alone, there are in fact 5,040 logically possible combinations (and 13,700 if we allow for combinations of less than seven). Government can combine these instruments in several ways.

First, it can combine several types of information-dispenser *simultaneously*, so that they reinforce one another. For example, when there is an outbreak of cattle plague or an epidemic, or if a major change in social behaviour is required (such as a switch from driving on the left to driving on the right, as in Sweden in 1967, or the introduction of a new currency system such as the euro in 2000), government may want to pull out all the stops, and is likely to employ every means available to put its message across. It may track down particular individuals who have been exposed to infection in order to warn them of their danger, mount special approaches to inform members of relevant groups, and at the same time launch a propaganda campaign in the hope of alerting the general public. Even in less extreme cases – for example, when government interests itself in protecting the consumer – a variety of information-dispensers are commonly linked together.

Second, government can combine its information-dispensers in time, by using them in sequence. Once public attention has been caught by propaganda, it may be possible to offer further information by different means. For example, if government wants to set up a lottery, it may seek to attract punters by propaganda in the form of widespread popular advertising, stressing the large prizes to be won and the joys of affluence that lie in store for the lucky winners. Those who are 'hooked' by such a message may then be informed further by the self-serve method, inviting them to check the website, phone the call centre or pick up the leaflet for a description of the lottery scheme. For those who are lucky enough to win a prize, the mode may then switch to privished messages or to direct notification, depending on how the winners are to learn of their success. Even then, government will need at least one further information-dispenser to handle unclaimed prizes or untraceable winners.

Third, information-based tools for detecting can be mixed with those for effecting. Indeed, when government requests or demands information there is often an accompanying propaganda campaign explaining why the information is needed. Failure to send in a compulsory return may trigger a reminder from government, directly notifying the individual offender; or those who have difficulty in completing the returns may be referred to such-and-such a website, helpline number or an explanatory leaflet, on the self-serve principle. The enquiry office producing prompted or unprompted query responses is invariably a two-way street in information traffic.

Fourth, the combinations can be extended to space *and* time as well as nodality-based tools for detecting and effecting. They can also be extended to include combinations of other types of tools (authority, treasure and organization), which were introduced in Chapter 1 and will be discussed in the chapters that follow. When we start to think of coupling information-dispensers with government's other classes of tools, the number of possible combinations takes a quantum jump, from thousands to billions.

Nodal tools in the digital age

So what difference has information technology made to the use of tools of government based on nodality? Most of the nodality-based tools for detecting have been transformed by internet applications. Email, for example, provides another cheap and at least superficially anonymous channel for unsolicited tenders, although in fact mobile phone and email traffic records are a potentially huge vein of 'by-product' information available to government that can be searched electronically. As mentioned earlier, technology-based information-processing systems, such as road-pricing and ticketing, offer new possibilities for government to obtain useful citizen-based information as a by-product. Websites provide government with a new generation of 'ear trumpets' that provide a modern form of the Venetian State Inquisitors' letter boxes. Certainly there are now more free media for government to scrutinize than in pre-internet days, though the effectiveness of such scrutiny depends on the use of search engines. Similarly, new and cheaper modes of direct inquiry become available, through online opinion surveys for example, although such methods may fail to reach groups such as the poor, the elderly, the alienated and the followers of alternative lifestyles. Similarly some of the nodality-based tools for effecting become sharper in the internet age while others may be less effective than before.

Suppression of information, as in the example from China given earlier, may demand more technical ingenuity for government (even IT-savvy states like Singapore have found it an uphill task) and central management of information may be more challenging in a world of multiple dynamic websites even within government. Email obviously lends itself to 'leaking' information because of its 'one-to-many' facility but equally presents a huge challenge to government information management because of the ease with which emails can be unintentionally broadcast with embarrassing consequences. Geospatial innovations publicly available on the internet, such as Google Earth, make it more challenging to keep secret the locations of nuclear installations, causing the President of India to express concerns that the online mapping tool posed 'a significant security risk to the country' (*Technology News* at www.physorg.com/, 10 March 2006).

As far as direct information is concerned, the digital age seems to have heralded a new type of group-targeted message and a tendency for messages at either end of the spectrum from 'bespoke' to 'broadcast' (the 'most bespoke' and 'most broadcast') to become more difficult. In the middle of the spectrum, websites have transformed information dissemination by government as well as other organizations by providing repositories for vast quantities of information that government agencies need or want to make generally available online. A generation ago individuals who wanted information about a registered company or about birth, death or marriage details of their ancestors had to visit the relevant registry, or call or write to obtain the information they needed. Today such information is increasingly available online, and the marginal costs of additional online users are much lower than when dealing with letters, telephone calls or office visits. Providing 'privished messages' to specific groups also takes a new and distinctive form with web-based technologies, because such messages can be provided via a website with simple password access, on an intranet available only to employees of an organization or via a 'secret' URL only known by a small group of people.

Thus web-based technologies have transformed and in many ways enhanced government's ability to make 'packaged self-serve' and 'prompted query response' information available in a new form of 'group-targeted message' – with ever greater capacity for targeting more specific groups. For instance, many websites allow users to key in a zip code or postcode to receive very specific information about that immediate locality. Such facilities allow a new mix of nodal tools, somewhere between a prompted query response (in that they rely on citizens actively visiting the website) and packaged self-serve information – because the government does not have to 'touch' the information to deliver it to any individual citizen. This form of information provision is popular among organizations of all kinds because once the information is made available, there are low marginal costs for additional users. But by the same token, bespoke messages of the direct notification type tend to become proportionally more expensive.

This new form of group targeting has the potential to greatly enhance government's capacity to propagate information directly, but brings new problems too. For example, aiming to cash in on the popularity of family history, the UK Public Record Office launched an online version of its 1901 census in 2002 amid much publicity, resulting in an even more publicized 'meltdown' of its site which received 1.2 million hits per hour, about 25 times the traffic for which it was designed. The site crashed on its first day and was taken down for many months, before being relaunched with minimal publicity. Learning from the UK's lesson, the Canadian equivalent was specifically designed to be more difficult to use and the National Archives of Canada 'purposely buried the online launch' (*Edmonton Journal*, 31 May 2002).

Other drawbacks include the fact that such channels tend to be open to all potential users, some of whom might have quite different intentions from those envisaged by the architects of the system. For example, the US Federal Office of Pipeline Safety spent years developing an internet program that allowed users to log on, type in their zip code and find out whether they lived near a gas pipeline. But after the al-Qaida attacks of 11 September 2001 on New York and Washington, officials closed the site, concerned that a terrorist could use it to locate a pipeline and blow it up (*The Denver Post*, 1 October 2001).

All these applications of internet technology, however, depend on the existence of a group of citizens who have access to the necessary facilities and are motivated to use it actively to pick up information from government. As noted earlier, in the many circumstances when these conditions do not apply, for instance the unconnected (who tend to be disproportionately from disadvantaged groups), the disaffected or just plain uninterested, the limits of self-serve or responsive tools, based on the internet or anything else, are reached.

While messages in the centre of the spectrum from 'bespoke' to 'broadcast' seem to have been facilitated by internet-based technology, those at either end seem to have become more problematic. Technically, direct notification might be easier using internet-based tools, for instance by automatically generating personalized information by scanning internal databases. But it seems that governments often make far less use of such facilities than private sector customer-facing organizations such as banks (see Dunleavy and Margetts, 1999, 2002), finding it particularly difficult to resolve the identification and authentication issues that such techniques require. And in any case, as noted above, the more heavily charged and tailor-made the message, the less suitable it may be for digital delivery. When the government pursues an individual for failure to pay a fine or tax, more personalized and 'non-virtual' forms of notification are soon employed, such as recorded delivery mail and ultimately a personal visit from government officials.

At the other end of the spectrum, the digital age brings a new challenge to a government's ability to broadcast messages via propaganda. Widespread use of the internet introduces new competition for public attention, with government lagging behind the private and voluntary sectors in its provision of timely information. For example, the *Washington Post* noted, after the terrorist attacks of 11 September, 'while government websites stayed eerily static for hours after [the] attacks, private companies and non-profits swiftly ripped up their home pages to focus on the tragedy' (*Washington Post*, 13 September 2001). Indeed, another type of competition for nodality on the internet comes from the widespread use of search engines like Google, which work using a combination of word searches and page-ranking algorithms, the exact nature of which is a closely guarded secret. Private sector organizations devote considerable resources and develop strategies to manipulate these algorithms to maximize their own visibility in Google searches. Governments are less likely to employ such strategies, meaning that their own information may be less likely to reach public attention.

In addition to the internet, the proliferation of other media channels (television, radio and print press) in the digital age also makes the task of putting a message out to the public at large more difficult, as there are so many alternative places for public attention to be. A striking example of this kind of competition occurred after a massive tsunami hit South East Asia on 26 December 2004. In Western countries, concerned individuals automatically turned to their governments for information about missing relatives who had been travelling in affected areas, but many found that other governments were providing more reliable information (Swedish and British governments in particular were criticized for reacting 'way too slow' (*Los Angeles Times*, 31 December 2004). Indeed, it was internet bulletin boards, operated by voluntary organizations such as the International Red Cross, private sector travel organizations such as Lonely Planet and media organizations that became widely used sources of information for those seeking news about foreigners in affected countries, operating as a huge information exchange between those on the ground and those seeking news of relatives from afar.

Selecting nodal tools: the wider social context

'Wider social context' is used here to mean the cultural climate in which government operates. What circumstances might affect the type of information outlet – or mix of outlets – that government uses? When would we expect each tool to be used? Many characteristics of the cultural climate might affect such a choice, but here only three main elements will be discussed. They are the size of population, the extent to which government rules with the broad consensus of its citizens and the degree of attention of the informee population.

Size of population The relative cost to government of particular as against general messages is likely to depend to some extent on the size of the informee population. When that population is very small, it may be no more costly to use particular messages than to use general ones, and indeed the latter might well tax government's bureaucratic resources more heavily than the former. Moreover, as the previous section has argued, the development of information technology has greatly reduced the cost of sending particularized messages to large numbers of people, where the information involved is routine or clear-cut enough to be programmable, and the intended recipients are connected enough to be easily reached through low-cost information channels. Government, along with marketing organizations generally, can now send bespoke messages of this type at relatively low cost. The predecessor to this book (Hood, 1983) pointed to the difficulty of operating a railway without any published timetables, such that each prospective traveller had to be told personally about trains and times for his or her particular trip, and used that as an example of the potentially high costs of producing bespoke information for large numbers of people. But over the intervening two decades, it has become eminently possible to provide precisely that kind of information, through computer-based web or call centre enquiries.

But as soon as the information concerned is not readily programmable or the recipients not really reached by standard non-face-to-face communication channels – for instance, if government is trying to track down and inform individuals who might have been exposed to a disease such as rabies in a particular spot during a summer holiday period – the costs of bespoke messaging become very high as the population grows larger. Certainly, giving out *all* of government's information by waiting for unpredictable and heterogeneous enquiries and then delivering tailor-made responses according to the circumstances of each particular case would become enormously expensive as it went beyond computer-programmed responses. 'Direct notification', where government actually tracks down each informee, may also take a heavy toll of government's bureaucratic resources when the population to be informed is large and cannot be reached through standard channels.

By and large, then, government is likely to try to confine bespoke messages to relatively small informee populations, extreme situations, or to a back-up or long-stop role. When the informee population is large, government is likely to look to 'broadcast' or 'group-targeted' messages. It will try to pre-package information in some way, before a mass of enquirers actually turns up on its doorstep. Similarly, governments will use passive rather than active detecting tools as the population size increases.

Consensus A key element of the cultural climate in which government operates is the degree of consensus or general acceptance of its right to rule on the part of its subjects or citizens. In general it may be supposed that, as the degree of that consensus or general acceptance declines, the emphasis will shift in the direction of propaganda and unprompted query responses – and possibly of direct notification, too.

This is because individuals are likely to be less inclined to take up advertised information from the authorities when their loyalty and trust in government decline. But at the same time they may be more inclined to find out government's secrets and to press it for information which it is not eager to give out in a pre-packaged form, or indeed in any form. To the extent that the public at large displays increasing attention and interest in information which government is trying to hide, more load may be thrown on the unprompted query response form of information outlet – a device which, as was noted before, is expensive for government to use in large quantities unless it involves the dispensing of information that is readily reducible to algorithms by computer programmers.

Just as a social context of 'low consensus' will cause attention on the part of the public to increase in relation to some kinds of information – the kind government wants to hide – that attention will *decrease* in relation to the messages that government wants to put across. Those information outlets that rely on 'take-up' by the public, such as self-serve or prompted query methods, will prove less effective. Even groups such as the news media or pressure groups are likely to become less reliable and amenable as information conduits. Government may therefore find increasing pressure to use the propaganda instrument in an attempt to put its message across in a general way. Of course, in a context of declining consensus or acceptability, even this instrument may come to have diminishing or negative returns, as Tony Blair's once-famed New Labour spin doctors discovered in his government's second term. Credibility sinks to the point where anything that government chooses to say to the public at large is ignored or automatically dismissed as lies. If government really wants to get a message across in those conditions, it either has to rely on the work being done by an independent source or to inform each person individually using the face-to-face form of direct notification – the most expensive way for government to dispense information in large quantities.

Hence, at the very point where it might be most important for government to communicate effectively with individuals, it is likely to be both over-informing and under-informing them, snowing them under with propaganda while at the same time blocking their demands to know its secrets through unprompted queries. It is likely to be increasingly thrown back on its most 'expensive' information outlets. Indeed, there is a point of social pressure at which government is likely to switch the emphasis away from information and to lay more emphasis on its other main effecting tools.

Degree of attention A third element that is likely to affect the mixture of information-propagating tools is the degree of *attention* that is manifested by the informee population. Where attention is high, government need not employ tools such as direct notification and propaganda, any more than a business firm with eager customers need resort to heavy advertising of its products. Its citizens will actively look for information, triggering unprompted query responses and being alert for privished messages. For example, governments in Europe are mandated to advertise tenders for government contracts over a certain size in the *European Journal*, and have little need to advertise anywhere else (in spite of the decidedly unappealing format of the journal) because all prospective bidders will routinely scrutinize that source for potential contracts. Little 'spoon-feeding' of information will be necessary in those conditions.

Attention is, of course, a function of interest and specialism. When our interest is focused on a certain topic – for example, our occupational specialism, scarce goods or services that we wish to obtain, the health of our children, prizes we hope to win, our other interests and hobbies – we will be highly receptive to messages within that field. We may well be on a 'rumour circuit' which informs us of approaching events long before any formal announcement is made. When the relevant group or individual is hanging on government's every word, it is a waste of effort for government to 'shout' or to buttonhole its listener. It need only whisper or let slip the most cryptic hint into the information network for the message to gain immediate currency. But government will find that it needs to move more in the direction of direct notification and propaganda when it is operating outside or cutting across established information networks, or when it is trying to reach individuals who are not consciously involved in the matter in question. The whispering gallery effect ceases to operate. For example, there was no need for the British government to go to great lengths to announce Queen Victoria's death in 1901 to the citizens of London, who were mostly 'tuned in' to the royal happenings through direct observation, rumour and newspapers. But the government had to send a special gunboat to proclaim the queen's death to the remote Scottish island of St Kilda (the inhabitants of which had been unaware of Queen Victoria's accession for a year after she came to the throne in 1837

(Steel, 1975, pp. 33–4)). And degree of attention is not, of course, only or necessarily related to geographical remoteness.

Conclusion

This chapter began by examining ways in which government can use nodality as a tool for obtaining information and then looked at some of the variety of information that modern government purveys to individuals – from the ponderous to the trivial, from the abstruse to the everyday. It only takes a casual look at the websites that have largely replaced the government bookshops of yesteryear to underline the point. Information from government is not only a form of 'effecting' tool that we find in use all around us; it often comes early in the sequence of government's responses to a problem. For instance, one of the British government's first moves on the outbreak of war in 1914 was to appoint a Director of Propaganda (Clark, 1971, p. 24); one of the US government's first responses to the suppression of trade unions in Poland in 1981 was to stage a one-hour television spectacular entitled 'Let Poland be Poland'. After the lack of immediate governmental response to the al-Qaida attacks of 11 September 2001 on the USA as noted above, the federal government portal firstgov.gov rallied well, detailing information about government agencies' response to the attacks and providing links to a wide range of information and advice to individuals. In the following days and weeks the Microsoft search engine referred more visitors to Firstgov than any other website (*Newsweek Business Information*, 8 October 2001).

We have suggested that the digital age has brought a move away from both ends of the spectrum of nodal effecting tools and a blurring of boundaries between the tools in the middle of the spectrum. It has become technically more difficult to suppress information held in digital form and direct notification has become disproportionately more costly, apart from the hitherto few instances of automatic bespoke messaging noted above. There has been a dramatic rise in the potential for a new kind of information provision, on the cusp of prompted query response and packaged self-serve information. Meanwhile, at the other end of the spectrum, it is more difficult to achieve universal coverage with propaganda. The provision of 'packaged self-serve' information has become easier, but organizations of all kinds are innovative in providing it and the local or national government is no longer so likely to be the first place that occurs to citizens (or, indeed, Google) when they need to find something out. There are just too many alternative information sources, and too much competition for nodality.

Using information as an effector has the advantage of not necessarily laying government's authority on the line. 'When arguments are used, authority is left in abeyance' (Arendt, quoted in Wrong, 1979, p. 32) and the same might be said of information dispensation in a broader sense. But in many situations, of course, there comes a point at which other instruments must be used – orders, threats, bribes, physical coercion. Mere communications – words – are not enough. Other kinds of government tools will be needed.

Chapter 3

Authority

. . . and that's official.

(Common daily phrase)

One of the four basic resources of government that were discussed in Chapter 1 was legal authority. This is the ability to command and prohibit, commend and permit, through recognized procedures and identifying symbols, for example the Great Seal of the United States, the vermilion pen used by Chinese emperors in selecting the top candidates in civil service examinations, official rods, maces and chains of office, and the many other devices employed by governments to lend 'officiality' to their pronouncements.

We will not concern ourselves here with the *source* of government's authority, whether it be popular election, the presumed will of God, or the many other doctrines on which governments base their claim to rule. What is of interest here is the way in which government *uses* authority as an instrument for detection, obtaining information by requisition or as an effecting tool. It 'spends' this resource in the form of what can be called *tokens of authority*.

A token of authority can be thought of, metaphorically, as a piece of paper with an official stamp on it, although in reality such tokens need not take that literal form and nowadays many may take the form of digital signatures or internet passwords that translate into authority to use some digital government service, or smart cards conveying entitlement. The term is perhaps somewhat over-portentous for the mundane reality of many of the devices that convey government's authority, which are often far removed from the *lettre de cachet* or the imperial decree. But there is no satisfactory word in English that can serve as a generic term to cover official tokens of all kinds. The German word *Schein* perhaps comes close to it.

As with government's messages and payments, its tokens of authority are ubiquitous both for gathering information and changing behaviour. Orders, bans, requisitions, vouchers, warrants, coupons, licences, quotas, certificates (digital or otherwise) – once you start looking, you see them everywhere. They are intended to convey authority, not simply information, to the outside world.

Indeed, it often happens that a mere piece of paper with an official stamp or signature on it may be extremely valuable and eagerly sought after: for example, government guarantees for bank loans or operator licences for air routes, broadcasting or telephone franchises (as with the huge sums paid in the auctions for '3G' mobile phone licences in Germany and Britain in the late 1990s). Other kinds of official token, such as tax forms, requisition orders or military call-up papers, may be considerably less welcome.

In another sense, of course, the official token is 'no more' than a metaphorical piece of paper with an official stamp on it. Naturally, legal authority may not be sufficient in practice to ensure that government's official tokens are automatically obeyed or respected. Government's citizens may well decide to ignore the intendedly authoritative pieces of paper that it issues. In fact it happens quite frequently. In such circumstances, government must look to a different set of tools if it wishes to obtain information or make any impression on the world outside.

The first part of this chapter looks at requisitions, government's detecting tools based on authority. The second part of the chapter discusses some of the different kinds of official tokens available to government as effecting tools, beginning with low-constraint 'directed' tokens and concluding with high-constraint 'blanketed' ones. In the third part of the chapter, the contexts and combinations in which government uses official tokens and the impact of digital-age technologies will be explored.

Detecting tools based on authority: requisitions

The main type of detector based on government's resource of legal authority can be labelled 'requisition'. Instead of obtaining information by nodality or by exchange, government requires it, under threat of sanction for non-compliance.

As with nodality, there is a spectrum from 'passive' to 'active'. One common passive method can be termed the *obligation to display.* Here government requires subjects of certain classes or types to display identification symbols so that they can be spotted or counted by the use of fairly passive methods (there is, of course, a fine line between requiring others to display and government doing the marking itself). Government may oblige the population at large to carry identity symbols in the form of cards, papers, bracelets and the like.

Personal identification is a highly charged issue. But the device also has more humdrum applications, as when airlines require us to put identity tags on our luggage. Motor vehicles are required not only to be registered with the government (a process that will be discussed shortly), but also to have their registration numbers prominently displayed so that the number can be seen from a distance. In most countries discs or stickers denoting payment of tax or safety inspections also have to be displayed on the windscreen or registration plate. Other applications of the principle are the transponders that must be carried by aircraft, the load lines that must be displayed by merchant ships, the registration numbers that must be displayed by fishing boats, or the house names or numbers that must be displayed so that government can know where we live.

As in the latter case, obligation to display is closely linked to the use of tokens of authority to compel individuals and organizations to display certain information, such as food ingredients or the kinds of chemicals being carried by road tankers, to the general public (as distinct from the forces of government alone). The two often overlap, and indeed such an overlap may sometimes strengthen government detection. Simon *et al.* (1950, p. 479) describe how persons allocated extra fuel rations on account of their occupation in the USA during the Second World War were obliged to paste a sticker on the windscreen of their car, in the hope that anyone who was not really entitled to such extra rations would be betrayed to the authorities by his or her neighbours.

Obligation to notify

A more common method by which government can obtain information by requiring it under threat of sanction, while still retaining a relatively passive detection stance, is the *obligation to notify.* Government insists on certain items being brought to its notice, as opposed to having symbols displayed in case it chooses to notice them. For example, it may require people in a certain age group to register for military draft purposes.

There are many varieties of this device. Sometimes we are required to give government prior notification of a course of action that we plan to take, as applies to alterations to land or buildings. Sometimes we are required to notify government post hoc, telling the authorities about some event after it has taken place. The 'notifiable incident' is an information-gathering tool in very common use by government, applying to items such as transport and industrial accidents, mishaps at licensed nuclear installations and even, in the case of cattle plague, to mere suspicions, which British farmers have long been obliged by law to report to the police. It was widely used by 'quarantinist' regimes in the battle against smallpox in the nineteenth century (see Baldwin, 1999, p. 532) as a means of targeted intervention less costly and drastic than mass vaccination or infrastructural change. As in that case, notification requirements typically act as triggers for a different mode of information-gathering to be set in train.

Public registration is an example of the 'obligation to notify' tool which goes back to very ancient times. The most familiar example (because everyone is involved in it at some time in their lives) is the registration of births, deaths and marriages. Traditionally, such registers were compiled in Europe by the local clergy but in many countries church-based registration has been superseded by government-operated civil registration systems over the past two centuries, for instance in France from 1792, the Netherlands from 1811 and the Ottoman Empire from 1839. In many countries residents are also required to register their current address with the local police.

Registration schemes in fact exist throughout government's sphere of interest, sometimes extending into less familiar areas. Registration is commonly applied to cars, boats, planes, guns, dogs and bicycles, and has even extended to prostitutes in some countries, including France and Germany in the nineteenth century. An example from the USA is the requirement for foreign lobbyists to register with the Justice Department, as a means of identifying public relations firms and consultants purveying propaganda and 'disinformation' on behalf of foreign governments without revealing the identity of their paymasters. Most schemes of business regulation include as part of their standard equipment a requirement that firms operating in the industry concerned must register with government; and, in the extreme case, government may require certain types of information to be submitted to itself and to no one else. For example, during the Second World War the British government prohibited employers from notifying job vacancies to any source or medium other than government labour exchanges (Barnes and Reid, 1980, p. 9).

Registration in this sense does not necessarily carry any 'enablement', in the sense that eligibility for some benefit flows from the information supplied. In practice, of course – as a 'social exchange' theorist would be quick to notice – some compulsory registration systems are deliberately mixed in with other types of government benefit, so that in reality there is some element of indirect reward for registration. For example, without registration of birth it is difficult to claim government cash benefits or tax offsets in respect of children, and without registration of death it is similarly difficult to claim death benefits or to dispose lawfully of a dead person's possessions. But registration is not invariably linked to direct rewards for the informant in this way, especially when the informant is an organization rather than an individual, and government can thus tap into standard operating procedures in a way that may make 'cover-ups' expensive (see Hood, 1976, p. 126). For instance, the 2005 European Union Savings Directive mandated member states to require all banks and building societies operating interest-paying accounts in their jurisdiction to report certain information (identity and residence of the account-holder and the interest paid) to government, which in turn provides this information to the tax authorities of the state of residence of the account-holder.

Returns

A further tool by which government may require information from the world outside is the *return,* as in the case of returns for tax or the obligation for charities or companies of a certain size to produce annual reports. The term 'return' implies a request for information in a specified form to be returned to the relevant government office by the individual or organization involved. Returns are very closely linked to obligation-to-notify and compulsory registration systems as information-gathering devices, so that it is difficult to draw a precise boundary.

Part of the distinction between returns and other forms of requisitioned information lies in the frequency or regularity of the process. The term 'return' is often used to mean obligations to notify government of the state of some system at regular fixed intervals, as in the many cases of monthly, quarterly or annual reports of information that government requires. They can be distinguished from those obligations to notify that are only triggered if and when certain events occur, as in the case of births, deaths or certain types of accidents. Many types of government register operate on the irregular, event-triggered, obligation-to-notify principle rather than on returns.

Returns do not only differ from inertia-based, obligation-to-notify systems in the matter of regularity. They are also typically different in that government takes a more active part in the scrutiny process by sending out standard forms to be sent back by the informant. This is the other sense of 'return'. The classic or textbook case is the income-tax return that many governments traditionally sent out to citizens or residents. In such a case the revenue authorities were clearly taking a more active part in the information-gathering process than, say, the registrars of births, deaths and marriages, who required others to make the first approach. But the degree of activity involved is still limited: the return mode still lays on the informant the onus of obtaining and producing the information that government desires.

Interrogation and inspection

Information-gathering involves a greater degree of active search when government not only signals to the informant that information is required (rather than leaving it up to the informant to approach government in certain specified circumstances), but also itself takes on the task of ferreting out the information. All that we, government's citizens or subjects, are required to do is to make ourselves (or it may be our property, papers and so on) available to government for examination.

Two broad types of such information-gathering can be distinguished, differing in terms of the location in which government and its citizens meet. One mode, here termed *interrogation*, requires us (or our property) to attend on government for examination. 'Interrogation' can be used in many different contexts and with varying levels of intensity. It ranges from cases such as the testing of returning nationals for HIV (as in Cuba, China and Iran) to Spanish Inquisition-type processes of the kind portrayed in such books as *Nineteen Eighty-Four, Darkness at Noon* and *The Brothers Karamazov.* Government may demand to see our papers or our persons for tax purposes. Its Official Receivers may summon us before them if a bankruptcy petition has been filed against us.

A final type of compulsory government search involves an interrogation process that is still more active in a locational sense – a process that is here termed *inspection.* 'Inspection' involves government playing away from home. It waits on the informant, rather than vice versa. Government may go out compulsorily to inspect factories, retail stores, food outlets and other businesses, sometimes in the form of unannounced 'dawn raids' to catch us unawares. It may seek to locate and compulsorily interview individuals such as bankrupts or schoolchildren (for whom compulsory medical inspections were introduced in the early twentieth century in many US states, Canadian provinces and the UK), or even a large part of the adult population, as in the case of the traditional government census, as administered for some eight hundred years in Ancient Rome. If it takes prisoners of war, it may legally demand certain personal details from them (under the 1949 Geneva Convention). It may compel drivers to submit to a breathalyser test if there is reason to suspect they are driving under the influence of alcohol or drugs, or even submit drivers to random spot checks. Similarly, it may apply this type of scrutiny to goods or animals rather than to individuals. For example, in the 1840s the British government began the compulsory scientific testing of imported tobacco for adulteration, so as to prevent importers from adulterating imported tobacco for re-export and thus fraudulently claiming repayment of customs duties from government while retaining a portion of the original tobacco for sale in the domestic market (Crombie, 1962, p. 159).

Inspection is a type of information-gathering that corresponds in some ways to the 'direct inquiry' and 'propositioning' modes of inquiry, except that in this case the informant is legally required to answer government's questions, rather than simply invited to tender information on a voluntary basis or offered a reward for doing so, or simply inspected involuntarily. Failure to cooperate, for instance in responding to census questions, can and sometimes does result in legal penalties (though such penalties are of course hard to impose where information refusal is widespread).

Inspections, like interrogations, can vary widely in frequency, mode of selection and intensity. They range from the routine and predictable mode of government visitation to the raid or sortie, involving intensive search parties coming from out of the blue (as in the case of sudden tax raids, random checks on vehicles or drivers, snap inspections of bank reserve assets, sorties by fishery cruisers, spot searches and locker checks in prisons).

Effecting with authority: tokens of authority

Governments can use authority as an 'effecting' tool – to change behaviour – as well as a tool of information-gathering. When it comes to effecting with authority, the basic instrument is some sort of demand or prohibition linked to a token of authority.

As a way of indicating some of the different tokens of authority that government can wield, two basic distinctions will be made in this chapter. The first is the distinction between 'particular' and 'general' applications, which by now will be becoming familiar. Particular kinds of tokens – here called *directed tokens* – are those which relate to specific and named individuals, places, organizations or objects. Operators' licences that are people or place specific, such as licences for street or subway musicians, are a case in point. By contrast, official tokens which are general – here called *blanketed tokens* – apply to anyone or everyone. Traffic lights or 'no smoking' notices are examples.

The other distinction relates to the degree of *constraint* that official tokens seek to introduce into the behaviour of government's subjects. Low-constraint tokens merely approve or recommend; high-constraint tokens order or forbid. An example of the former is the US Navy's 'E' award, which was given to factories with high production in the Second World War (Simon *et al.*, 1950, p. 472). An example of the latter is government's exercise of its power of 'eminent domain' (that is, the legal power to compel the sale of land for government purposes). In between is a set of tokens, such as bargains and permits, which involve an intermediate degree of constraint.

Directed tokens

Certificates are perhaps the least constraining form of directed tokens. A 'certificate', in the sense used here, is essentially an authoritative declaration about the properties of an individual or object, often in terms of fitness or unfitness. This is necessarily 'particular' and it involves low constraint in that it need not of itself convey any privilege or sanction. It is a mixture of giving information and wielding authority.

The most straightforward kind of certificate is that which states the facts of a case in an (intendedly) authoritative way. Many organizations – not just government – use a host of stamps, cards or seals to officially identify employees, documents or other items. Familiar examples are the detective's card, the bank teller's stamp or even the stamps that organizers of some events or entertainments put onto the wrists or hands of customers who have paid to allow them re-entry to the venue. A similar example, incorporating an element of organization as well as authority, is the finger dipped in indelible ink that shows that citizens have voted in an election or referendum, a traditional device of electoral administration (see Mackenzie, 1958 p.125) that was applied to voting in Iraq after the 2003 war.

Somewhat less straightforward are certificates which attest to less matter-of-fact properties. Examples are government's certification of trade unions as independent (as opposed to the 'bogus' creations of employers) or its certificates of academic or technical achievement, such as seamen's proficiency certificates or certificates of achievement in public examinations.

There are at least three circumstances in which government need look no further than certification in its toolkit to find an instrument for influencing social behaviour. First, the need for some common or approved standards may be sufficient to give government's certificates a value, for instance in officially certifying the fuel efficiency of each make of car, to provide 'authoritative' figures for consumers. In such cases government does not tell us which car to buy; it simply provides official statements about one of the properties of the different models available.

Second, and closely related, the award of government's 'seal of approval' may be prized and eagerly sought after as intrinsically desirable. Government's honours and medals are perhaps the clearest example: many of them involve little or nothing in the way of concrete privileges and so amount to little more than official certificates of merit to individuals, from the official heroes of the former Soviet Union to the older chivalric orders in long-established monarchies such as Japan or the UK. Similarly, companies in Britain have long valued the social *cachet* that their products can acquire as a result of displaying the 'royal warrant'.

Government's 'seal of approval' is often valuable to businessmen and traders, as a means of inspiring confidence among their customers. For example, in many countries farm producers apply to be certified for 'organic' status, complying with the standards set by some governmental or non-governmental body in order to appeal to consumers wishing to avoid the potential affects of pesticides and fertilizers used in the production of fruit and vegetables and artificial additives in animal foodstuffs. Many roadside petrol pumps in Britain were voluntarily submitted for testing and certification by the Board of Trade long before that process became compulsory in 1926 (Llewellyn Smith, 1928, p. 164).

Third, we may want a certificate from one government to get

something from another government. For instance, we may need our home government's certificates of specifications or other documents if we are applying for patents from another government; we may need to get official certificates of purity to export livestock or animal products to another country; or, if we are moving between countries with reciprocal arrangements for state medical benefits, we will need a certificate of entitlement from our home government. In 2006, the US government compelled all those wishing to travel to the USA without a visa to possess a biometric passport complying with US standards, thereby not only obliging US-bound travellers to obtain such passports but also requiring 'visa-waiver' countries to introduce them.

In such circumstances, government may be able to rely on the instrument of certification alone, without needing it to invoke any element of compulsion. In other cases, of course, government may be able to do *no more* than offer certificates in the hope that they will have an effect. Certification must serve *faute de mieux*. For example, government may find itself unable to guarantee work to the unemployed, but it can give such people official certificates to prove that they have been on a government training course or job-creation project. It may not be able to forbid young children to cycle on the street without a permit, but it can encourage them to take cycling tests to obtain certificates of competence from the police.

Medium-constraint varieties

Certificates are 'directed tokens' involving low constraint on the behaviour of government's subjects. Before coming to the high-constraint variety, we will discuss an intermediate category of medium-constraint directed tokens. Within this category fall what we can call *conditional tokens* and *enablements*.

Conditional tokens A conditional token is an undertaking (promise, threat) by government to do *x* if *y* happens. Of course, many official tokens have conditions attached to them, but in the pure case of the 'conditional', events or behaviours other than *y* are not prohibited (except, perhaps, by ordinary rules such as laws of fraud or contract). We can take government's deal or not, just as we choose. The outcome depends explicitly on the turn of events or on the behaviour of others with whom government is dealing. That is why conditionals can be considered as involving a middle level of constraint.

Government guarantees are perhaps the best example of the pure conditional. Most governments have schemes for guaranteeing approved exports against default by overseas clients, or for guaranteeing overseas investment against political risks such as revolutions or *coups d'état*. Governments may guarantee insurance contracts for business firms faced with threats of terrorism, or the loans made by private banks to particular institutions. Dramatic examples from the USA are the so-called 'Lockheed loan' of $250 million in 1975 and the 'Chrysler loan' of $1,000 million in 1980. In fact, these were not loans at all as far as the US government was concerned. All that passed between the US government and these companies was an official slip of paper saying that the federal government would guarantee bank loans up to the stated amount. That was the only 'constraint' needed to prevent the firms concerned from going bankrupt, because it allowed them to borrow money on the private market on terms that would otherwise not have been available (Lowi and Stone, 1978, p. 22).

Enablements Conditional tokens such as bonds, guarantees and contracts may be constraining in the sense that they convey 'an offer you can't refuse', but there is no formal prohibition on unlicensed activity. You are not forbidden from exporting or borrowing without government guarantees if you can do it. By contrast, an 'enablement', as it is termed here, is a token which permits you to carry on an activity which would otherwise be prohibited. Alternatively it may convey rights of allocation or exemption from some government rule or payment that would otherwise apply. 'Enablements' belong in the medium-constraint category because they only allow, but do not *compel*, you to undertake the activity in question.

Like certificates, enablements are a commonplace device in every organization. Outside government we find them everywhere; the security pass, the parking permit, the railcard, the boarding card. For government itself, enablements are a long-established instrument. Governments have always been in the business of issuing licences, charters and letters patent granting privileges of a variety of kinds. Traditional examples include licences for traffic, for markets and fairs, and 'patents' in the modern sense of licences granting a temporary monopoly to inventors. Sometimes such enablements conveyed coercive powers, such as letters of marque (licences to commit piracy on foreign merchant ships) or the powers obtained by the London Fishmongers' Company in the seventeenth century to enter and search shops and to seize and dispose of any fish found to be bad.

Today, government enablements cover a bewildering range of activity. For example, if you want to run a zoo, an employment agency, a taxi service, a casino, a slaughterhouse, an animal experiment laboratory, a pharmacy or a databank on individuals indicating their creditworthiness, you will need permission from government in most countries (a process that can be extremely laborious, as Hernando de Soto's (2000) experiments with attempting to set up a bakery shop in different countries have shown). The list can seem endless, extending to such things as permission to marry and have children, as in the Chinese tradition. Nor, apparently, is there any escape in fiction: even Ian Fleming's famous secret agent '007' had to be 'licensed to kill'.

Enablements are 'everywhere' partly because, like certificates, they are one of the most basic tools used to regulate business. Government may require you to be licensed for a certain *activity* – when you are importing or exporting food, say, or armaments on some official list of strategic goods. It may require you to be licensed to trade over a *period*, as typically applies to taxicabs. It may require you to ask its permission to *change* your activities or standards of service. Arguments constantly go on as to whether government should use licensing to regulate this or that trade or activity: sex shops, private security firms, marriage bureaux, DNA testing services, material provided on the internet, or whatever the current political argument is about.

Enablements go under many different names in practice, such as licences, warrants, quotas, coupons, vouchers, permits, exemption certificates. The differences in terminology are often misleading. But there are real differences in the way government can go about giving enablements. For example, they can be limited or unlimited, qualitative or quantitative. A brief comment will be made on each of these types.

First, the difference between limited and unlimited enablements. Sometimes official permissions to carry on an activity are issued in restricted quantities rather than without limit to anyone who qualifies (such as driving licences). Examples of the former are casino licences, work permits or immigrant admission vouchers, even vehicle licences in the crowded city state of Singapore. Limiting enablements to a fixed number may sometimes make them valuable and so give an incentive to permit-holders to police their privileges themselves, for example by informing on illegal activity or 'cowboy' operations. Most of the examples that have been discussed so far are discrete or qualitative, like a certificate (either you get the token or you don't). But some government enablements are quantitative. They specify a quota or a point along a scale. A common example is the production quota, which allows a particular undertaking to do so much and no more. Such quotas are widely used in controlling farm produce, fishing catches, even land development, in those cases where official permission to develop is accompanied by a limit on the size of building that can be erected on any particular site (so-called 'plot ratios'). More recently, tradable emissions quotas as permissions to pollute the atmosphere up to a certain point and no more have been introduced with the aim of reducing overall pollution. Emission-trading systems have been introduced both at the international level (for example, the Kyoto protocol which entered into force in 2005 allows those of the 164 participating nations that emit less than their quota of greenhouse gases to sell emissions credits to polluting nations) and within nations or regions (for example, the US state of Illinois in 1997 adopted a trading programme for volatile organic compounds in most of the Chicago metropolitan area, a scheme later extended to 100 major sources of pollution in eight Illinois counties).

Most of the examples of enablements given here have been in the realm of business regulation. Of course, the device is used in many other contexts: for instance, the tokens which grant parole or bail to prisoners, or the tokens which entitle individuals to obtain money, goods or services from government or from some other source. Ration cards or old-age pension order books are examples of the latter; and the development of the modern 'welfare state' has been accompanied, as we will see in Chapter 4, by the heavy use of enablements of this kind.

Constraints The term 'constraints' stands, in a self-explanatory way, for the most constraining form of directed token. Constraints, in contrast to certificates, conditionals and enablements, positively demand or prohibit an activity.

Constraints can be negative or positive, sometimes both at the same time. Negative constraints are prohibitions laid on particular individuals or items. A well-known example is the 'cease and desist' order which the US Federal Trade Commission can apply to firms engaged in trade practices deemed to be 'unfair'. More drastically, in 2002, the government of Zimbabwe, acting under amendments to its controversial Land Acquisition Act, ordered 2,900 farmers to halt their operations and leave their farms (see *Daily News*, 26 June

2002). Though that example is extreme, it is by no means unique (see, for example, Self and Storing, 1962, p. 111).

Constraint, of course, is used extensively to maintain law and order in most societies. Virtually all governments use constraint in the endeavour to prevent or at least minimize murder, manslaughter, violence, drug-dealing, burglary, theft and a raft of other activities deemed to be against the law. Those individuals who engage in such activities are liable to experience a hard edge of governmental authority, through the police and judicial and prison systems, not usually felt by law-abiding citizens. Of course constraint in the form of authority will often need to be supplemented by other instruments, such as treasure or nodality for gathering information and organization to haul people off to gaol. But the application of directed tokens of authority usually forms an important part of the process.

The other side of the coin is the order that requires positive action. Governments in most countries require us to see that our children go to school. Government may call us up for military service or billet troops or evacuees in our households. It may order the slaughter of diseased livestock or the felling of trees affected by pests as happened in Ghana (then the Gold Coast) in 1947, a decade or so after the cocoa swollen shoot virus (CSSV) had first been officially identified in the country's cocoa farms. It may require the repair, demolition, sale or evacuation of specific buildings. It may issue compulsory cropping orders to raise the output of agricultural land, as happened in Britain in the Second World War. It may order us to undergo specific medical tests before we can get married, as applies in both parts of Cyprus at the time of writing in relation to the gene that causes thalassaemia, a serious inherited blood disease.

Indeed, government may sometimes choose to combine prohibitions and positive injunctions in a double-barrelled operation. For example, government may both order the broadcasting authorities to desist from transmitting specified material *and* require certain material of its own to be broadcast by them.

A variation on the theme is what may be called an 'arbitrament'. In this case, government uses its official authority to constrain against a background of conflict – or at least of potential conflict – between two or more parties. It sets itself up as an appeal court against the actions of other individuals, agencies or organizations. Arbitraments go back to royal involvement in quarrels between powerful barons. When the royal bureaucracy had grown larger, the device was in turn taken up by the king's servants, and it is still sometimes found today. For example, government arbitration in labour disputes was compulsory in Britain during the Second World War, when strikes were officially prohibited; and government arbitration of a compulsory type is found in numerous other states, including Singapore (which had not had a strike for twenty years at the time of writing), South Korea and Namibia.

Group-targeted tokens

The kinds of official tokens that have been discussed so far are all 'particular', in the sense that they apply to specific individuals, organizations or items. In the next section we will look at more general types; but before passing on to that it is worth noting very briefly that government sometimes chooses a halfway house between general and particular, using the medium of *groups* – just as applies to its other kinds of effecting tools.

For example, government often conduits its certificates and enablements through organized groups. In the days before 1994, when the UK had laws restricting trading on Sundays, traders certificated as bona fide Jews by the Jewish Board of Deputies were exempted from those laws (Alderman, 1982, pp. 99–104). Similarly, government may enable certain certificated groups to perform actions that others may not, such as the ability of certificated doctors to prescribe drugs or sign death certificates or lawyers to draw up wills or covenants. It may give voluntary organizations the authority to act for individuals applying for some benefit or allowance, as discussed in Chapter 2.

Similarly, government sometimes applies constraints to groups at least in a sense, though such constraints are more common in authoritarian states than in liberal democracies. Such constraint was approximated in Australia in the 2000s, when government prevented individuals on a registered list of sex offenders from travelling abroad as the phenomenon of 'sex tourism' became evident and available and some Asian countries were being advertised in some circles as places where underage sex was available. In the so-called pillarized societies associated with the 'consociational' approach to governance (Lijphart, 1968, 1977), where public services are organized by the various social groupings in a divided society, confessional or linguistic groups may also be treated as a unit in the use of public authority. Group-directed applications of conditional tokens are by no means uncommon, when governments offer threats or promises to use their authority in ways that depend on the behaviour of organized groups, for example in offering pro-labour measures in exchange for wage restraint by labour unions or wage controls if pay claims go above a certain level.

Blanketed tokens

Blanketed tokens are official tokens that are 'general', applying to the world at large or to whomever it may concern. Each of the 'targeted' types of token discussed earlier can be translated into a general or 'blanketed' form. A very brief discussion must suffice.

Certification in its general form can be termed *standard approval*. This denotes those tokens used by government to lend its authority to certify or approve, but without necessarily implying constraint or entitlement. There are two ways in which certification can be 'generalized'. One, the weaker sense, is to make certificates transferable, as applies in those cases where a certificate may be transferred on a change of ownership, as with roadworthiness certificates for cars and airworthiness certificates for aircraft.

The other way is for government to approve or lay down targets or codes of good behaviour – standards which are not legally binding but are self-consciously 'official'. An example is 'government time', the official measurement of time and its accompanying conventions such as putting clocks back and forward in autumn and spring in order to save daylight, as was adopted in many countries away from the equator in the twentieth century. No one forces us to use 'government time' in our own private affairs, but most of us do. Similarly, government may choose to issue codes of good conduct in matters such as driving behaviour or labour-management relations – codes which are not legally binding but which bear a heavy stamp of official approval (perhaps suitable for production as evidence in court). This kind of standard-setting takes us on to the interesting borderline territory between the token of official authority and the information-dispenser.

Open compacts The general form of the 'conditional' token may be termed an *open compact*. This is used by government to offer a bargain, not to specific individuals or groups, but to whomever the matter may concern.

A well-known example is the amnesty, a device that is used commonly enough for tax defaulters, for the illegal possession of weapons, and even for overdue library books. Traditionally, for example, all incoming French presidents with a majority in the French parliament have begun their reign with an amnesty for some petty crimes such as traffic offences, though this tradition of 'Republican amnesty' has become increasingly criticized as an invitation to lawlessness. An amnesty means a government guarantee that it will not try to punish anyone who declares past misdemeanours or hands in proscribed items. But amnesties are usually linked with threats of heavy penalties against future offenders, of course.

Indeed, the promise 'to pay the bearer on demand', quaintly preserved on British paper money even now, is a relic of an 'open compact', although it is an obsolete and empty one, as anyone who presents banknotes to one of the note-issuing banks (in the hope of obtaining gold in return) can discover.

Open permits Enablements in their general form might be termed *open permits*. Enablements, like certificates, can become generalized if they are transferable; and indeed many enablements that are particular in the sense that they apply to a named object, organization or animal may also be 'general' in the sense that they are transferable among people. Entitlement is then a matter of the document or of the number of government vouchers that you can produce, not of 'who you are'. Private sector equivalents are trading stamps, 'packet-top' offers and the like (as distinct from loyalty cards, which in principle are particular to the person holding the card).

Permits for land development, production quotas for agriculture and fisheries (such as milk quotas in the European Union or tradable fishing catch quotas introduced in New Zealand in 1986), permissions to drive in cities (such as Mexico) that depend on car registration numbers, and, increasingly, tradable emissions quotas are examples of permits that are open in the sense that they are transferable even if they begin as person- or firm-specific allocations. Even production quotas can sometimes take this form. For example, in the late 1920s any farmer who wished to start growing hops in Britain could only do so by buying the necessary tokens from other farmers who already held hop quotas (Self and Storing, 1962, p. 89). On occasion a lively market can develop in open permits, as with milk quotas on farms in the European Union.

Another application of open permits is to sanction activity which government normally forbids: for example, if government lifts its normal evening curfew for everyone on the occasion of a holiday or relaxes city car-parking restrictions during a train strike.

Standard constraints Constraints in their general form might be termed *standard constraints,* those compulsory edicts of government that apply to the world at large, or to whomever it may concern.

Like their 'directed' equivalents, standard constraints can be negative or positive. Examples of the negative variety are not hard to find. Governments often issue general prohibitions of certain products or activities, as did the EEC when it banned the import of leather treated with whale oil in 1982 or as did the late Saparmurat Niyazov, President-for-life of Turkmenistan, in his various bans between coming to power in 1991 and his death in 2006. Beards, video games, ballet and opera were some of the things banned by presidential decree at the time of writing (see http://en.wikipedia.org/wiki/saparmurat_Niyazov). Less dramatically, water authorities may forbid the use of hosepipes to water gardens or wash cars in times of drought. Fishing agencies may ban certain types of fishing or fishing equipment. Agricultural agencies may ban livestock movement in order to prevent the spread of animal disease. No named individual, of course, is involved in any such prohibitions, though there may be exemptions for named individuals.

Equally common are standard constraints from government which require action of a more positive kind. Government often sets standards, not in the non-mandatory 'standard approval' form, but by demanding that the standards be observed by anyone who wishes to undertake a certain activity. We may not be obliged to observe 'government time', but we are obliged to observe government's speed limits. Government may demand that all petrol be stored in containers of a certain type or material. It may demand that all houses be built of brick or stone. It may set minimum or maximum prices at which goods may be sold. It may even prescribe which side of the pavement pedestrians have to walk on, as traditionally applied in some German cities (to the amusement of J. K. Jerome (1998, p. 264).

Another application of standard constraints, touched upon in Chapter 2, is the requirement sometimes laid by government on those whom it may concern to transmit a message to the public, as a way of saving government from having to do the job itself. An example from the 1850s is the government requirement that limited liability companies add a word to their names (such as 'Inc.', 'Ltd', 'PLC', 'AG') to signify their status. Indeed this administrative invention was regarded by the British administrator Llewellyn

Smith (1928, pp. 165–6) as a masterstroke, since it conveyed a public warning at no cost to the government.

Since the nineteenth century, this application of standard constraints has been greatly extended, becoming almost a commonplace of government administration today. If we are learning to drive, we may be required to signify the fact to other road users. If we are an undischarged bankrupt, we may be required to signify the fact when obtaining credit. Tobacco companies almost everywhere are required to display government health warnings on cigarette packs and food manufacturers to display details of their products on the label. Advertisers of medicines may be required to include a 'data sheet' giving factual information about their medicines and at the time of writing much is being talked about imposing similar requirements on those selling food to display fat or calorie content, in the context of concerns about increasing obesity in Western countries. It costs government little to slap standard constraints of this type on to anything it chooses, since the compliance costs are in large part met by others. But of course those affected may complain of the compliance costs loaded on to them, at least in the kinds of regime where such concerns can be voiced.

The toolset in context

The catalogue set out here is only a rough and ready one, intended to show some of the broadly different ways in which government can deploy its 'authority' as an instrument. There are, of course, cases that do not fit neatly into one category or another. For example, is a passport to be interpreted as a certificate (of identity and nationality) or might it really be counted as an enablement? Strictly, only a visa might be held to amount to an enablement to enter or leave a specific country, where that is otherwise forbidden. But in practice international travel without passports is difficult even where it is not forbidden, and some governments (such as that of the former USSR) require passports to be used for internal travel. Or again, some purists might interpret a passport as a standard constraint – an order to let the bearer pass 'without let or hindrance', as the British passport 'requests and requires' of those whom it may concern.

Leaving the inevitable difficult cases aside, however, the final part of this chapter follows the pattern of the previous one in attempting to set government's tokens of authority into context.

Combinations, linkages and substitutions

It will be clear by now that even a small set of basic instruments can produce a large number of combinations. Like its other tools, government's tokens of authority are most commonly used in combination, not in isolation. They can be 'coupled up' in at least three ways.

One way is to combine official tokens in a simultaneous compound. For example, official permission to carry on some activity commonly derives, not from a single token, but from the combination of several different official tokens, all of which must be held at the same time. To operate a passenger vehicle, vessel or aircraft, government may require us to have an up-to-date certificate of road/sea/airworthiness, to possess a licence to operate over that particular route, and to employ operatives who have the specific qualifications required. Only when these tokens are added together is the relevant permission obtained.

Another way is to make the combination sequential rather than simultaneous, with government requiring one token to be produced before it will grant the next one. For instance, government commonly requires a certificate to be produced before it will grant an enablement. For example, you typically have to produce your birth certificate before government will give you a passport, or produce your car's roadworthiness certificate before government will give you a vehicle licence. Frequently the chain is longer than this (see Simon *et al.*, 1950, p. 472).

Third, just as tokens of government's authority may be linked with one another, they are everywhere linked with the other main types of government instrument discussed in this book. They 'key in' to the movement of money and physical operations by government. They are frequently linked up with government's information-dispensers and detectors. Roadside speed cameras involve a mix of authority and organization; and they are also a hybrid of detecting and effecting tools, as every driver knows when the line of traffic they are in all slams on the brakes at the sight of a camera. And government amnesties are often linked to large-scale propaganda campaigns. A different kind of example of chaining of instruments is the official procedure for winding up a dead person's estate in the common-law jurisdictions: before you can legally transfer a dead person's property, you need an enablement from government in the form of a certificate of probate (which itself must be preceded by production of a valid death certificate), and applications for such certificates automatically alert government's tax collection detectors to examine the estate.

It has been noted already in several places that government's instruments can sometimes be substituted for one another as well as combined; and the point applies to official tokens just as much as to government's other main types of instruments. For instance, standard approvals and standard constraints may often be substitutable to some extent. The same applies to certificates and enablements; and government may also have a degree of choice among directed, group-targeted or blanketed tokens in order to do a job. For example, if government wishes to restrict exports or imports, it might impose a general ban on certain types of products, or alternatively it might issue import licences or quotas (which themselves could be made either transferable or non-transferable).

Again, there may on occasion be scope for substitution or trading off between government's tokens of authority as a group and other kinds of government instruments. As we have seen, government can choose between using its own information-dispensers and using tokens of official authority to require others to put its message across. Similarly, there are often possibilities for substitution between tokens of authority and physical operations. Government may regulate business by a set of certificates, enablements and requirements, or it may decide to set up in business on its own account. It may forbid trespassing, or employ physical devices (walls, ditches, barbed wire) which make trespassing all but impossible. It may approach labour-management disputes by information-dispensing, that is, 'counselling', to find common ground between the parties, or by arbitraments which impose a binding solution.

Simon *et al.* (1950, p. 11) present a dramatic example of government using official tokens instead of other instruments. Inconvenienced by coal miners' strikes during the Second World War, the US government could have responded with a number of instruments, for example information or propaganda, money incentives, coercion or physical operation of the mines by government. Instead, it chose tokens of authority: an official 'seizure' of the mine. All that this seizure meant in practice was a formal declaration and the Stars and Stripes flying over each mine. But this pure exercise of authority, mixed a little with a 'broadcast' message, was sufficient to end the strike.

Tools of authority in the digital age

In one sense, technology makes no difference to authority as a resource held by government. For example, when government requires internet providers or mobile phone companies to keep records, the basic authority instrument is no different from obligations on innkeepers to keep a register of their guests as has been as required in many European countries from the eighteenth century at least. But digital technology has to some extent changed the tokens of authority that are used, and the relative ease with which government may issue them.

Digital technologies have changed the way government can requisition information, particularly the development of more sophisticated 'passive' methods such as 'obligation to display'. Some such obligations relate to the person, as in the case of the Bluewater Shopping Centre in Kent, England, which in the mid-2000s banned users from wearing baseball caps and hooded jackets which might obscure their faces from CCTV cameras (news.bbc.co.uk, 19 May 2005). The development of roadside cameras (and associated tax and driver-control regimes) can bring more demanding and technologically sophisticated 'obligations to display' for vehicles, as in Singapore where all cars must be fitted with an 'in-vehicle unit' to be picked up by road-pricing gantries located at all entrances to Singapore's central business district and along roads with heavy traffic.

The operation of 'obligation to notify' has also become more sophisticated in the digital age. First, in those countries where government can have reliable electronic records of all its citizens, governments can automatically 'know' when some event becomes due (such as a child reaching the age where school or military service is compulsory), rather than requiring individuals to come forward with the information. Second, it is only the fact that all organizations of a certain size maintain large amounts of information electronically that make obligation-to-notify data-sharing initiatives, such as the EU directive on interest-paying bank accounts noted above, possible to implement.

While the more passive methods of requisitioning information have been transformed in such ways, requisition at the active end of the spectrum seems to have changed less and indeed, it could be argued, to have become more challenging in the digital age. After all, the internet offers a major new forum for economic and social activity which is technically difficult to inspect even for the most well-resourced and ambitious of governments. And more efficient, digital methods of reducing some types of fraud have pushed 'cyber-criminals' to new levels of sophistication on the internet, often including major fraud on government's treasure and tokens of authority.

When it comes to using authority as an effecting tool in the digital age, we see new and cheaper ways of implementing group-targeted tokens, as for nodality. Certain categories of taxpayer or benefit claimant may be more easily identified electronically by some code on their record and automatically issued with a token, like an obligation to file or an obligation to supply additional information. Such notification may appear to be directed by some human intelligence because proper names appear on communications but in fact may have been carried out automatically in a 'zero touch' way, requiring far fewer resources than directed tokens.

As for nodality, therefore, we might expect to see a movement towards a mixture of the general (blanket tokens) and the specific (directed tokens). Take the example of the application of authority to road traffic, to which we have already referred. In the weakest form of direction, speed limit signs can light up as your car approaches at more than the prescribed maximum speed after crossing a cable in the road, replacing 'blanket' static road signs indicating a speed limit. In a stronger and more directed form, roadside cameras register your driving misdemeanours (such as speeding or jumping traffic lights) and automatically communicate with a system which imposes penalties on the registered owner of the car you are driving. In countries where photographs of the driver are taken (in addition to the registration number), the constraint is even more closely directed. The very specific tokens of the kind that were the main means of enforcement in many countries up to the 1980s, for example individual police officers measuring the speed of drivers, stopping them with sirens blaring, examining their papers and requiring them to present themselves to a police office on a subsequent date, have now been supplemented (and in some cases, replaced) by a range of these authority-based technologies. In effect, the same has happened to barriers and gates, with systems in which gates open or barriers sink in the ground when approached by vehicles carrying the appropriate transponder (ambulances, fire trucks, police cars, taxis) but block the way for everyone else.

There are several other ways that digital technologies may be used to target groups for 'special treatment' in the use of authority, both desirable and undesirable. For example, for over ten years the US Immigration and Naturalization Service has operated an automatic teller machine for frequent international travellers to insert an ID card, put their hands in a slot and (if recognized by the system) be cleared in thirty seconds, dispensing with normal security procedures. The system later became the 'blue lane' expedited services for those US-bound passengers who gave passport information to laptop-equipped airplane personnel for transmission via the internet to inspectors at the port of arrival (Koslowski, 2002, p. 20; Koslowski, 2005) and by 2005 had been upgraded to use biometric data. A perhaps less heart-warming example is the use of electronic devices to target groups of prisoners convicted of lesser offences in many countries, who can be released into the community from prison with an electronic tag that allows their whereabouts to be tracked and the conditions of their release strengthened or loosened. Such a device acts as a detector and effector rolled into one, collecting information about the prisoner but also acting as a kind of 'virtual' chain on their activities.

Tokens of authority: the wider social context

Finally, what factors may prompt government to use certain kinds of official tokens rather than others? Many factors, particularly culture, may affect such choices, for instance in opposition to compulsory identity cards in countries such as the USA, Australia and UK, in contrast to their acceptance in other countries such as Germany. However, only two shaping factors will be considered here, both of which have been used earlier. These are the size of the population involved and the degree of overall consensus or acceptance with which government operates.

Size of population As we have seen with other kinds of government effector, some forms of official token are likely to be more 'expensive' for government to use than others. The greater the particularity of any token, the more discriminately can government wield its authority; but at the same time the greater is the bureaucratic input involved. Rationing schemes that involve the allocation of individual vouchers or coupons, for example, are notorious for the staff time and effort they require on the part of government. Breyer (1982, p. 267) makes the same point for business regulation.

Hence, when the population involved is large, a government interested in limiting the load on its bureaucratic system must use directed tokens sparingly. It is likely to find itself having to balance the control advantages of directed tokens against the bureaucratic costs involved. Sometimes government may be able to lighten the load by decreasing the frequency with which directed tokens have to be renewed, for instance in extending the renewal interval of identity cards (as was done by the former West German government) or extending the renewal interval of driver licences (as the British government did in 1976 when it moved from three-year driving licences to licences that remained in force until the age of 70, unless the driver concerned was disqualified or suspected by a law court). (In Northern Ireland, fixed-term driving licences continued, though they were extended from three- to ten-year intervals after 1984).

Another way of lightening the load is the development of digital methods which ease the use of directed tokens, aided by new and less resource-intensive methods of requisition. Renewal of documents such as passports, identity cards and driving licences can be less resource-intensive for government online (although it does not necessarily reduce the time cost to individuals and may indeed greatly increase costs, stress and frustration for the latter). Electronic identity card schemes are generally linked to national registers which may then be used to facilitate the use of other directed tokens: the Belgian identity card, for example, allows a single sign-on to digital applications used by departments across local and central government. Digital technologies also offer another way of coping with the size problem for group-targeted tokens, particularly for those groups where internet penetration is very high, such as students or large businesses. However, size can matter even for centralized databases and at the time of writing even the more developed countries with larger populations (such as the UK, the USA and Japan) were less likely to have nationwide interlinked systems in operation for directed tokens.

Where digital methods are not available, the only way to lighten the load is to move away from directed tokens altogether. Government can sometimes do this by switching to group-directed or blanketed tokens. For example, in the USA general rules have long been laid down by government for income tax liability: individuals determine their own tax liability, and the government limits itself to a checking-up role. Up to 1996 the UK operated a different system whereby individuals were obliged only to supply information about their finances to government, which government then had to transform into a directed token in the form of an individual tax assessment signifying the sum for which each taxpayer is liable. The tax bureaucracy groaned under this burden, and government lightened its load (while correspondingly increasing that of taxpayers, of course) by switching over to a variant of the US system in 1996.

Given the continual pressure on government to apply its tokens of authority to ever-new contexts, government must rely in large part on general standards and 'codes of conduct' agreed with groups, if it is not to be swamped by issuing avalanches of individual licences, certificates, orders, prohibitions, and so on.

Of course, there are occasions when governments may prefer blanketed to directed tokens for reasons quite other than that of economy. Sometimes the attraction of blanketed tokens lies precisely in the fact that they afford less discriminatory control while giving the appearance of government activity and concern. For example, as part of an EEC system of economic sanctions against Iran in 1980, the British government banned any 'new' contracts for British exports to Iran, except under licence. But exporters *themselves* were invited to determine what constituted 'existing' trade contracts with Iran, which were therefore not subject to the general ban. This was described as an 'honesty' system, although 'dishonesty' might be closer to the mark, as so often applies to trade-sanction regimes agreed in international conclaves.

Consensus What is likely to be the effect of the overall degree of consensus, or satisfaction with government on the part of individuals, on the use of official tokens by government? In general, it may be supposed that as consensus falls, government may find itself moving from certification through conditional tokens and enablements to constraints.

When government is widely respected and accepted, the mere lending of its name to some individual, item or activity in the form of certification or standard approval may well be all that is needed to influence individuals. In such circumstances, it might be wasteful and unnecessary to use other types of tokens. Where consensus is low, however, government certificates and declarations may not merely decline in their efficacy; they may come to have a negative value, being seen as badges of shame rather than of glory. A mild case of this process occurred in the United Kingdom in 1966, when the government chose to bestow medals on the Beatles, then a controversial pop group, causing a number of war heroes and other traditionally minded individuals to send their hard-won medals back to the government in disgust.

Even conditionals and enablements may start to falter at some point of low consensus. The power of conditionals will wane as the promises and threats of a government perceived to be shaky or untrustworthy decline in authority. Offers from government may become increasingly refusable. Its amnesties may be ignored. Even its currency, as a general guarantee of exchange value, depends for its operation on a climate of general confidence in government. When foreign currency becomes the chief medium of exchange in a country – as happened in Argentina in the early 1990s, when the US dollar started to replace the austral – something has gone very wrong with this type of token.

As consensus declines, government's enablements are also likely to come under pressure, making it difficult to enforce the prohibition on those without enablements. The limited-edition type of licence or franchise system (such as applies to oil-drilling sites or broadcasting channels) may come to look attractive to a government under pressure, since such devices are to some degree self-policing. But even if that continues to apply *in extremis* (which is unlikely), a government which puts too much weight on this device may lose control over what is being done in its name.

Hence, as consensus declines, government has to put increasing weight on its most 'constraining' applications of authority, namely orders and prohibitions. The situation may start to approximate to that described in the grim joke about liberty under Italian Fascism: 'everything that isn't forbidden is compulsory' (Larsen, 1980, p. 54). For example, the orders compelling the destruction of cocoa trees affected by the CSSV in what is now Ghana between 1947 and 1962, as mentioned earlier, followed unsuccessful attempts to use less constraining forms of authority. There is perhaps a parallel with a hard-pressed superordinate who is finally obliged to tell a rebellious subordinate to 'do *x*, and that's an order'. But it is precisely at that point that the superordinate's authority is really 'on the line'. If the order is not respected, what happens next?

Clearly there is more than one possibility, as everyone whose orders to a child have at some time been ignored will at once realize. One thing that *may* happen is that at that point the difference between constraints and conditionals or open compacts starts to disappear as happened in the attempts of the beleaguered Nepalese monarchical regime to contain dissent in 2005. If our order has failed to have any effect, we may switch to bargaining, to the extent that we are left with any authority at all. If government orders a rebellious crowd to disperse and nothing happens, it may offer an amnesty instead. It may try to do deals with influential groups. But at the point when orders are merely a prelude to bargaining, government may be on very thin ice. Its tokens are becoming 'tokens of no authority'.

Alternatively, of course, the flouting of a constraint may cause government to switch away from 'authority' in any form to other kinds of effecting tools, such as information and persuasion or physical action. Indeed, to revert to the Ghanaian swollen-shoot disease example, the government orders to destroy the diseased trees in practice only became effective when government itself cut the trees down, and when the Ghanaian government attempted to revert to pure authority tools after 1962 (merely requiring farmers to destroy diseased trees), farmers ignored that requirement (see Olennu *et al.* (1989), p. 9).

Conclusion

Government's requisitions and tokens of authority are ubiquitous, appearing in everything from tax collection to farm subsidies, and constantly being applied to new contexts, as some of the examples in this chapter have shown. At least in their 'constraining' form, they reveal government at its most government-like, deploying its distinctive resources of legal or official authority.

But the concluding discussion of the decline in the standing of a government *in extremis* reverts to the point made at the beginning of this chapter: that government's tokens are 'no more' than self-proclaimedly authoritative pieces of paper or statements. If obedience or compliance is not automatic or readily forthcoming, the difference between betokening authority and dispensing information starts to disappear. Government's tokens are just so many pieces of paper. You might as well paper your walls with them. Some people did just that with the German banknotes that were produced by the Weimar government in the hyperinflation of the 1920s. To make its official tokens 'stick', government may have to use other kinds of effecting tools, such as financial incentives, as discussed in the next chapter. Ultimately, it will have to turn to 'direct action' tools, which are discussed in Chapter 5.

Chapter 4

Treasure

> Thus much of this will make black white, foul fair,
> Wrong right, base noble, old young, coward valiant.
> . . . Why, this
> Will lug your priests and servants from your sides,
> Pluck stout men's pillows from below their heads:
> This yellow slave
> Will knit and break religions, bless the accursed,
> Make the hoar leprosy adored, place thieves
> And give them title, knee and approbation
>
> (Shakespeare, *Timon of Athens,* Act IV, Scene iii; substantially the same passage is quoted by Marx and Engels, 1968, pp. 262–3)

After 'nodality' and 'authority', a third basic resource of government is 'treasure'. As was explained in Chapter 1, this term denotes government's stock of 'fungible chattels', in the sense of anything that can be freely exchanged. We use the term to denote whatever positive incentives or inducements government can use to secure information or change behaviour. Some of that involves treasure in the literal and traditional sense of bullion or banknotes, but there are other more subtle applications.

Of course, almost anything can be exchanged in some circumstances, and thus 'treasure' certainly overlaps at the margin with other resources of government that can be used for trade or exchange – such as official licences or certificates, pieces of information, titles and honours or anything else in the gift of government that is 'as good as money in the bank' to someone or other. But the discussion in this chapter is limited to what is *freely* exchangeable – monies or money-like substances.

The reader needs no lengthy demonstration of the power of 'treasure' in the hand of government, and so this chapter is fairly short. The official pen can sometimes be as mighty as the sword, especially when it is signing cheques or activating their digital-age equivalents. Treasure is what enables government to exchange, to buy favours, to court popularity, to hire mercenaries (see Lasswell and Kaplan, 1950, pp. 90–1) so it is not surprising that the power of treasure, dramatized in the epigraph to this chapter, is so often remarked upon. F. P. Dunne's Mr Dooley famously observed, 'The

American nation is a fine people . . . They love th' eagle . . . on th' back iv a dollar' (Dunne, 1899, p. 222), and that is hardly a distinctively American trait.

Governments have found it worthwhile to amass treasure since early times, and using treasure is an everyday feature of modern government. Government's dollars, euros and the rest find their way into almost every domain of our lives, and in many countries literally from the cradle to the grave: from the maternity benefits that may precede our birth to the death benefits that may come after our death. Nearly thirty years ago Richard Rose and Guy Peters (1978, ch. 3, pp. 65–85) showed that in Western countries almost everyone got his or her spoon into government's financial gravy at some point in their lives and at the time of writing it was probably no coincidence that the percentage of households that were in receipt of state benefits in Britain was uncannily close to the percentage of votes needed for a single party to win government outright.

The form of those payments can vary widely in detail. For example, governments across the world use treasure in a wide range of 'population policies' designed to raise or control birth rates. In Singapore at the time of writing families who have a second child within marriage before the age of 28 or a third or fourth child after that age receive a S$20,000 tax rebate. In France child benefit has traditionally been paid only after the second child was born (and in 2005 a new grant was offered for a third baby), while in other countries government child benefits have started with the first child. Nordic countries offer high quality childcare and extensive parental leave – rather than cash incentives – to create an environment 'conducive to higher fertility', while in Japan the government has used sponsored dating games and hiking trips and cruises for single people to encourage marriage and reproduction (Dixon and Margo, 2006).

Nor does the use of treasure end with welfare payments or subsidies to singles events. In most countries, government is by far the biggest single purchaser in the society. Much of what it buys comprises items that are not distinctive to government (such as timber, computers, boots or even currencies) but some of its purchases are government-specific (such as traffic lights, space rockets and warships). Murray Weidenbaum (1969, pp. 11, 35) has shown that purchases of goods and services from the private sector overtook wage payments to its own employees as the largest single category in the US federal government's budget after the Second World War, and that by the 1960s the federal government was buying over three and a half million separate items. Thirty years later, the federal government employed 142,000 workers dedicated to procurement, spending £200 billion annually and recording 20 million contract actions every year (Gore, 1994; Margetts, 1997, p. 55).

There are many other ways in which government can put its money to work. It may offer grants or concessionary rate loans for many purposes: for example, for moving a business to a certain favoured area, for starting up businesses (or closing them down, as with grants for scrapping fishing boats), or for environmental improvements. It may offer subsidies: for example, on exports, on agricultural produce, on fuel for favoured users such as farmers or fishermen. It may offer free bicycles and helmets to students to incentivize attendance and study, as has been tried in a number of US universities and summer schools. It may offer payments of a more venal or less mentionable kind: for example, a generation ago Harold Stockwell (1978, p. 246) observed that 'The US government, through the CIA, disburses tens of millions of dollars each year in cash bribes.' Treasure, in short, is often government's policy instrument of choice.

This chapter looks first at how government uses treasure as a detecting tool. In what ways can rewards be used to buy information? In the second section we briefly review some of the ways in which government can use its treasure as an instrument to try to influence the world outside, distinguishing general from particular applications of this instrument in the same way that we did for nodality and authority. Then we try to set 'money-moving' in a wider context.

Detecting with treasure: rewards

The term 'rewards' denotes information which government 'buys', offering some positive incentive. Often such incentives involve the use of government's 'treasure' in a strict sense, but rewards for information may be in forms other than straightforward cash payment.

Unsolicited propositions

As with the case of nodal receivers or requisitions, discussed in the previous two chapters, government may obtain information in exchange for reward in more than one way. The most passive mode is for government to wait to be approached by individuals or organizations offering information for a quid pro quo, as happens in those cases where 'supergrasses' or officials of potentially hostile governments offer to defect or to sell secrets in exchange for political asylum or other rewards. Inventors may offer to sell inventions to governments where they are likely to be of use only to public organizations. Computer services companies regularly lobby governments with new applications and hardware that they claim to be particularly suitable for public services. This type of transaction may be termed the *unsolicited proposition.* It differs from the unsolicited tender in that information is spontaneously offered to government, but only on condition that some 'price' is paid.

Advertised rewards and application

Somewhat less passive, and roughly corresponding to the 'ear trumpet' type of nodal receiver, is the case where government obtains information for reward by means roughly analogous to those used by mail-order firms and their digital-age equivalents on the internet – that is, by offering its wares and waiting for a response.

There are at least two forms of this approach. Government can use the straightforward device of *advertised rewards* for information. The term is self-explanatory, and the obvious case is the stereotypical 'wanted dead or alive' wall poster advertising a reward for information leading to the capture of criminals or outlaws, as in the Wild West. For example, in 2005 the Russian security services announced that it had paid an unprecedented $10 million to informers who helped track down a Chechen rebel leader (Aslan Maskhadov) and offered an identical prize for information leading to the capture of another Chechen rebel, Shamil Basayev (*The Associated Press*, 16 March 2005). Paid tax informers and other types of paid informers play a quantitatively small but qualitatively very important part in many types of government information-gathering, going all the way from informers on crime or welfare fraud to the sort of information that comes from paid subjects in government experiments. In some cases, of course, the 'payment' may be in a form more exotic than cash alone, as in the case of spies who are compensated with new homes, identities and positions in another country to protect them from reprisal. Indeed, in 2005 the Russian security services added plastic surgery to the

$10 million reward for informers leading to the capture of Shamil Basayev, as mentioned above.

A second device for drawing in information by publishing rewards is rather less direct. In this case information is obtained as a by-product, in that the bait being dangled or being sought is not specifically presented as a reward for information. This type of information is what government gleans from a variety of *applications*.

Information derived from applications is, of course, a commonplace in government, and it comes in many forms. To gain entrance to a country or to some particular government facility (such as an airport or a high-security prison or even, with the increasing ease of digital photography, a civilian department) government may photograph you as a condition of allowing entry. In extreme cases, government may require other kinds of information, including tests of your HIV status in some countries. If you wish to apply for a patent from government, you must produce extensive plans and drawings. If you are applying for welfare benefits from government you may be required in exchange to answer a battery of questions on everything from your educational qualifications to your sex life. In the 1970s the British government learned a great deal about the incidence of child handicap (a subject on which it was highly ignorant) by offering money to the families of disabled children and analysing the characteristics of those who applied (Bradshaw, 1980).

Indeed, whenever government disburses its treasure as 'contracts' or 'transfers', it typically requires the prospective recipient to supply information to establish qualification or eligibility. Government seldom gives out money 'with no questions asked', thus denying itself the possibility of obtaining information as a by-product. But such applications can, of course, be of varying spontaneity. The more government begins to prompt, with widespread advertising of the benefits that can be applied for and the like, the less passive the process becomes.

Information exchange and active propositions

A subtype of the use of reward for obtaining information, falling somewhere on the boundary of passive and active (and indeed of information-dispensers and detectors), is the *information exchange*. In this case, the sole reward for supplying information lies in access to the pool of data which is created by a number of individuals or organizations acting in this way for mutual benefit. The classic case of such an exchange, of course, is the marriage bureau or dating agency – normally a private sector activity, although the Singapore government has operated a form of dating agency for graduates since the 1980s, as a result of its concerns about the low incidence of female graduates in the island-state who were getting married and having children, and of a steep decline in population growth (*Wall Street Journal*, 1 February 2003). In the more conventional government sphere, the labour exchange or job placement agency is a somewhat similar device, to the extent (rather limited in practice) that it is a voluntary pool of information created by potential sellers and buyers of labour. A 'purer' type of this kind of information exchange is facilitated with digital technologies, on 'job search' websites where employers post jobs and employees post their resumés or curricula vitae. In Australia even by 1999 such a service was one of the most used websites in the country, while more recently the site EURES was claimed to aid job mobility across Europe, to the concern of some newer Eastern European states fearing that they would lose substantial numbers from their younger workforce. The pure information exchange is a rare tool in government, but approximations to it are not unknown and may be becoming more widespread.

Rewards as detecting tools become more active when it is government that approaches potential informants proffering gifts rather than vice versa. The analogy shifts from the mail-order house to the doorstep salesperson. The *active proposition* by government corresponds to the 'direct inquiry' mode in nodal receivers, except that in the latter case citizens are neither required to answer the questions nor rewarded for doing so. Direct inquiries rely for their effect on the informant's good nature, sense of self-importance, malice or hatred. When it uses active propositions, government is appealing to the informant's self-interest in a more straightforward way.

The term 'propositioning' has connotations of sexual advances in colloquial English, but it is here intended to be neutral and does not necessarily imply any kind of impropriety. Propositioning can take perfectly respectable and conventional forms, as normally applies when government seeks out particular individuals or organizations to offer rewards for consultancy or expert information. Even professors in their ivory towers have been known to be approached for information by government in this way. Of course, there *are* 'exotic' forms as well. Government may use sexual lures to obtain information, especially from foreign embassy staff (so-called 'swallows' in the argot of spooks and the intelligence world, as in the case of attractive hotel 'chambermaids' who were agents of the KGB in the days of the USSR, Cuban counter-intelligence prostitutes, and so on). All sorts of other rewards may be proffered in the cloak-and-dagger world of spies and defectors. Like the information exchange, active propositioning is not all that common in the whole range of government detectors, although it can be very important in some cases.

A more common way of government detecting with treasure is through opinion poll surveys, focus groups and even citizens' juries, where governments pay market research companies to find out what citizens think or how they act. In Britain the incoming New Labour government of 1997 paid the polling company MORI to set up a giant focus group of more than 5,000 people, grandiloquently labelled the 'People's Panel', purportedly to feed public opinion into public policy, at an average annual cost of £4.4 million from 1998 to 2001 (House of Commons, *Hansard Written Answers*, 20 Jul 2001, pt 1). As new Labour's long honeymoon came to an end, the People's Panel was replaced in 2003 by a so-called 'Big Conversation', a much cheaper exercise based around a website where citizens were asked to submit comments on a number of policy questions.

For eliciting information, treasure is a tool that government shares with other organizations, even if it puts the tool to government-specific purposes, such as bribes in exchange for the military secrets of other governments. But in circumstances where other basic resources of government, such as authority or nodality, do not secure key information, government will have to put more reliance on treasure for that purpose. And treasure often comes to be mixed with other types of detectors, for instance where a prize draw is combined with authority to sweeten the process. But as with authority, treasure reaches its limits as a detector just at the point where government's other tools have limited effectiveness, where the numbers who need to be paid to furnish any information start to get out of line with finite resources available, or where rival pressures make even lottery-win-type rewards ineffective. Such was the case with the $25 million the US government offered for information leading to the capture of Osama bin Laden in 2001, or the nearly £4 million (over US$7 million) at today's prices the British government offered for the information leading to the capture of Prince Charles Edward Stuart in 1746, both of which remained, at the time of writing, unclaimed. The same applies to treasure as an effecting tool, to which we now turn.

Effecting with treasure: from customized to open payments

When it comes to shaping behaviour as opposed to gaining information, government can use its treasure in two main ways. It can exchange it for some good or service. Or it can 'give it away', without requiring any further quid pro quo (or promise of such), to those whom it considers deserving, whose favours it wishes to buy, or who meet stipulated eligibility criteria. These uses can be hard to separate at the margin, and some specific methods for conveying treasure – grants and loans, for example – can be used in either way.

Similarly, government can give away its treasure in a highly particularized way – where the identity of the specific payee is crucial – or in a general way, where payment is made to those whom it may concern, with identity not of the essence. 'Particularizing' can also relate in some cases to the degree to which the manner of payment is one-off or specially contrived, even where the identity of the payee is not actually known – as in the extreme case where an (anonymous) blackmailer or kidnapper requires us to leave the money demanded in the form of used banknotes of stipulated denominations in a certain telephone box or hollow tree.

Customized payments

'Particular' forms of conveying treasure can be termed *customized payments,* and some such payments are indeed not far from the blackmailer or kidnapper example, in that they have to be elaborately tailored to the circumstances of a particular individual. As has been dramatized in many crime and thriller movies, government often needs to use precisely such methods for handing over money demanded by hijackers or terrorists in return for the release of hostages. It occasionally chooses to disburse treasure by elaborate ceremonies, by which payment is made in a special and formalized manner. For example, in 1981 US President Reagan personally presented a specially made outsize federal government cheque for $85 million to Mayor Koch of New York City, and variants of this approach are often used by attention-grabbing politicians in search of photo opportunities. And there are less dramatic circumstances in which government payments may have to be highly 'particularized', for example if police give 'first aid' money to cover the immediate needs of a person who has been robbed in the middle of the night.

Contracts The term 'contracts' can serve to denote payments that are customized or particular in the sense that they are paid to some specific individual or organization, and at the same time conditional in that they are made in exchange for some direct quid pro quo, the recipient being required to supply, produce or promise something. Sometimes the quid pro quo required may be a promise *not* to produce – a device that was satirized by Joseph Heller in his famous novel *Catch-22* and later become widely used in the EU as well as the USA:

> The government paid him well for every bushel of alfalfa he did not grow. The more alfalfa he did not grow, the more money the government gave him, and he spent every penny he didn't earn on new land to increase the amount of alfalfa he did not produce. (Heller, 1969, p. 94)

Government constantly uses contracts to shape behaviour for purposes both trivial and grave. As has already been mentioned, it is a buyer, lender and grant-giver on a huge scale. It uses contracts to encourage citizens both to do things that they may already be predisposed to do (such as improving their houses or upgrading their skills) and to do things that they would not otherwise dream of doing in the absence of government offers of payment (such as processing nuclear waste). And traditionally government has often used contracts to 'distance' itself from operations in which it does not wish to appear too closely involved. For example, a generation ago Stockwell (1978, p. 56) described how private air charter firms were used to transport stocks of foreign weapons to groups overseas in cases where the US government wished to mask its presence, and commented, 'even tighter security can be obtained by contracting with international dealers who will purchase arms in Europe and subcontract independently to have them flown into the target area'. A generation before that (though in a book that did not appear until 2002, having been blocked for publication by the British government since 1947), Mackenzie had written about the use of contracts in a similar way in the 1940s. And at the time of writing in 2006, the US Central Intelligence Agency (CIA) was accused of using private aircraft firms and front companies secretly to transfer terror suspects in violation of international law. The international human rights organization Amnesty International claimed to have records of nearly 1,000 flights where private organizations had been used to preserve the secrecy of 'extraordinary rendition' flights, most using European airspace (*Agence France Presse*, 5 April 2006).

The term 'contracts' is used here as a generic word to cover all payments made to a specific payee and with strings attached. Payments that are termed *grants* or *loans* would be included to the extent that government, in making such payments, requires conditions to be met, rather than offering a free gift or a no-strings loan. Indeed, it is rarely otherwise. Governments typically attach conditions to such payments to prevent recipients from relending their money in the open market and pocketing the profit, or from putting it to some other purpose not desired by government.

The quid pro quo for contracts can be substantive or procedural, and sometimes both. A common example of procedural conditions is the 'matching' requirement that the borrower or grantee finds a proportion of the money required for a certain project from his or her own resources or from some other source. The matching of other people's money with its own is widely used in government as a device for ensuring that the borrower or grantee has an incentive to avoid wasting money or to ensure that the project seems sensible to scrutineers from another money-providing source and is under surveillance from another quarter. A recent example is that of 'city academies', independent schools in disadvantaged areas of England for which sponsors from business, faith or voluntary groups provided 20 per cent of the initial capital costs (up to £2 million) to set them up and the government provided the remainder.

Of course, this tactic is by no means unique to government. Insurance companies work on exactly the same basis when they use excess clauses to require us to bear a part of any loss out of our own resources, to prevent carelessness and trivial claims. So do banks and other lenders when they require borrowers to have a personal financial stake in projects for which they seek a loan.

Naturally, the device has its limitations. There is the obvious likelihood of greater delay when such conditions are imposed, and of deadlock too, in that some projects may never be undertaken if government insists on a matching formula. Even if they are undertaken, there is no absolute guarantee against waste. For example, the contributions that the British government required from local landowners when it financed road- and bridge-building in the Scottish highlands in the early nineteenth century did not prevent conspicuous waste and failure, owing to the incompetence of the contractors in many cases (Haldane, 1962).

Transfers The other main way in which government gives its treasure to particular individuals is via what may be called *transfers*. When it uses transfers, government is not exchanging its treasure for a direct quid pro quo. In that sense, transfers are 'gifts'. They are made to people with whom government wants to curry favour (such as visiting heads of state) or to whom it is pledged to make payments (such as widows or the chronic sick). Sometimes they are used for more exotic 'slush fund' purposes, as in the case of money covertly paid by governments to organizations sympathetic to their aims. A famous – or notorious – example is the extensive military aid and other assistance (such as food and clothing) channelled to the Nicaraguan Contras by the US federal government during the 1980s in support of their fight against the Sandinista government which was itself aided by military assistance from the Soviet Union. Perhaps a less well-known case was the (then) secret US government funds channelled by the CIA after the Second World War into academic journals favoured by policy-makers in Washington and into organizations such as the Congress of Cultural Freedom and the National Student Association (see Colby and Forbath, 1978).

Transfers in this sense are not only 'unconditional'. They are also particular, in the sense that they are made one by one and that the identity of the particular person or organization with which government is dealing is of the essence. Government will not engage in these transactions with just anyone. At the least the payee will typically need a proof of identity of some kind (from a scribbled signature to full-on biometric identifiers) and in some cases the payment may be very much more particular than that.

Transfers are, of course, one of the commonest instruments of government. The modern era of government money payments to millions of individuals – such as pensions and welfare benefits – makes heavy demands on government's ability both to amass treasure and to disburse it effectively to the intended recipients, without losing too much to fraud or simple mistakes. The numbers involved typically require government to 'departicularize' the process of individual payment as far as it can, so that each transaction fits into an assembly line of similar transactions. Typically, just as banks and private firms use a variety of credit card schemes for clients to obtain cash and goods, government equips individual payees with tokens of entitlement (as was discussed in the previous chapter), from the traditional style of warrants and order books with tear-off slips to be presented to a cashier in exchange for payment to the modern era of smart cards and electronic fund transfers.

Naturally, there is a narrow line in practice between contracts and transfers. For example, the payments made as part of so-called 'population policies' which were noted above are not 'contracts' to produce children in the same sense as contracts to produce military supplies, but merely gifts as of right to those specific individuals who have produced children. But at the margin the distinction between the two types of payment becomes fuzzy, and their effects may be similar – just as payments to 'encourage' sympathetic guerilla groups may shade into the hiring of mercenaries, an allegation sometimes made against elements of Reagan's programme of military assistance to the Nicaraguan Contras during the 1980s.

Conduits

Conduits are ways of distributing treasure somewhat less particularized than the forms that have just been outlined. Conduits employ intermediaries to move treasure to its final recipient. They can be used both for exchanges and for 'unconditional' payments.

Just as we saw with group-directed methods of disseminating information in Chapter 2, the use of individuals or organizations as wholesalers in the movement of money is far from uncommon as a device of government. In taxation, the principle is very old, going back to the days when governments 'farmed' taxes, using outside contractors to collect tax payments from individuals and to hand over the proceeds to government in a lump sum. In a slightly different form the conduit principle is still widely used in taxation, with government using companies and organizations as the channel for collecting income taxes, social security taxes, sales taxes, oil taxes and so on. Its extension to paying out government money is perhaps inevitable in the modern context of credit card government and global IT corporations.

Government often finds it convenient to conduit payments in circumstances when, for good or bad reasons, it wants to avoid getting too closely involved in the decisions of how much to pay to whom. Hence many governments choose to conduit grants to individual scientists and artists through intermediary organizations in order to avoid close entanglement in what can be politically embarrassing questions of scientific or artistic merit. The same principle has been applied in Britain to the making of discretionary payments to assist asylum-seekers to mount legal challenges to deportation decisions, or to families of handicapped children, involving delicate case decisions (Bradshaw, 1980).

Conduiting of this kind is used for a range of other government payments through intermediary bodies. For instance, governments may decide to conduit compensation payments to farmers for bad-weather losses through farmers' associations or to conduit disaster-relief payments of other kinds. Governments will often channel aid to regions affected by natural disasters through aid organizations, particularly when local political conditions or widespread corruption mean that 'government-to-government' aid may not reach populations it is intended to help, as was the case in Indonesia after the tsunami of December 2004. They may decide to channel investment funds to companies through venture capitalists, as in the case of an 'Anglo-American Venture Fund' set up by the British government in 1980.

In some cases, of course, intermediaries spring up quasi-spontaneously as professional negotiators and agents, helping (at a price, of course) the lay public to get their hands on a basketful of government grants and loans with the minimum of vexation. Tax consultants and even 'ambulance-chasing' lawyers encouraging injured parties to sue for compensation are intermediaries of this kind. Although this is not quite 'wholesaling' in the same sense as the examples given above, it may come to approximate to it, and may indeed simplify the process of disbursal for government as well as the public at large.

In yet other cases, as has already been mentioned in the case of contracts, government may choose to work through intermediaries as a way of 'laundering' money payments that it wishes to conceal. For example, William Colby, a former director of the US CIA, whom we have quoted earlier, described how, in the CIA's operations in Italy in the 1950s, heavy use was made of secret funds channelled through intermediaries so as to conceal the source of the money from the world at large and even from the final payees themselves. As a case in point, he recalls that, during elections in 1955, 'I was authorized to fill the back seat of my Fiat with millions of lire and pass them on through my outside agent, an ostensible student' (Colby and Forbath, 1978, p. 125). And from the presidency of Charles de Gaulle until its privatization in 1994, the French oil company Elf Acquitaine is said to have acted as a secret arm of French government policy in paying sweeteners to foster relations with governments in francophone Africa (Global Policy Forum, 13 March 2003).

Open payments

The term 'open payments' is here used to refer to those cases where government hands over its treasure without much concern about the identity of those whom it is paying. This applies, for example, when treasure is used for casual purchases (without identifying the 'contracting parties') or in those publicity stunts when money is given away in the street to randomly selected individuals. One example might be the 'food drops' that are made to disaster-torn regions inaccessible to more systematic and equitable forms of aid distribution. Another is the introduction of free bicycles in cities, such as Copenhagen in Denmark or a number of US towns such as Denver.

Needless to say, government rarely disburses its treasure in this literal form. But it does on occasion make payments that are not tailor-made to the payee. The process is in some ways like a slot machine. You may, of course, press the buttons in such a way as to make a 'personal' selection, but the machine is designed to serve anyone who has the right coins or tokens.

Bounties The term 'bounty' is taken to denote a payment made in exchange for some direct quid pro quo, but which is open-ended in that the individual or organization which is to provide that quid pro quo is not specified. Anyone who produces the required goods or services gets the 'bounty'. An example is the reward that government may offer to anyone who hands over a certain criminal or outlaw (in contrast to the 'contract' approach of paying a particular person to do the job).

Government can pay bounties for many different purposes: for example, to encourage activities such as catching fish, growing crops or killing pests. Often it turns out that payments of this kind, precisely by their open-ended character, can influence the behaviour of government's subjects in ways that are not intended – a problem classically analysed in 1776 by Adam Smith (1910, vol. 2, pp. 18–20) in relation to the eighteenth-century British herring subsidies.

A more recent case of the same phenomenon can be taken from the period after the First World War, when the French government tried to support its ailing fleet of merchant sailing vessels by offering a subsidy for every nautical mile travelled by French sailing ships. The result was the temporary transfer of a large part of the world's merchant sailing fleet to the French flag, and the collapse of the subsidy scheme under the load. This is, of course, a story that is constantly being repeated in one form or another.

'Bearer-directed' payments The somewhat cumbersome term 'bearer-directed payments' must serve, in the absence of a better label, to describe the 'generalized' version of payments that do not involve an immediate quid pro quo, but are rather a consequence of eligibility of some kind. The bearer bond is, of course, the classic case of this kind of payment (hence the name used here). This type of payment features in innumerable thrillers, as for example in Dan Brown's 2003 best-seller *The Da Vinci Code* (Brown 2003, p.238) in which one of the key characters carries a suitcase full of large denomination bearer bonds drawn on the Vatican bank and negotiable as cash by whoever was holding them. But any kind of potentially transferable right to payment can operate in a similar way. For example, government will automatically pay us the prize when we produce the lottery ticket with the winning number on it. 'Who we are' is not especially important in such a case (which is why used lottery tickets are often used by criminals and racketeers to launder money). The payment might well be made by slot machines or computers if that were practicable.

The advantage of the bearer-directed payment is that it requires minimal discrimination on the part of government at the point of payment. Indeed, as has already been noted, many of government's welfare state payments operate like this at the point where money actually changes hands. This is done by concentrating the 'particular' part of the process on the issue of official tokens, such as food stamps and vouchers, which then serve as 'coins'. Such tokens have the added advantage that recipients can be given a choice of suppliers but are restricted to a specified range of goods and services. Both vouchers and stamps are used extensively in the US welfare system, particularly for housing (housing subsidy recipients can use vouchers to rent a unit even outside the jurisdiction of a local housing authority) and food (at the time of writing, the food stamp programme served about one in ten Americans with an annual cost of around $25 million; each food stamp had a set monetary value and could be used in some 215,000 different food outlets). Despite the enthusiasm of their proponents, however, vouchers can lead to an increase in demand, engendering rising caseloads and programme costs, while fraud has always been an issue with food stamps – recipients can sell stamps on the black market and claim they have been stolen, while vendors have an incentive to accept vouchers for unauthorized items (Hall and Eggers, 1995).

The toolset in context

At the end of the last chapter, we saw how, by mixing the tools up, a wide range of possible combinations could be produced; and how the tools could on occasion be substituted for each other and for other classes of effector. We considered how governmental use of authority had changed in the digital age. And we explored some of the possible circumstances that serve to shift government's emphasis from one kind of tool to another. Exactly the same questions can be asked for treasure.

Combinations and substitutions As we saw for information-dispensing in Chapter 2, government can link together its different ways of dispensing treasure, meaning there are many combinational possibilities. For example, in the days before overfishing was widely perceived as a major policy problem, government might seek to assist fishermen by a mixture of bounties (for every unit weight of fish caught) and contracts (loans or grants to individuals for building or improving boats) as well as other non-financial measures such as rescue services and weather forecasting. Typically it assists the unemployed by a mixture of transfers (welfare payments to individuals), contracts (grants to organizations promoting schemes for temporary employment and grants to students aiming to upgrade their skills, as with the British government's ill-fated 'Individual Learning Accounts' scheme of the early 2000s), and perhaps also conduits (grants to 'talent-spotting' intermediaries).

Government can also *substitute* one method of dispensing treasure for another, or indeed substitute money-moving as a whole for other kinds of effectors. An example of the former is the substitution of conduits for customized payments, for example in channelling international aid payments through non-governmental organizations (NGOs) and aid organizations rather than directly to the target individuals or groups. The advantages of these two methods can often be finely balanced, for instance in war-torn or politically sensitive countries where both NGOs and governments find it hard to operate.

As far as the second kind of substitution is concerned, it is almost in the nature of treasure to be substitutable for other kinds of effector, and in many 'normal' circumstances that will indeed be the case. For example, subsidies or cash incentives may be substitutable for exhortation or propaganda. The same may apply to money incentives as against orders based on authority. Government may conscript troops or recruit them on the open market, matching the financial incentives offered by other potential employers. It may offer payments to its citizens not to produce commodities that are in surplus, or simply impose production quotas. It may use authority in the form of guarantees or tax concessions, which may do exactly the same job as actually handing out its treasure, even though no money changes hands in a literal sense, and are conventionally known as 'tax expenditures' (Heald, 1983, ch. 2). And in the 'population policy' noted above, there is the well-known case of China where (working in the opposite direction) the government has relied on authority rather than treasure in its endeavour to reduce population growth by prohibiting families from having more than one child.

Similarly, treasure is substitutable for 'organization' over a wide range of applications. The credit card or cheque book is often a substitute for doing it yourself, for government as well as for individuals. Just as 'cheque-book journalism' means paying people in the news to reveal their stories in an exclusive way as kiss-and-tell 'confessions' and the like, instead of having journalists go to the trouble of ferreting out the relevant facts themselves, so government can use 'cheque-book government' instead of organization and direct action.

Military supply is one well-known case of such substitution. Before the nineteenth century, there was no military–industrial complex (in the sense of a defence 'sector' of semi-independent companies producing armaments and other supplies for the armed forces) on anything like the present scale in countries like Britain and the USA (Hood, 1976, pp. 30–1). Government made all of its own armaments and most of its military equipment, even down to items such as military uniforms. In the nineteenth century many states moved from building their own warships (as in the case of the famous Venetian arsenal) and making their own war material to contracting with private firms and just using its credit card or cheque book for the purpose. A dramatic recent example of such substitution occurred when the Russian submarine *Kursk* sank after an accident in the Barents Sea in 2000 and had to be raised by foreign contractors rather than the Russian navy (*Kursk*, built to attack US aircraft carriers, had once been the pride of the Russian fleet). Exactly the same happened with most kinds of government IT systems and equipment in the twentieth century (Margetts, 1995, 1999). Today the bulk of these items are made by multinational corporations. Government just writes the cheques.

The same applies to a large range of other activities for which government can choose between paying others to perform the task in question or carrying it out 'in-house'. For example, government can make its money and medals by manufacturing them in its own mints, or contract such production to others (private firms, other governments). It can dredge fishery harbours itself or pay others to do the job. And so on, for everything from security patrols to garbage collection.

Treasure in the digital age

In the earlier version of this book, this chapter on treasure was headed 'cheque-book government' and we have used the term at various points in the book. Indeed, cheques have been in use, on some accounts, for many centuries, originating from the Arabic *Saqq* in the ninth century, a written vow to pay for goods when they were delivered to avoid money having to be transported across dangerous terrain (*The Independent*, 11 March 2006). But in the digital age, cheques are becoming a thing of the past. In many transactions that individuals regularly undertake in digital societies, electronic payments systems that have developed since the 1970s have all but replaced paper-based instruments of transferring treasure such as cheques and order books. By 2005, in many industrialized nations even signatures were becoming far less prevalent, as 'chip and pin' technology in bank cards was widely introduced.

In principle the digital age can revolutionize government's ability to transmit treasure to its citizens, with digital methods offering the beguiling prospect of a high volume of individualized transfers at higher speed and lower cost than traditional treasure-transfer technology allowed for. That is why the US Debt Collection Improvement Act of 1996 provided that all US federal government payments except tax refunds were to be made by electronic transfer by 1999. In practice, there are some inevitable limits to such a switch and some that seem to be prevalent even if they are not inevitable. Even in the most digital societies (those where internet penetration is over 50 per cent) there seems to be a lag between government's electronic processing of treasure and that of other organizations, a phenomenon observed in the USA in the mid 1990s (thirty years after the world's first cash dispenser had been launched):

> For 15 years electronic funds transfers have been widely used. They cost only 6 cents per transfer, compared with 36 cents per check. Yet each year, Treasury's Financial Management Service still disburses some 100 million more checks than electronic funds transfers . . . Fewer than one in five Supplementary Security Income payments and one in ten tax refunds are transferred electronically. We have only begun to think about combining electronic funds transfers for welfare food stamps, subsidies for training programs, and many other government activities. (Gore, 1994, p. 121)

Similarly in the UK, research in 2005 suggested that while 87 per cent of internet users had bought or looked for goods and services online and 45 per cent used online banking services, only around 6 per cent had paid any government fine, tax or service online (OXIS, 2005, p. 25). These figures appear to hold true in general internationally: in 2003, 37 per cent of European internet users (18 per cent of all European adults) were using online banking (*OUT-LAW News*, 21 March 2003), while a global study of e-government found that across 32 countries in Europe (21 countries), North America and Asia Pacific only 8 per cent had 'transacted' financially (that is, involving bank or credit card details) with government online (Taylor Nelson Sofres, 2003, p. 8). But there are some exceptions, particularly Singapore where a concerted and resource-intensive e-government initiative was used to kick-start e-commerce in the 1990s.

A further barrier is the persistent aversion on the part of a small but significant subsection of the population even in the most advanced nations against having a bank account. Even in digital-age USA, over 10 per cent of the citizens remain 'unbanked', even in the face of heavy blandishments from government to encourage them to get and use bank accounts (Prescott and Tatar, 1999, p. 51). The reasons for this continuing aversion to bank accounts in spite of the apparent convenience and attractions of using such facilities probably include fear of attachment, tax evasion, avoidance of means-testing of welfare benefit and hiding income from other people in the household (Prescott and Tatar, 1999, p. 61). Moreover, even if those individuals (most of whom have low incomes) could be induced to make the switch to becoming 'banked', there would still need to be some significant exceptions, for example in government payments to informers who would be most unlikely to want their payment to be electronically recorded (Prescott and Tatar, 1999, p. 63).

Looking to the future, however, it is clear that there is great potential for digital technologies to change government processing of treasure through new scope for group-targeted payments. Digital technologies do not make highly individualized payments (such as rewards) any cheaper. That may be one reason why the UK Child Support Agency (created in 1993 to calculate and collect maintenance payments for children due from one parent to another after divorce or separation and formally scrapped in 2006, to be replaced by another agency) in 2005 spent much more money on collecting money from absent fathers than it disbursed, in spite of a myriad of expensive computer systems. Neither do they affect the cost of open payments, such as food drops to disaster-torn regions or free bicycles in cities. But information systems can greatly enhance government's ability to identify certain categories of citizen eligible for benefits or tax credits, which are calculated according to a range of characteristics and specific needs, and then paid electronically in a 'zero touch' way.

Information systems of this kind can also be used for differential pricing in transport systems. For example, once electronic card-based ticketing systems have been introduced they can be used to incentivize citizens to use public transport at certain times (making it more expensive in the rush hour, for example) or to vary costs for different types of traveller, such as students, older people or tourists. Such mechanisms are possible with more manual ticketing systems, but they can be far more easily changed in response to changing conditions and policy requirements if they are electronic. Likewise, variable road-pricing systems can be used to reduce traffic congestion, as they are in Singapore. At the time of writing, insurance companies in the UK have started to experiment with transponders fitted on vehicles to offer 'pay-as-you-go' insurance, whereby groups considered to be higher-risk (younger male drivers, for example) pay less insurance if it can be established via the transponders and satellite navigation systems that they did not drive after 11 p.m. It is conceivable that the more digital of governments could use such applications as a new form of universal road tolls with prices dependent on congestion levels.

Treasure-based tools: the wider social context

The previous two chapters concluded with a discussion of the circumstances in which government is likely to have to switch its emphasis from some kinds of information-dispensers or authority to others, and from information-dispensing or authority as a whole to other kinds of effectors. The same pattern will be followed here, but in a much briefer and more tentative way. Here we comment on two possible factors bearing on government's use of treasure. These are the size of population with which government is dealing; and the degree of consensus with which government operates.

Size of population It was suggested in the last chapter that the more 'particular' forms of information-dispensing would typically tax government's bureaucratic resources more heavily than more 'general' types, at least when the population to be dealt with was large. The same applies to the dispensing of government's treasure. The more that government cashiers or their digital-age equivalents have to take account of the particular identity and circumstances of each person to whom they must hand out money, the more laborious the process will be. In principle the computer age might be expected to reduce the absolute cost of making individualized payments, but the relative costs are still likely to be higher. Certainly, if all payments to individuals had to be *totally* 'customized' – through formal presentation ceremonies or special conditions of payment – government would quickly grind to a halt.

Of course, there are some types of money payment that can never be standardized or channelled through intermediaries. But wherever the client population is large or where payment is repetitive, the bureaucracy-intensive character of totally customized forms of payment will lead government to look for means of making life easier for itself in some way. As we have seen, this often means turning transfers into a form of bearer-directed payments. Similarly, conduit payment has been used by governments for a long time as a way of saving the bureaucratic effort involved in transacting individual payments, and it will come almost instinctively to the administrative mind in some cases. Much administrative skill in this age of cheque-book or credit card government goes into devising bureaucracy-saving conduits and standard payment systems.

Consensus The great advantage of cheque-book or credit card government, as opposed to the other kinds of effectors available to government, is that it can be used to further purposes which government cannot completely specify – not merely to secure obedience or compliance, but to induce people to act positively or creatively or to choose the best means of achieving some broadly specified goal. Government's other effectors may on occasion be used in this way as well, but they do not lend themselves to it so readily. In principle, treasure is an elegant effecting tool capable of being wielded with great finesse to achieve a finely balanced incentive structure.

Perhaps this is the reason for the apparently growing emphasis on cheque-book government in some countries, a phenomenon to which we will be returning at the end of the book. But there are some obvious limits to the extent to which government can retreat into the role of a banker, controlling society solely by its ability to offer money or to cut it off. Even in the best of circumstances, there are service and manufacturing operations that must be under government's direct control in order for it to *be* a government.

Moreover, it is in the nature of treasure – unlike nodality and authority – that, once spent, it has to be replenished. Outside the world of legends and fairy stories, treasure does not renew itself; and refuelling its stores of treasure can make heavy demands on government's detecting apparatus as well as on its effectors based on authority and organization. Treasure can therefore be a costly instrument for government to use (and that applies to 'tax expenditures' as well) unless it brings immediate money returns in forms such as interest payments. The implications of this are explored in Chapter 7.

Moreover, as government comes under pressure and encounters increasing resistance to its regime, the more difficult it is likely to be for government to direct its treasure accurately, and the more expensive the process of replenishing its stocks of treasure is likely to be. 'Directionality' (the capacity to move treasure accurately to a specific target) is lost and immediate money returns are less likely to flow in, as payees default on debts, renege on contracts, or put government's money to purposes quite other than those officially intended. Even to be seen personally receiving government's treasure may become dangerous, so that government has to switch away from customized payments to conduits or open payments, even if that means diminished control and more unfairness.

Similarly, as the pressure mounts it may become costlier for government to renew its treasure. Growing disobedience by subjects may make loans to government dry up, except on punitive conditions, and may mean increasing resistance to taxation and its analogues. At the same time, larger money rewards may be needed to maintain loyalty and to perform important tasks as the 'price' of compliance goes up. In circumstances such as these, the role of a mere banker becomes harder for government to sustain. Coercive force, if it is strong enough, can always be used to secure treasure; but cheque-book operations will not necessarily buy physical support.

Hence cheque-book government may have something of the character of a 'fair weather' instrument. It is likely to be a lead policy instrument of government in a fairly consensual society, or at least in a world in which individuals are able to be highly receptive to the short-term balance of financial advantage, so that they are prepared to respond readily to the money incentives offered by government and to use the funds more or less as government intends. There is some parallel here to nodality, as explored in Chapter 2 – another resource which appears to become harder for government to lean upon as social hostility rises.

Of course, even in fairly high-consensus circumstances, the payments that government offers may not achieve the desired result. Dishonesty, incompetence and malign chance will always take their toll. But treasure may be increasingly unreliable when government is *in extremis*. When it is our lives rather than our bank balances that are at stake, we may become decreasingly responsive to the cheque-book mode of government. Lasswell and Kaplan (1950, p. 93) quote Solon's telling comment on the wealth of Croesus, which can serve as a counterpoint to the epigraph at the beginning of this chapter: 'If another king come that hath better iron than you, he will be master of all this gold.'

Chapter 5

Organization

> I was trying to get more people in. And another concern of mine was if they gave my National Guard to the Department of Defense General, they might then consider that all the force that I was going to get, and I needed more people. I needed more people. I needed a lot of people.
>
> (Governor Kathleen Blanco, Witness to the Hearing of the Senate Homeland Security and Governmental Affairs Committee on 'Hurricane Katrina: the Role of the Governors in Managing the Catastrophe', Washington, DC, 2 February 2006, p. 55)

Government uses nodality, authority and treasure as the mainstay of many of its activities. But these are not, of course, the only resources available to it for detecting or effecting purposes. There is another shot in the locker. The final resource of government that was considered in Chapter 1 is 'organization' – a label for a stock of land, buildings and equipment, and a collection of individuals with whatever skills and contacts they may have, in government's direct possession or otherwise available to it. 'Organization' betokens capacity and capability – armies in government's own service instead of mercenaries.

For some people, 'organization' in this sense might be held to be a compound or derivative of nodality, authority and treasure: a subset rather than an element of the same set. But it is treated here as a quite separate resource from the other three. As has been mentioned earlier, it is perfectly possible to derive nodality, authority and treasure from organization rather than the other way round. Indeed, historically many governments come into being through precisely that process. It is, after all, an ancient dictum that 'Money can be used to get men and men to get money'.

For that reason alone, even in what is often said to be an age in which governments do much of their work at second or even third hand, for instance in working through contractors and subcontractors, or funding organizations to fund other organizations, we might expect government to maintain organization in some quantity. The US federal government, for example, is an employer and landowner on a massive scale: in 2004, directly employing nearly three million people and owning over 650 million acres of land (US

Census Bureau, 2006, pp. 459–89). And there are still many instances where government operates directly through organizations rather than dealing through contractors or intermediaries, as in the case of the government-run food stores (offering cheap food) run by the government of President Hugo Chávez of Venezuela in the run-up to his re-election in 2006.

This chapter has the same format as the last. The first part looks fairly briefly at detectors based on the resource of organization, here labelled ergonomic detectors. The second part explores effecting with organization, giving some indication of the range of 'treatments' that can be applied by government, beginning with treatments that are particular and working through to more general ones. The third part comments briefly on ways in which treatments are put to use, linkages and substitutions, and explores some of the circumstances in which government applies treatment in different forms. It also investigates the impact of the digital age on the organizational capacity of government.

Detecting with organization: ergonomic detectors

Government's organization, just like its other three basic resources discussed in previous chapters, can be used as a basis for detecting or information-gathering, and, as in those cases, a variety of information-gathering devices can be identified. Information-gathering tools drawing mainly on government's resource of organization – notably equipment and trained staff – may be termed *ergonomic detectors*. Instead of relying mainly on nodality, authority or rewards, government can put the emphasis on physical or mechanical (that is, 'ergonomic') devices for obtaining information involuntarily or without the cooperation of the informant. Indeed, it has no alternative but to use such means when the object of scrutiny is non-human, or when there is no human medium through which the information may be obtained. Examples include land surveys, forensic science and the observation of weather patterns.

Turnstiles and fixed scanners

To look for passive modes of collecting information involuntarily is to move on to rather more slippery ground than for the three other main types of detector. But in one sense one can conceive of passive applications, to the extent that government is strategically placed to watch from a fixed point, even if the strategic placing involved requires the sort of labour and effort needed to put up spy satellites or watchtowers.

The most passive device for involuntary data-gathering is here termed a *turnstile*. This is a detector that is placed in such a way that it is difficult to avoid going past or through it. Modern surveillance systems for the frail elderly in sheltered housing depend on a strip placed under the floor at a key point in such a way that a switch is automatically triggered when the individual under surveillance is active, thus cancelling an alarm signal that would otherwise be sounded after a given period. Many similar examples could be given. Of course, not all 'turnstiles' depend on complicated technology. A traditional example is the gangway system for customs and immigration checks at airports, which simply relies on the routeing of travellers through a bottleneck or turnstile at which government officials sit.

Whereas a turnstile is a detector so placed that the informant more or less involuntarily goes through, past or over it, a *fixed scanner* is simply a device for convenient observation over some field of potential activity. In that sense it involves a fractionally more active search process than in the case of the turnstile. Effective surveillance from a watchtower (the traditional form of fixed scanner) requires an active lookout, whereas a detector at a turnstile has virtually no option but to record the passing of traffic. Just as in the case of turnstiles, the fixed scanner comes in many forms. Some are very simple, such as the large convex mirrors employed by retail stores to help their security staff to catch shoplifters. Others are more technically sophisticated, such as CCTV cameras that are now ubiquitous in the UK, but are being introduced (with more controversy) across other countries in the industrialized world. Like turnstiles, fixed scanners are an involuntary information-gathering device, in that even if we know that they are watching us, we can only avoid scrutiny by considerable ingenuity or by putting ourselves to some degree of inconvenience.

Mobile scanners and hidden scanners

As has already been indicated, even tools of the type described above can only be termed 'passive' in a certain sense. But they are somewhat more passive than the *mobile scanner*. This is a detector which requires the forces of government to move about in order to conduct involuntary detection. Examples include helicopter surveillance of riots or motor traffic, the roving warships, photographic spotter aircraft and fishery cruisers which governments use for detecting breaches of fishing limits and regulations, traffic wardens patrolling the streets looking for illegally parked vehicles, or observers sitting in parked cars conducting traffic censuses. We can in principle observe such detectors in action if we bother to look, know where to look, or recognize what we are seeing. But, like the fixed scanner and the turnstile, the mobile scanner requires no active cooperation from us. Indeed, such detecting devices are operated on the basic assumption of non-cooperation from the informant.

The final type of detecting tool considered here is the *hidden scanner.* The term refers to detectors that are unobtrusive or deliberately concealed from the informant, like the secret investigations mounted by insurance companies searching for evidence of fraudulent claims (*The Times*, 6 January 1972). Government may choose to steal or copy key documents without the owner's knowledge. It may obtain information through spies and through agents provocateurs, as in the case of test purchases of regulated goods, test bets with bookmakers, or inquiries by social security 'snoopers' posing as relatives of those whom they are investigating. In the 1960s 300 officials of the US Federal Bureau of Investigation infiltrated and spied on the 2,500 or so members of the Trotskyite Socialist Workers Party (Lowi and Stone, 1978, p. 27).

Other forms of hidden scanners are secret recorders, hidden cameras, telephone taps and similar devices, which involve some sort of 'plant' on the part of government operating outside its own official domain, and are in that sense rather different from the fixed scanner or turnstile. When government uses hidden scanners, it is active in that it attends on the informant, just as in the case of inspections, propositions and direct requests. The difference is that in this case the obligation to supply information is an involuntary one.

As we shall see later, involuntary detection in the present day draws heavily on digital-age technology replacing the traditional approach of placing watchtowers and officials at the gateways of walled towns or at key ports and harbours. But involuntary detection is an instrument that goes back into the very distant past. Governments have always secretly opened mail and listened at keyholes. Indeed, the traditional government monopoly of the carriage of mail was said, on the establishment of a regular post office in England and Wales in 1657, to be 'the best means to discover and prevent any dangerous and wicked designs against the Commonwealth' (Committee of Privy Councillors, 1957, p. 8).

Effecting with organization: direct action or treatment

When it comes to instruments for 'effecting' rather than detecting, organization is what enables government to act directly on individuals, their property or their environment. In that sense, it is the 'business end' of government. It is the seat of government's 'defining' (Rose, 1976) or 'last resort' activities – suppression of rebellion and resistance to enemy attacks – as well as of a great variety of miscellaneous activities.

For effecting, government 'spends' its resource of organization in the form of *direct action* or *treatment,* and 'treatments' commonly appear in its repertoire. Government may forcibly arrest us, throw us into gaol, even execute and bury us. It may collect, manufacture, treat, distribute, provide. As with the other effecting tools we have discussed in previous chapters, these treatments range from those targeted at specific individuals to those that are applied to the world at large.

Individual treatment

The term 'individual treatment' is used to refer to all those cases where government acts directly on the persons or property of specific individuals or organizations. Treatment comes in at least four main forms. It may consist of *marking* an item, for example in marking the houses of victims during a plague or trees that are found to be diseased. It may consist of *storage,* as in the case of government-bonded stores or strategic reserves of food or fuel. It may consist of *moving* or *distributing* some item in a physical sense, for example when government transports convicts or refugees. Or it may consist of *processing* an item, changing its state, as government does when it vaccinates beasts or humans against disease. Each of these applications will be discussed briefly.

Marking Marking is (usually, at least) a mild and almost necessarily particular form of treatment. It has a range of applications, many of them humdrum and many linked to the use of authority in some way. In many cases marking is done indirectly, through the use of authority, as in the case of the numerous European states which in the 1990s required specified types of dangerous dogs (particularly pit bull terriers) to be tattooed with a unique identifier. But in some cases government does the job itself. For instance, government may colour alcohol or oil fuels to show that tax has been paid, just as in former times it put seals on rolls of imported tobacco that had been through customs. The same principle has often been applied to agricultural subsidization and disease control, for instance in marking farm animals as a means of preventing them from being presented for subsidy twice over. Older people in Britain can remember a system of government marking of individual eggs between 1957 and 1968 (Giddings, 1974, p. 201), which was also a means of preventing subsidy from being paid on the same egg twice over.

Other applications of marking do not quite have this everyday character. For example, government sometimes marks the very persons of its subjects, for instance when it brands them as a form of punishment or when, as noted in Chapter 3, it physically marks voters with (supposedly) indelible dye after they have cast their ballots, to prevent or at least limit multiple voting. In the developed countries government tends to 'mark' people in less direct ways, either by using its authority to require citizens to signify the characteristics in question, as noted earlier, or by issuing them with special clothes, identity cards or discs.

Storage and custody Storage and custody is another form of treatment which has a range of applications from the mild or everyday kind to more coercive or repressive uses.

The former type is manifested in the many cases when government offers custodial or storage facilities on a voluntary basis to particular individuals. For example, government in numerous countries has operated as a retail banker, offering citizens custody of their money. In 1945 the French government took over the country's four largest commercial banks and most of the remaining ones in 1982 (only to start privatizing them again in 1987). Government may even offer its services as a manager of our investments, as did the British Public Trustee Office throughout the twentieth century, originally as a backdoor measure to enable married women to keep their property independent of their husbands.

Sometimes the storage or custody that government offers is of a more physical nature. For example, many governments, notably that of the USA, maintain substantial strategic oil reserves and historically governments have often maintained granaries and stores of other strategic items. Government may maintain animal quarantine stations as a means of helping livestock exporters to meet the quarantine requirements of overseas governments. Government may provide voluntary custodianship over individuals, such as refugee camps or hostels for the homeless.

Frequently, of course, government storage or custody is not offered for us to take up or not as we wish, but is compulsorily imposed upon us. For example, compulsory storage was a traditional method used by government in the United Kingdom for enforcing excise taxes; government also kept the keys for methylators to control the 'denaturing' of spirits, and maintained bonded stores for untaxed products, on which duty had to be paid as the product left the store.

Government applies this form of treatment more coercively when it is persons rather than property or things that are compulsorily detained. As with marking, custody is sometimes provided indirectly through the use of authority or treasure. But in most countries governments directly operate substantial numbers of prisons, detention centres, juvenile correctional institutions and mental hospitals for those defined as criminally insane. They may choose to set up internment camps for imprisoning those perceived as potential dissidents or threats to the regime, as did the US government to Japanese Americans during the Second World War, the British government in Northern Ireland from 1971 to 1975, and the US government since 2001, using a naval base outside the United States (at Guantánamo Bay in Cuba) to imprison persons alleged to be militant combatants captured in Afghanistan and Iraq.

Involuntary detention by government is a form of treatment that can be applied over a range of coerciveness, from children's homes and open prisons to padded cells and establishments such as the notorious arctic death camps of the former Soviet regime (Conquest, 1978). Some governments, of course, are much more heavy-handed with such forms of treatment than others; none does without them altogether. Governments also vary in the extent to which they use compulsory detention as a policy tool. By 2005, a 'league table' of the world's prison population (Kings College London, 2005) showed that the USA had by far the highest rate of imprisonment globally with 714 per 100,000 population followed by Belarus, Bermuda and Russia (all 532). The figures for Western Europe were much lower, topped by England and Wales (at 142) and tailed by Scandinavia (Norway and Sweden were at 65). Governments have tended to increase their use of this tool over time (the 2005 report showed that prison populations had risen in absolute terms in almost three-quarters of the world's countries, with the biggest increases in Japan, Brazil and Mexico) (*Daily Telegraph*, 27 June 2005; *Guardian*, 27 June 2005; Kings College London, 2005).

Compulsory detention is not just used for dealing with those who have committed crimes, but extends to applications such as quarantine or asylum. Indeed, in the late nineteenth century the British Home Office even went so far as to extend the approach to alcoholism, by establishing special government reformatories to which habitual drunkards could be sentenced, involving the compulsory deprivation of alcohol for as much as three years. Needless to say, the scheme was a total failure (Troup, 1925, p. 182). Nineteenth-century governments often placed considerable reliance on quarantine (and even compulsory treatment, as in the case of Sweden) to check the spread of killer diseases of that day such as cholera and syphilis (see Baldwin, 1999). Similarly, in China today, drug addicts are required to receive rehabilitation in drug-relief reformatories under police departments; those who fail to abandon drugs are supposed to stay in such reformatories for up to two years. In 2004, there were over a quarter of a million drug addicts receiving compulsory drug rehabilitation across the country (*Global News Wire*, 26 June 2005).

The keeping of individuals under some form of constraint is a form of treatment which tends sorely to tax capacity (the limit of 'organization'), especially when large numbers are involved; but such trends as those discussed above do not suggest it is likely to disappear as an instrument of government.

Transportation and distribution A third method of treatment is transportation and distribution, the latter in the sense of direct physical allocation rather than in the tokens-of-authority sense of quota enablements.

Governments often involve themselves directly in physical removal and distribution activity. For instance, garbage collection is often conducted indirectly, with contractors paid out of local taxes, but government sometimes performs the operation itself, as did the Singapore government after independence in 1959, since control over the unionized garbage-collection workers had been a potent political weapon in that tropical city during the 1950s, and turning a key group of garbage workers into civil servants meant they were forbidden to strike. Similarly, government may supply individuals with building materials for putting up houses and farmsteads in remote areas. It may physically distribute ballot papers to each registered voter in an election – a device originally introduced in the nineteenth century to prevent abuse of the secret ballot in the form of bribing voters to deposit in the ballot box voting papers that had been marked outside the polling station (Etzioni-Halevy, 1979).

Government frequently uses transportation and distribution as a front-line instrument for tackling natural and other disasters when it moves items like blankets, food and medical supplies to the victims. Governments have distributed food and grain to their subjects from their storehouses during times of shortage since the days of the ancient oriental despotisms (Wittfogel, 1959), and modern governments may find themselves undertaking physical distributions in a variety of 'crisis' situations. For example, the Spanish government distributed large quantities of cooking oil after many of its citizens had been poisoned by contaminated cooking oil in 1980, and the Hong Kong government distributed blankets to the elderly during a period of cold winter weather in 1999.

Civil emergencies of a rather different kind may also cause government to draw on its organizational capacity for transportation and distribution. Governments may choose to move important supplies as a means of strike-breaking, as did the British government when it moved food from the docks during the General Strike of 1926 (and it has used similar treatment in response to a number of subsequent strikes). The Venezuelan government sent troops to secure petrol distribution plants and seize tankers during a massive strike which closed refineries and ports and paralysed the Venezuelan oil industry in December 2002 (*The Australian*, 13 December 2002). Governments may also try to achieve the same result in a less direct (but still organizationally intensive) way by offering companies armed protection to break strikes, as did the military government of Nigeria in the mid 1990s to Anglo-Dutch Shell, its main oil producer, during a strike of oil workers.

Sometimes it is people rather than goods that government chooses to move and distribute, whether in the form of evacuation of stricken populations after disasters or the movement of people for less humanitarian reasons. From the time of the loss of its American colonies until 1867, the British government transported convicts to Australia. In many cases, of course, government causes people to move by means of official tokens such as deportation orders. But, if only as a last resort, government will sometimes do the job itself. Even the most liberal of governments will from time to time have to undertake the forcible deportation of individuals who do not find favour with the authorities.

Processing A fourth major way in which government may apply treatment is to change the state of something rather than to mark, store or move it. This, too, is applied by government in a wide range of circumstances, from more or less unexceptionable everyday services to repression of the most outright kind.

An example of the former type is the role sometimes taken by government in destroying wasp nests, insect infestations, rats, mice or more exotic creatures in those circumstances where using authority, in the form of orders on the relevant owners or occupiers to clear their property of the pest in question, will not do the job for one reason or another. For example, in 2005, with signs of a bird flu pandemic spreading rapidly across the world, 1,700 officials backed by armed police were sent to slaughter all poultry in the Liaoning province of north-west China.

Sometimes it is propagation rather than destruction that government seeks through treatment. Many governments at one time ran their own stud farms, for instance in Russia, Spain, Britain and France, where such farms were established by Colbert in 1665. At such farms, individuals could, on payment of the appropriate fee, send horses of either sex to be mated with government's breeding animals. In the early 1980s the French government had over 1,500 breeding stallions for this purpose (*The Times*, 11 July 1981). Such operations were a survival from the days when many governments took a close interest in the breeding of bloodstock to ensure a supply of good-quality horses to serve as cavalry mounts in time of war, but government stud farms still exist in many countries, including France, the UK, Ireland and Spain.

From government processing of goods or animals to processing the persons of its individual citizens is a step which begins to take us away from common or garden government services. But even here there is a range of applications, from the prison haircut or the vaccination through compulsory treatment for traditional forms of sexually transmitted disease in the Swedish tradition (see Baldwin, 1999), compulsory sterilization or frontal lobotomy to the firing squad or the disposal of the dead in government crematoria and cemeteries.

Some kinds of public health measures, such as compulsory vaccination and the punishment of those defined as criminals or deviants in processes of law enforcement or political repression, typically make heavy use of this form of treatment. All governments must be equipped forcibly to arrest their own or other countries' citizens in certain circumstances, if only to enforce the judgments of law courts. Beyond that, governments vary enormously in their use of such instruments. Over the past century or so some governments have chosen to execute their subjects in massive numbers – a process too depressingly familiar to need extensive illustration. The million or so executions carried out in the People's Republic of China between 1945 and 1953 and the million or so carried out during the Cultural Revolution of the 1960s (Rosenberg and Young, 1982) are just two of the well-known examples.

Variations in the use of this kind of processing are not only a matter of the differing readiness of different governments to reach for weapons to punish their political enemies. The point at which such treatment is triggered also varies widely. In the former Soviet Union, to take an extreme case, those who committed crimes such as 'economic sabotage' in the form of corruption or fraud were liable to be executed by the government. Those, such as Alexander Solzhenitsyn, who criticized the government in public might find themselves subjected to a course of 'psychiatric treatment' in a government mental hospital (since public criticism was seen as a clear sign of insanity).

There is, in fact, a grim catalogue of such 'treatments' by government, which includes flogging, mutilation and prison punishments – the modern-day equivalent of the treadwheel and the crank, formally abandoned in British prisons in 1898. The international human rights organization Amnesty International periodically gives examples of such punishments in a wide range of countries including torture, bodily mutilation (such as cutting off thieves' hands) and flogging of children for 'immoral behaviour' used as judicial corporal punishments in Saudi Arabia; torture at detention centres throughout Egypt, Indonesia and China (see Amnesty International, 2003); and numerous examples of torture and abuse of detainees in US-controlled detention centres in Afghanistan, Guantánamo Bay and Iraq. In a world of international treaties against torture, governments do not readily admit to using this instrument, in contrast to the days of the seventeenth century, when using the thumbscrew on suspected conspirators was regarded as a legitimate instrument of government. But what is admitted and what is practised are not the same; and, at the least, diminutives of torture are used by all governments.

Group treatment

The last section discussed the application of government treatment to the persons or property of particular individuals. That discussion was intended to convey some indication of the range of applications to which government's 'organization' can be put, stretching from the comparatively trivial to fundamental matters of life and death. Of course, government can apply treatments in a more general way as well; and, just as has been shown for other kinds of effectors in previous chapters, there is an intermediate point at which government may direct its efforts towards groups rather than to particular individuals or to the world at large. *Group treatment* is something practised by governments since very early times, for instance by the burning or destruction of a whole settlement as a form of 'group punishment' for the acts of some of the inhabitants, as in the days of colonial rule in British India when villages were built for defence against tax-collectors and land revenue was sometimes collected by regular sieges and with the aid of field guns (see Baden-Powell, 1907, p. 68). It is by no means in desuetude today, and there are many applications, as an example or two can indicate.

One instance is group transportation. For good or bad reasons, governments sometimes transport social groups rather than aggregations of individuals. Governments often find themselves involved in evacuating refugee groups from a place of danger or deprivation by means of airlifts and the like. The British government's first experience of this kind of activity in modern times came in 1930, when it evacuated the entire population of the remote Scottish island of St Kilda, using a naval vessel (Steel, 1975). And in recent years perhaps the most dramatic example was the mass evacuation (at first voluntary but later mandatory) of nearly all the 500,000 residents of the US city of New Orleans in 2005 after Hurricane Katrina triggered massive flooding in what became the costliest natural disaster in US history (*Chicago Tribune*, 31 August, 2005). A week after the hurricane struck there were over 60,000 National Guard and military personnel in the region and the handling of the disaster involved massive use of organization by state, local and federal governments for purposes such as evacuation, transportation and distribution of food and the identification of around 10,000 government-owned properties within 500 miles of New

Orleans which could be made available to public housing residents forced to evacuate their homes. Widespread and worldwide condemnation of the relief effort (the federal government in particular was criticized strongly for its late, uncoordinated and inadequate response), which left thousands of the city's residents trapped in a superbowl stadium for many days waiting to be evacuated, shows some of the challenges that governments even in developed and wealthy countries face in using organization effectively for group treatment.

Another example is crowd control, in which government applies treatment to a group as an entity, rather than to any particular individual, employing methods such as police baton charges, tear gas, water cannon and plastic or real bullets fired into the crowd. But there is, of course, a narrow line between 'treating the group' and treating the world at large.

At-large treatment

'Group treatment' is a halfway house between the general and the particular. *At-large treatment* is treatment applied by government to the world at large or to whomever it may concern. Examples of 'at-large treatment' are the traditional mantrap (and its modern equivalents) and involuntary methods of disinfection (such as footbaths built into the entry to swimming pools or disinfecting pads placed across farm gateways to prevent the spread of animal disease). Other examples are the putting of fluoride in domestic water supplies or all the grisly techniques that modern governments are able to deploy for large-scale homicide, from neutron bombs to biological weapons. Such applications of organization are in a sense 'general' and thus loosely correspond to general applications of other basic government resources, such as propaganda or standard constraints, which have already been discussed.

Government may 'treat' us in the mass by altering the physical environment in which we operate rather than by getting to work on us as individuals (one of us has termed this approach 'ergonomic control': Hood, 1976, pp. 118–20). Government may provide for the welfare of its citizens in general by providing facilities such as parks, gardens, bridges, dykes and dams. It may cover the landscape with towers and gateways, roads and barriers (Lasswell and Fox, 1979). It may exhibit its collections of art treasures, documents, property, land or animals, for anyone who wishes to see them.

Similarly, governments have always employed construction projects, altering the world at large, as part of their basic equipment for coping with enemies or insurgents or reshaping their environments. Modern governments have experimented with methods of 'weather control', by cloud-shepherding and the like, have reversed the flow of rivers (as in Stalin's USSR) and have extended their own territory (as with the extensive reclamation of land in post-independence Singapore). A more traditional example of at-large treatment is the government wall designed to prevent escape or invasion, such as the Great Wall of China, the Roman walls, the Flodden Wall built round Edinburgh in the sixteenth century, the Berlin Wall of 1961 to 1989 (the 'anti-fascist protection wall', in the language of the former GDR) and the wall built by Israel between Israel and Gaza in 2004.

Wittfogel (1959) controversially argued that at-large treatment in the form of big construction projects was one of the most basic instruments used by the great oriental despotisms of antiquity. Wittfogel's argument has been rejected by many other scholars, but most governments rely heavily on this device at least from time to time. Even in the USA with its cultural suspicion of direct bureaucratic action, many kinds of physical development, particularly dams and water projects, have been carried out by the Army Corps of Engineers, and indeed it was the Corps of Engineers that repaired the damaged levees of New Orleans after they were breached by Hurricane Katrina in 2005. In Britain, after defeating a rebellion by Jacobite forces in 1715, the government undertook a massive road-, canal-, fort- and bridge-building programme in Scotland, in the hope that such developments would enable government to defeat future rebellions more easily. The programme was carried out entirely by government's own troops until 1790, after which government adopted the more common modern practice of relying on outside contractors for construction projects (Haldane, 1962, p. 19). In other words, there was a switch away from 'organization' to 'treasure' for the job.

The architecture of 'defensible space' (Newman, 1972) as a means of general treatment is basic to government, but new applications are constantly appearing. For example, the upsurge of rebelliousness by university students in the 1960s led several governments to search for ways of moving away from the traditional one-campus physical layout of universities to make it more difficult for student revolutionaries to paralyse the organization by seizing a single key point. Similarly, from the 1970s some governments started to become more self-conscious again about incorporating crime prevention into the architecture of public places, and thereby rediscovered some of the architectural principles of eighteenth century 'police science' such as Nicolas Delamare's 1713 *Traité de la Police*, for example by brightly lit wide open spaces with no hiding places, no paving stones for rioters to tear up, and vandal-proof street furniture. And the digital age has brought new applications of that approach (so-called 'digital architecture') by the integration of technology into physical construction, particularly via the use of CCTV cameras in public spaces of all kinds as a device for surveillance and crime prevention.

Much of government's at-large treatment is, of course, fairly humdrum: clearing snow, treating sewage, lighting streets. Often, however, such physical operations may form the keystone of a wider administrative arch. A well-known and traditional example is the device of the fiscal monopoly, in which government monopolizes the production of a key item like tobacco or salt or alcohol as a revenue-raising device (instead of granting licences to others to do so, as in the tax-farming mode). Sometimes such monopolies are highly specific, resting on a narrow point or 'handle' in the production process. A telling case in point is an early attempt to impose taxes on playing cards in Britain, which involved printing the ace of spades separately at the government printing office. The penalty for anyone using an ace of spades other than those printed by the government was originally death (Olmstead, in Herman, 1967, p. 139), though the sentence was later reduced to transportation, and later still, in 1861, to penal servitude for life.

The toolset in context

From the comments that have been made about other classes of government's tools in previous chapters, readers should now be well primed to notice several things themselves about the use of treatment by government.

The administration of treatment

The range of examples in the first part of the chapter was intended to convey an impression of the variety of ways in which government can put 'organization' to work. 'Treatment' or direct action is an everyday tool of government. It figures, of course, in most if not all of government's operations as the 'long-stop' or final stage of physical law enforcement. Apart from that, its use varies widely from one area of policy to another. Some domains of government operation tend to be heavy on treatment (such as public health, where government may be involved in emptying cesspits and septic tanks, removing refuse and night-soil, sweeping streets and processing sewage, providing public lavatories and baths, and so on); others tend to be light (such as the control of charities or financial institutions, which typically requires no more than an occasional invoking of physical law enforcement, such as dawn raids and the like *pour encourager les autres*). Other areas may involve heavy resort to treatment only intermittently (such as labour relations, where, as we have already noted, government may periodically become involved in breaking strikes and taking over the jobs of strikers).

However, in some ways government's use of treatment is a little different from the effectors considered in the last three chapters, especially those based on nodality and authority. As we have seen, these are employed by almost every government agency to some degree and may be inextricably tangled up with one another, so that the same agency or government official might continually turn from using one tool to another, just as the surgeon must be able to turn readily from probe to scalpel to forceps.

There are, of course, exceptions, as has already been noted. But treatment, by and large, is not like that. Many government agencies, such as regulatory offices, which rely principally on nodality and authority to perform their tasks, do not use it at all. Many if not most direct government employees never perform any treatments at all (Simon *et al.*, 1950, p. 443). The use of violence and the physical treatment of individuals (in prison, for example) tend to be concentrated in units that are separated from general-purpose bureaucratic operations even in quite early systems of government (Fagen, 1966, pp. 131–2, n. 5). The same often applies to uses of treatment in other, less dramatic ways, which are often concentrated in 'common service' agencies or units rather than deployed directly by all government agencies.

Combinations and substitutions

Another theme which is by now familiar is government's ability to link different kinds of effecting tool together. Government can combine treatments, both sequentially and simultaneously, in many different ways for the tasks it wishes to carry out. For example, it may respond to natural disasters such as floods, earthquakes or landslips by individual treatments (distribution, processing), by group treatment (such as evacuation), by at-large treatments (remodelling the landscape), or by some mixture of all three. It may repress dissent by treating 'dangerous' individuals, by concentrating on groups, or by at-large treatments such as the erection of defensive walls.

Equally, government may substitute one kind of tool for another at two levels. First, it may substitute one form of treatment for another. For example, when government physically alters capital cities or football stadia to make crowd control easier (such as by digging a moat or building a wall around a football field, or by caging spectators with chain-link fences to stop them from running on to the field to attack players or the referee), it is using at-large treatment in an attempt to take some pressure off group and individual treatment.

Second, direct action may be substitutable for the other types of effectors that have been discussed in previous chapters. In Chapter 2 an example was given of government to some extent substituting information-dispensing for direct action in the policing of an unruly crowd. Indeed, there are many cases where the effective use of information may make treatment unnecessary. But the opposite is also the case. Instead of using nodality to influence people's minds, government may use treatment to change their bodies or their environment. For example, instead of exhorting motorists to drive slowly through residential streets, many governments have built speed bumps built into such roads so that high speed can only be achieved at the cost of a heavy toll on the drivers' nerves or expensive wear and tear on their cars. Instead of trying to persuade squatters to leave the property they are occupying, government can cut off the water, electricity and gas supplies to vacant properties. Instead of propaganda campaigns to encourage children to take care of their teeth, government can fluoridate the water supply.

Direct action may similarly be substitutable for the use of money or tokens of authority. The choice for government between contract and 'do-it-yourself' was discussed in Chapter 4, and even 'treasure-heavy' governments may want to choose the latter in some circumstances. As we have already noted, the US Army Corps of Engineers often undertakes difficult or dangerous civil engineering work itself where no tender for the job is forthcoming at a reasonable price, and most US federal prisons are still run directly by the US Bureau of Prisons even in an age when the state is often said to have been hollowed out by privatization and outsourcing.

The same goes for tokens of authority. For example, instead of forbidding grafitti in public places, government can coat the relevant walls with a surface on which it is impossible to write, or from which writing can easily be erased. Instead of forbidding glue-sniffing, government might treat glue in such a way as to make it unattractive to sniffers. It can require unfit meat to be stained or do the job itself, just as it can operate its own slaughterhouses or set standards for the slaughtering of meat.

Organization in the digital age

Of all the NATO tools, it is perhaps for the tool of organization, in its most literal sense, that the digital age has brought the clearest change. From the days when computers were first used for the carrying out of bureaucratic operations in government (the 1950s for some industrialized countries such as the USA and UK), they have been justified as a way of reducing staff numbers in public organizations. Digital technology has also been claimed to have transformed government operations. By the twenty-first century, the tool of organization – which we defined earlier as the possession of people, skills, land, buildings and equipment – generally involves fewer 'people' and more 'skills' and 'equipment' than in the pre-digital era. The 'automated state' has long been portrayed as even more faceless than the stereotypical view of bureaucracy, from the technologically aided Orwellian Big Brother of the 1940s to the 'virtual organization' of business management textbooks in the 1990s. Even the least technological of government organizations is liable to consist of at least one major computer system as well, and some kind of internet-based front-end, if only a simple website. This injection of digital technology into governments' organizational capacity strengthens some forms of direct action.

In detection, there has been a trend towards sophistication in turnstiles. Turnstiles, customs points and ticket barriers increasingly comprise technological devices which count and record some kinds of data and may check against other data. Borders themselves have been 'digitalized' in some of the more hi-tech regimes: in the USA at the time of writing, there are more than 10,000 motion sensors buried beneath crossing points and trails; when crossed, vibrations from footsteps trigger an alarm at border patrol stations, creating a kind of electronic wall with the capacity to detect as well as effect. A commoner form of hi-tech fixed scanner is the CCTV camera, as discussed earlier, though this technology is by no means confined to government and it is strongly resisted in some countries, just as identity cards are resisted in others. Some of the older types of mobile scanner have been displaced by more sophisticated fixed scanners – as with the case of radar 'speed guns' once used by traffic police to monitor speeding drivers. But other mobile scanners have become far more sophisticated through the use of satellite navigation systems allowing locations to be pinpointed precisely and remotely. And to revert to the US border control example (where even between 1994 and 1999 the US Border Patrol increased its equipment spending from $2 million to $90 million), modern night-vision scopes and goggles are used to detect heat and spot objects as small as a mouse from an elevated position.

Effecting with organization has also changed. As with our other tools, digitalization seems to bring a move at both ends of the spectrum towards group treatment. Devices which were previously fixed and at-large, such as walls and barriers, may be targeted at specific groups. Take speed bumps and road barriers, mentioned earlier as a classic case of at-large treatment. With in-car transponder devices, it is possible to have such obstacles which are lowered for some vechicles but not others, such that ministers' limousines, fire trucks or other favoured individuals get through but not the rest of us. And while individual treatment such as punishment, imprisonment or transportation remains highly costly for governments to use, the identification of groups for such treatment may become easier. For example, governments are less likely to have to expend resources on stopping and searching car drivers if registration plate recognition systems are used to flag up vehicles of which there are specific reasons to be suspicious.

In general, therefore, digital technologies allow government to use its organization more precisely and discriminatingly than ever before. And as noted above, if previously 'unintelligent' forms of physical effectors such as walls and barriers are embedded with detection capabilities, government can use them to pinpoint specific individuals or groups. Similarly, at least since the Vietnam War of the 1960s, arms manufacturers and governments have sought 'smart munitions', using the power of the computer age to get a degree of scalability and directionality into military operations that is potentially far removed from the sort of 'carpet bombing' that was conducted by forces on both sides in the Second World War. But this beguiling prospect has proved somewhat elusive in practice. Part of the problem seems to be that the supposedly 'smart' devices are far from infallible, as was shown for example by the accidental bombing of the Chinese embassy in Belgrade by a US 'J-STAR' surveillance plane (the technological flagship of the US airforce at that time) during the Kosovo War in 1999, based on topological mistakes by the National Geospatial Intelligence Agency (*Seattle Times*, 1 July 2004). But a probably more important reason why the promise of scalability and directionality is often not delivered in practice is the equally 'smart' but often low-tech strategic responses to such technology by hostile forces. For instance, directional weapons might have worked well enough for US forces during the 2003 Iraq War if Saddam Hussein's regime had conveniently located its elite forces and air defence weaponry in isolable locations. As it was, the regime chose to put those items next to places identified as 'non-targets' by US intelligence forces (schools, hospitals, orphanages and embassies), thereby cancelling out the greater potential directionality of US weapons.

The same problems also arise in other domains when digital technology in principle offers government the possibility of using its organization more precisely – for example, in electronically extracting the taxes we owe from our bank accounts rather than sending in the bailiffs or debt-collectors, or in using the electronic engine management systems in our cars to make us obey speed limits rather than relying on exhortations or speed bumps to slow us down. Such systems may add significant directionality and scalability to government's organization where we choose to be compliant (or grumble ineffectually). But such systems depend, in the first case, on taxpayers choosing to have electronically accessible bank accounts in their own names and keeping money in them; and in the second case, on drivers using modern electronically controllable engines in their vehicles and not tampering with those electronics. As soon as such assumptions cease to apply, the promise of greater directionality and scalability through digital technology will start to evaporate.

A further change to organizational capacity is that as society moves online, government's treatment has to move online too, particularly when it comes to dealing with new forms of 'cyber-crime' and tackling the evident suitability of the internet for terrorist purposes. That means that government's organization increasingly needs to contain the knowledge and skills to tackle internet-based frauds and scams and new forms of money-laundering (as with the 'cyber-division' of the US Federal Bureau of Investigation (FBI), designed to achieve on the FBI's three top priorities, namely to 'protect the US against cyber-based attacks and high technology crimes' (FBI website at http://www.fbi.gov/priorities/ priorities.htm). Similarly government organization needs to develop ways of taxing electronic money flows in a world of increasingly electronic commerce and banking where the entitlements of national authority may be unclear and individuals and businesses may move money around the world with ease.

Treatment and direct action: the wider social context

What circumstances may cause government to switch its emphasis from one kind of treatment to another, or its overall emphasis on treatment relative to its other effectors? No general answer can be attempted here; but as in previous chapters, two main factors will be picked out as liable to influence government's treatment 'mix'. They are the size of populations involved, and the extent to which government operates within consensus (or the opposite).

Size of population By now the reader will be accustomed to the idea that (ignoring any revenue or output effects and looking only at the absolute administrative costs) some tools may be more expensive for government to use than others, in terms of the administrative effort and cost involved.

Just as applies to the government instruments discussed in previous chapters, 'particular' types of treatment will tend to be more expensive for government to use than 'general' types where the population is large. Where the numbers involved are very small, it may well be less expensive for government to operate on the individuals concerned than to change their environment in a general way. But there is likely to come a tipping point at which the balance of advantage is reversed, and government then has to weigh up the extra discrimination among its citizens that may be achieved by using individual treatments against the extra bureaucratic effort that is involved. As we have seen, capacity is heavily taxed whenever government tries to imprison large numbers of people, and the same goes for many other kinds of individual treatment.

Moreover, for reasons that will be explored more closely in Chapter 7, if revenue effects are laid aside, direct action or treatment is in some ways a more expensive instrument for government to use than instruments based on nodality or authority, since like treasure it rests on a resource which in its nature has to be resupplied or replenished as it is used. Possibly for this reason, government is often on the lookout for ways of substituting other tools for treatment, and indeed that has been a marked trend in government over the past two decades.

For example, from 1919 until 1971, the British government itself disinfected all imported goat hair and goods mixed with goat hair as a means of preventing the deadly disease of anthrax. At its height, this was a major factory operation, handling millions of pounds in weight of goat hair per year. But in 1971, when looking for ways of cutting costs, the government switched to a different instrument, replacing organization with authority. It simply banned the import of goods such as goat hair that were liable to be infected with anthrax unless they were sent for disinfection to private sector factories approved by government (*Department of Employment Gazette*, 1971, p. 819).

Consensus The degree of consensus within which government operates is also likely to affect the mix of tools that government adopts, as we have seen in earlier chapters. Thus in conditions of consensus or of general acceptance of its regime, government may be able to use direct action tools sparingly. Information, official tokens or the cheque book will often suffice as effectors in these circumstances. Government can reserve the typically more expensive tools of direct action for the emergency, the exceptional case, or the activity especially dear to its heart. Many have remarked that government, certainly on the modern scale, would be impossible if no activity could be induced from its citizens except by applying coercion to each individual. For instance, Margaret Levi (1988) bases a major theory of revenue collection on the idea of 'quasi-voluntary compliance'.

As consensus and acceptance decline, however, government will be decreasingly able to rely on its other effectors alone. Indeed, as we have seen, there comes a point at which government's official tokens and demands for payment are flouted, its messages fall on deaf or hostile ears, and its cheque book or credit card fails to buy physical support. In those circumstances, government has to switch increasingly to direct action tools, being obliged to turn to the most expensive kinds of instruments just at the point when its resources are likely to be under the heaviest pressure. Nor is relief necessarily to be expected from the hi-tech digital forms of organization discussed above in those circumstances because those applications also rely on compliance. For instance, an individual who aims to escape paying taxes at all is unlikely to do so electronically, and is unlikely to hold bank accounts from which tax may be automatically extracted.

Moreover, as government comes under pressure, experiencing increasing resistance to its regime, it may find itself having to turn from individual treatments in the direction of at-large ones. As the pressure mounts, discrimination may become decreasingly possible. The innocent must be lumped with the guilty, the bystander with the committed rebel. Instead of individual treatments, government may come to place more emphasis on treatments that address the populace in the mass, dealing with crowds or groups in military-style operations or undertaking general environmental changes to influence social behaviour by 'ergonomic' means. In times of general compliance, digital technologies can allow the pinpointing of organizational resources in the ways outlined above, but in times of conflict, civic unrest and natural disaster these methods tend to break down too. When asked about the communications system in the aftermath of the New Orleans disaster referred to above, another witness to the US Senate hearing quoted at the start of this chapter responded: 'My head of the National Guard might as well have been a Civil War general for the first two or three days . . . He did have helicopters instead of horses, so it was a little faster, but the same sort of thing.'

Of course, a switch to at-large treatment in those conditions may serve to reduce still further the overall level of social acceptance within which government operates. This is partly because in such circumstances government is no longer distinguishing effectively between its enemies and its friends or non-combatants, and partly because activities such as the ones mentioned above may bring the darker side of government's toolbag into greater exposure. Such exposure can be dangerous for government. Governments like to be coy about their use of violence against the person, even though that is an inescapable and indeed defining part of the activity of any government. Often it is kept out of sight or obscured by such euphemistic phraseology as was noted in Chapter 2 (for example, the British government forces deployed to quell riots in prisons were once termed, with perhaps a touch of irony, 'Minimum Use of Force Tactical Intervention Squads'). But when direct action becomes government's mainstay or its only usable instrument, this side of its activities becomes harder to conceal.

Direct action, in the form of the use of force against their citizens, is said to be 'the last argument of princes'. But it is a very expensive way for any government to argue. And it is expensive in a sense rather different from the bureaucracy-intensive costs of using tools such as customized payments or direct notification. That is precisely because it *is* the last argument of princes. If the final shot in government's locker fails to go home, nothing else remains.

Chapter 6

Comparing the Tools of Government

What's the good of the pipe if it's not played on?

(Irish proverb)

What can we do with the toolkit approach? In the spirit of the proverb quoted above, this chapter looks at one way the framework can be used to make sense of the complexity of contemporary policy-making: by making comparisons. There are at least three ways in which we can use the toolkit approach for comparative analysis. We can compare the way government uses those tools as against other kind of organizations. We can compare the way the tools are used across different governments, levels of government or government agencies. And we can compare the use of the tools over time. At the end of the chapter, we discuss how such comparisons might be quantified, as the next stage in developing the analysis of government's tools.

Government tools or tools of government?

One kind of comparative question that we touched on briefly in Chapter 1 but did not develop is: what is so special about *government's* tools? Are they qualitatively different from those used in the world outside government, and so amounting to some sort of specialized 'government technology'?

In some ways the answer is no. Many, perhaps most, of the tools used by government are not in any way special or unique. As we saw in the previous four chapters, government's attempts to make an impact on the world outside do not, much of the time, differ from those of other organizations in terms of the basic tools of the trade. Government is not using especially unusual tools when it seeks to persuade or to propagandize, when it buys or sells or gives money away. Government's tokens of authority, as we saw in Chapter 3, have parallels in many cases with instruments used by organizations outside government. Private or independent organizations issue certificates, franchises, licences and guarantees. Again, much of government's direct or physical operations on the world at large and its means of obtaining information have parallels with instruments used by other organizations. Even quite specific activities which one might think of as peculiarly 'government-like', such as the minting of coinage or the provision of lighthouses, have private sector parallels (see Binney, 1958, p. 31).

Some government tools, on the other hand, *are* certainly special: they are specifically government tools rather than common-or-garden instruments that happen to be used by government. Government's requisitions for obtaining information from the world outside (other than as a contractual condition or within the confines of an organization) are one case in point. So are government's official tokens in the form of orders and prohibitions of a 'general' type. These tokens are not really paralleled by trade union 'licences to work' and the like.

Moreover, there are differences, not so much in the basic instruments used as in the emphasis and the specific application, especially when it comes to authority. Government in the past has sometimes used tools other than 'organization' to provide prisons or other custodial services, making use of private organizations instead. That approach came back into use in the later twentieth century, with so-called 'privatized' prisons in the USA, Australia and the UK. But the authority to compulsorily detain or punish prisoners, or to classify citizens as mentally unfit to be at large in society, is peculiar to government and such authority is typically exercised by government officials directly, often in conjunction with 'group' forms of authority. For example, to compulsorily detain someone in a psychiatric facility in England, a police officer has to be present (along with a general practitioner, a psychiatrist and a social worker). The task may be referred to a judge in other countries (Spain and Argentina, for example).

Indeed, the power to commandeer private facilities or organizations is itself a distinctive tool of government, as happened when the UK government requisitioned merchant ships in the 1982 as part of its combined forces to retake the Falkland Islands or Malvinas which had been seized by Argentina. (That case was later used in arguments in favour of protecting the British shipping trade, with parliamentarians claiming that it would not be possible, ten years on, as there were insufficient merchant ships registered in the UK (*House of Commons Hansard Debates*, 9 July 1992, column 558).) And, as has already been noted, sometimes nominally 'private' organizations turn out to be front organizations for government, as in the case noted in Chapter 4 of 'private' charter airlines conducting 'extraordinary rendition' of political prisoners to countries that practise torture.

Finally, it is clear that government may apply its instruments on a scale or across a range that is unique. For example, a criminal or terrorist organization may well illegally use government-like instruments ('contracts' by hit men, detention by kidnappers, licences to operate under protection), but only an extraordinarily sophisticated one – indeed, one which was practically a government in its own right – could match government's range.

Tools of which government?

Of course, the distinctiveness or otherwise of government's tools depends heavily on which government we are speaking of, or which part of what level of government. Indeed, once we start to disaggregate government – that is, to distinguish its separate parts and levels – the toolkit approach can be used for other kinds of comparisons. First, different levels of government use different tools and it is rare to find the full range of government tools being deployed at the extreme 'ends' of government. At the most parochial level of government, the village committee or commune, the instruments in use – such as the village or town drummer who roused the inhabitants from their sleep in the mornings before the age of cheap and reliable timepieces in many countries – may often amount to little more than information-dispensers, relying mainly on nodality and with little or no use of instruments based on authority, treasure and organization. At the other end of the scale, institutions of international government are also typically limited in the tools they can use. Even the European Commission, which has pretensions to being a relatively strong supranational government institution, has little in the way of 'organization' at its disposal. It employs around 25,000 staff, about the same as a medium-sized city council in Europe. It has to rely on nodality, authority and treasure, and even then it does not make heavy use of some of the important instruments based on those resources, such as propaganda. And the use of authority to regulate many aspects of commercial activity with little or no direct organization means that enforcement of such regulations is inconsistent across member states.

It is in between these two ends of the scale, at central and intermediate levels of government, that we are likely to find all of the tools of the bag in use. Differences here are likely to be more a matter of emphasis or of application, more of subcategories than of the main classes of government tools. In federal states in particular we will also find different allocation of the tools across national and regional jurisdiction. In Spain, for example, regional governments, particularly that of Catalonia, have relatively more authority, treasure and organizational capacity at their disposal for interacting with their citizens than does the Spanish national government. The same goes for nodality too, and it is no accident that Spanish tends to be the last language (after Catalonian, French and English) on official notices. The same point could be made about other strongly regionalized or consociational countries such as Belgium.

When we turn to comparisons among national governments, we tend to find the whole toolkit in use to a greater or lesser extent, but there is great variation in resources available, state–society relationships and the environmental and technological context that shapes the way the tools are used. For instance, the wealthy OECD countries mostly have relatively benign fiscal environments in comparison with the rest of the world in the sense of highly monetized economies with a relatively small farm sector and a large proportion of employment and retail transactions in the hands of organizations above the family-firm level and therefore capable of being harnessed as conduits for tax collection. But they vary greatly in the way they use treasure, from a tax base of around 12 per cent of the GDP in many of the 'tiger' economies of South-East Asia to 60 per cent or so in Sweden, reflecting enormous differences in the extent to which government uses treasure for purposes such as welfare state payments to citizens and protection of the environment.

When it comes to the developing world, the situation is very different. Treasure by definition is in much shorter supply for purposes such as agricultural subsidy and governments are far more likely to have to resort to their other tools – yet those tools are also often problematic. For example, organization is likely to be thinly stretched, and low levels of literacy and poor lines of communication prevent use of nodality in ways that are familiar in developed countries (such as phones or the internet). And when it comes to 'predatory' or 'failed' states, we typically find both that there is little organization other than that in the hands of the government and that organization, and 'group treatment' often in the form of collective punishment, is a favourite government tool – as in the case of Robert Mugabe's Zimbabwe, noted in Chapter 3, where government directly destroyed over 2,000 houses in 2005. Indeed in communist Albania, under the iron Stalinist heel of Enver Hoxha from 1944 to 1985, there was no real equivalent of money in circulation and state vouchers were the main official bases for transaction in society.

Inside government: comparing government agencies

As noted earlier, the way tools are used does not just vary across governments but also varies among the different parts and pieces of government. For example, a defence ministry in any country is likely to use practically every tool in the bag, from publishing magazines for would-be soldiers, through wielding the 'legitimate use of force' to physical bombardment and alterations to the landscape. In contrast, a department of foreign affairs is likely to be more heavily reliant on nodality, relying on its place in social and informational networks across the world for the ability to pick up information and exert influence. How far treasure is used is likely to depend on circumstances – in the rich Western countries treasure in the form of overseas aid is a major tool of foreign policy, since threats to reduce or cut off aid payments can be used as a way of exerting influence, but in the majority of the world's countries such an instrument does not loom large in foreign policy. Organization will often be smaller too (most governments have fewer spies and diplomats than they have soldiers), though tokens of authority such as passports and visas are heavily used.

Thus the toolkit may be used to compare agencies as well as governments. Although most agencies will use all the four NATO tools at least to some limited extent, the two examples given above show how the emphasis, mix and context of application varies from case to case and comparing government agencies in terms of the tools they use is one way of bringing out what is distinctive or otherwise about the 'production function' of any given agency. To illustrate this point, Table 6.1 shows how the main classes of government tools discussed in this book might be applied by three different government agencies: an agricultural agency, a department of commerce and a tax collection agency.

For these three fictional agencies, the agriculture department would probably put roughly equal weight on each of the four 'NATO' elements, making for an unusually broad-based 'mix'. The commerce and tax departments, by contrast, would probably put proportionately more weight on authority-based instruments and relatively less on the other three. When it comes to the use of organization-based instruments, the tax and agriculture departments use them for both effectors and detectors, while the commerce department uses it for neither.

Of course, making comparisons at an 'agency-wide' level still involves a fairly high level of aggregation. We can get a different picture if we take the next step and look at the constituent units within agencies. For example, suppose that the tax collection agency was divided into a section dealing with customs duties and a section dealing with all other taxes, as happens in many countries. The tool-using differences between the two sections might then be just as marked as those between the three separate agencies. We could expect the customs section, in the nature of its work, to make much heavier use of organization, both for effecting and detecting, than the other section. Customs detection typically makes significant use of the whole battery of 'ergonomic detectors', heavily using turnstiles and fixed, mobile and hidden scanners and ever more so with advances in digital technologies. Such devices would be unlikely to be so heavily used by the other section. We could also expect direct action to figure much larger in the 'effecting' operations of the customs section than in those of the other section, with the much greater emphasis typically involved in customs work on direct pursuit and seizure, on processes of sealing and marking and bonded stores. Most other kinds of tax operations – the province of the other section in this imaginary agency – make authority relatively more important, for both detecting and effecting.

The 'cells' of government institutions could, of course, be split into progressively smaller subunits and, indeed, the results of organizational comparison are often highly sensitive to the choice of the level or unit to be compared. The advantage of the analytic approach set out in the previous chapters is that it can be applied at an increasingly disaggregated level from the government as a whole or top-level departments down to individual public officials or contract workers.

TABLE 6.1 *Applying government's tools: three (fictional) government agencies and some of their tools*

	Agriculture *Agricultural services*	**Commerce** *Services to trade and commerce*	**Tax** *Tax collection*
(1) Nodality-based instruments			
Effectors	Advice to farmers broadcast and tailored	Advice to exporters and inward investors; trade promotion	Tax reminders
Detectors	Receipt of information about animal or crop disease	Receipt of complaints about unfair trading	Receipt of malevolent information on tax evasion; scrutiny of free media & internet
(2) Authority-based instruments			
Effectors	Certification of healthy stock; import and export licences; prohibition of animal movements (disease control); orders to destroy weeds	Certification of successful export companies; import and export licences; grant of patents; tariff orders	Clearances for customs and probate certificates; licences for excise traders; tax assessments; tax amnesties

Detectors	Registration of farms; notification of animal diseases; farm inspections	Registration of companies, trade marks, hall marks; investigations of bankruptcy	Tax declarations and returns; registration of taxable traders (for sales and excise taxes); tax inspections and raids
(3) Treasury-based instruments			
Effectors	Grants, loans, subsidies to farmers	Grants to organizations for trade promotion, etc.	–
Detectors	Information from applications	Use of consultancy services	Paid tax informers
(4) Organization-based instruments			
Effectors	Marking of subsidised animals; stud farms and artificial insemination centres; vaccination and slaughter of farm animals; destruction of pests; plant and animal quarantine	–	Stamping of legal documents (for stamp taxes); marking of spirits; bonded stores; arrest and seizure operations; tax inspections and raids
Detectors	Research farms, satellite surveys of crops		Traffic scrutiny at ports and airports

Retooling: change over time

Organizations rarely stand still. Often we want to compare over time as well as cross-sectionally. Looking back to see the various instruments employed by governments from time to time to tackle some problem or other can have the same fascination for the student of government administration that the engineer gets from early cars or bicycles. It may also provide some clues about future patterns, if we can identify trends in the use of tools and draw conclusions based on the sort of tools governments are using, for instance if they put more emphasis on treatment of individuals through custodial sentences or if they develop military and nuclear capacity, as with India and Pakistan from the 1970s onwards.

One fairly common type of transition runs from reliance on nodality alone to instruments based on other resources (see Lowi, 1969). Governments may move from military recruitment propaganda to conscription, from exhortations to save fuel to fuel-rationing, from persuasion to force. For example, during a sustained period of drought and water shortage across parts of Europe during the early 2000s, governments in many European countries started with raising public awareness through general advice and guidance on how to save water. The next stage consisted of various prohibitions and restrictions applying to some 13 million people in 2006 and including bans on hosepipes, sprinklers, car-washing and the filling of swimming pools. In some countries such prohibitions were accompanied by nodal detection, as individuals were asked to report on neighbours breaking the bans. Government's organization tools began to come into the picture in the worst-hit countries too, for instance with water police patrolling farms to enforce water restrictions in France (*Agence France Presse*, 14 June 2006) and plans for water tankers organized or operated by government distributing the available supplies to firms and households.

Another fairly common type of transition runs from reliance on authority alone to the use of treasure and/or organization. A typical example, relating to one of government's long-standing activities, is the prevention of the spread of disease in animals, particularly where they have the potential to spread to or cause illness in humans. For example, when government in Britain began to interest itself in preventing the spread of cattle plague (BSE), the first step was to deploy official tokens, ordering farmers and landowners to slaughter diseased stock when the occasion arose. Late in the nineteenth century, government moved into the business of slaughtering diseased animals itself and compensating the owner for the loss (Winnifrith, 1962). The same sort of development has been seen recently with the tools used by governments to deal with the spread of avian influenza, particularly in South-East Asia. Mandatory notification was replaced by compensation for slaughtered animals in Hong Kong and China, with a gradual ratcheting up of treasure as it became clear that inadequate compensation was leading to under-reporting and the selling on of birds where problems had already been spotted. And as noted in Chapter 5, organization was eventually added to the mix in China, as state officials were brought in to slaughter all live poultry in one province.

Similarly, an early attempt to tackle the problem of overcrowding in the slum tenements of Glasgow in Scotland relied solely on authority, in the form of official quotas which specified the maximum number of people permitted by government to inhabit each house (Mitchison, 1970, pp. 403–4). Detection was by periodic police inspections, during which the 'surplus' population of each house took refuge among the chimney stacks, just as surplus passengers dismount when overloaded buses approach police checkpoints in some of the poorer countries of the present day. But later approaches to the 'overcrowded housing problem' in Britain and other countries supplemented official quotas by the use of treasure to subsidize low-income housing and even on occasion by the use of organization to provide housing directly.

The tools used by government may also alter with regime change (for instance, with the removal of extensive secret nodes, as in East Germany after the demise of the GDR), although extensive carry-overs can apply as well, as Alexis de Tocqueville (1945) detected in the move from the *Ancien Régime* in France to the new regime after the 1789 revolution. In other cases governments may turn from one instrument to another without much evidence of a 'linear' progression, either because the 'problem' is stubborn to attack (crime control, drug addiction, promotion of economic development, environmental protection) or because the context is highly contentious, or both. It is like trying to modify a child's behaviour by switching the emphasis from reasoning to peremptory commands, bribes or physical coercion without settling on any of these methods for long. As every parent knows, this strategy is not without its problems.

Frequently there are dilemmas involved in the choice of instruments by government (Hood, 1976; Dunsire, 1978). That is, using one instrument may well bring about undesirable side effects; but the alternatives may be similarly attended by unwanted by-products. The more active government becomes (and the more complex the social problems that arise), the more manifestations of such dilemmas may develop. The way government changes its approach to policy problems over time, turning from one instrument to another, has been termed by Guy Peters and Brian Hogwood (1980) as 'policy succession', to distinguish it from the entry of government into completely new social territory or, conversely, the total departure of government from some field of activity. Peters and Hogwood argued plausibly that as government activities came to embrace more and more aspects of social life, there was less virgin territory for government to move into. With the 'ending of the frontier', so to speak, government's 'policy space' becomes crowded with agencies and programmes. Hence, argued Peters and Hogwood, government is likely to be increasingly concerned with policy succession. It will be trying to react to the dilemmas created by unwanted or unanticipated side effects arising from the use of government instruments in an ever more crowded policy space (Offe, 1975, pp. 88–9; Wildavsky, 1980). It will be searching for new packages of instruments to apply to areas where the set of instruments originally chosen does not seem to answer the purpose.

Peters and Hogwood may have underestimated the extent to which new technology and social development create new virgin territory for government to deal with (as in cases such as the internet, biotechnology or new diseases such as AIDS and BSE). But in another sense, their notion of 'policy succession' points to the complexity of the concept of novelty in the sphere of government's tools. As has already been stressed, most of the generic instruments used by government have a long ancestry and new instruments of the same order as nodality, treasure and organization are unlikely to appear. The basic toolkit – the NATO tools and combinations thereof – is intended to be exhaustive. But, as we have also seen, it is in a sense true *both* that there is nothing new under the sun *and* that there is vast scope for innovation in the use of government's instruments. Provided there is a mechanism for generating variants – mutations or innovations – complex evolutionary processes can operate on the basis of a relatively fixed population of basic types. The interesting question, of course, is what *are* the mechanisms for generating innovation in this case? There is now a large and growing literature on innovation in government (see Cabinet Office, 2003; Black *et al.*, 2005; Hartley, 2005) but broadly, when novelty is generated in government instruments, one or all of three things may be happening.

First, an old instrument may be applied in a new *context*. Deployment of old instruments for new problems or in different places is something that happens all the time, often through a process of imitation (Simon *et al.*, 1950, p. 38; Nelson and Winter, 1982). As we saw in Chapter 3, government is forever wheeling out old stand-bys such as compulsory registration or licensing schemes in new contexts. Imperial licences for the operation of printing presses are translated into the present-day system of government licensing of broadcasting stations (Enzensberger, 1970, p. 13) and may come to be applied to the internet as well. Procedures for closing canals are translated into procedures for closing railway lines (Dunsire, 1978, p. 93). Procedures for government control over railways are translated into procedures for government control over aviation (Breyer (1982, p. 6) shows that the 1938 US Civil Aeronautics Act was indirectly modelled on the 1845 British Railway Act). Very simple applications of authority, such as traditional 'tall chimney' requirements as a means of controlling pollution, may be replaced by more complex applications to cope with an era of 'acid rain' and the like (Knoepfel and Wiedner, 1980, p. 97). Old instruments can also be applied in new contexts when one government borrows or imitates instruments used by another, often under the label of 'policy diffusion', from stamp taxes in the seventeenth century to online tax filing in the late twentieth century.

Second, an old instrument may change in salience as a result of technological change. As discussed in each of the NATO chapters (2–5), digital technologies allow government's tools to be reshaped and some tool combinations become viable for the first time. As we have seen, in government detection, the 'ear of Dionysus' of classical times and government's traditional monopoly of the carriage of mail (enabling it secretly to read its subjects' letters) have been transformed by technological change into the electronic scanners of our own day, such as internet search engines, lie detectors, CCTV and speed cameras, and wiretap technology for fixed and mobile phones. And we have already suggested that in the case of information-dispensers, the development of computerized records makes some kinds of direct notifications (such as reminders tailored to individuals) less expensive for government than would be the case if government had to use old-fashioned manual methods. Even treatment may change in character as a result of technological change. At one time, madmen and some of government's more implacable enemies had to be kept in chains or cages, there being little in the way of alternative instruments open to government apart from torture or execution. Modern government still uses incarceration on a large scale, but it has a wider range of possible alternative treatments at its disposal, such as frontal lobotomy, electronic tagging, implanted microchips or the administration of behaviour-modifying drugs.

Third, novelty may mean a *combination* or *mix* of instruments different from what existed before. The ingredients are the same but the recipe is different. It is very common, as we have already seen, to find government shifting the balance from one tool to another without abandoning any of them completely. An example is the constantly changing balance of information-dispensing, tokens of authority (including tax exemptions) and money-moving that governments deploy in the hope of directing business investment. Another is the restless search for policy initiatives which combat environmental damage, with nodality, authority, treasure and organization (such as environmental information dissemination, regulatory instruments geared at cleaner industrial activity, 'green' taxes as financial incentives and clean-up operations in the event of environmental disaster) deployed to varying degrees by different governments at different times.

Thus, even with an unchanging repertoire of basic instruments, a powerful potential for generating novelty is afforded by context, combination and technological form. Of course, it may take a certain touch of 'administrative genius' to realize this potential – to spot a 'niche' or a new combination or to see how an instrument can be carried over from one context to another. Not everyone can do it in practice. But at least the process can be understood.

The measurability of the toolkit approach

The move from qualitative judgement to expressing things in numbers can transform the way we see our world and the sort of questions we are prompted to ask about it. Give a child a bicycle and he or she would certainly be aware of differences in speed – fast down hills, slow going up, somewhere in between on the straight. Put a speedometer on the bike and the child gets a quite different perspective on speed: for instance, if he or she notices that there is a 20 per cent variation in the speed recorded going down the same hill on the same bike, the question about what accounts for such variation arises, that would never be raised in the absence of a speedometer.

So, how far can we, like the child with the bicycle speedometer, move from qualitative comparisons of government's toolkit, as indicated above, into quantitative comparisons? Twenty-five years ago, when an earlier version of this book first appeared, data on government activity were far sparser than they are today, meaning that the scope for quantitative comparison was limited even if the conceptual difficulties of measurement could be overcome. In the early twenty-first century, things seem to be very different, at first sight anyway. Over the past two decades there has been a huge, apparently exponential, increase in quantitative data on government performance and activity both at national and international level. Ever-growing enthusiasm for indicators, benchmarks and international rankings by bodies such as the World Bank, the United Nations, the OECD and the World Health Organization means that we are drowning in data on what government does today. So we seem to have gone from relative data poverty to an embarrassment of riches over that period. But can these data be turned into effective measures of government's toolkit as described in this book?

A sceptical response to this question might argue that data are not information, that the apparent embarrassment of riches is an illusion, and that the quality – as opposed to quantity – of public sector data has by no means improved. The sceptic might therefore argue that meaningful quantitative data about the use of government tools may be no more plentiful in practice than they were two decades ago. And that sceptical argument can certainly not be brushed aside. Measuring how government uses its tools is not as simple as fitting a speedometer to a bike. In addition to simple measurement error (to which even a speedometer is subject), there are major problems in categorizing cases in different languages and state traditions (try looking up 'nodality' in a few dictionaries translating English into other languages). And gaming comes into the picture too. There is not much reason to tamper with a bike's speedometer (except in exotic circumstances), but when it comes to data on government activity, the players often have every incentive to suppress or distort data even on apparently matter-of-fact things like public employment or spending, particularly when the data produced are going to be used for international league tables of saints and sinners or for allocated debt relief and aid money by international bodies. And it is certainly not only poor countries that cheat when the stakes are high. Nevertheless, even if we accept the sceptic's argument that the underlying data may not be much different in quality from those of twenty or thirty years ago, the accessibility and manipulability of such data as there are have greatly increased in the digital age, particularly with the advent of the internet and search engines. Public sector data just are more readily available to a far greater range of people and the transaction costs of processing them to produce proxy measures for government activity drastically reduced.

Treasure is probably the tool that is most easily turned into numbers, and indeed has long been used as a way of comparing what government does over time or across countries or policy sectors. Even a century ago military spending across countries was much studied and as far back as the 1960s Frederick Pryor (1968) produced a path-breaking analysis of public spending in communist and capitalist countries. However, even now cross-national data on expenditure are more developed and readily available for policy domains such as health than they are for domains such as transport and crime and security. And governments often have strong incentives to massage or manipulate their public spending figures, responding to pressures to put spending off budget or to comply with international regimes such as the European Growth and Stability Pact (see Savage, 2005). Nevertheless, the development of common international accounting conventions, particularly the European Union, probably makes it easier than it used to be to compare the amount of money dispensed to individuals across different countries.

Authority and organization present greater challenges for measurement, both because less reported data are available in comparable format and because the conceptual difficulties of measuring authority are severe. It is true that some political scientists have counted number and length of laws passed as an index of legislative use of authority (see, for instance, Huber and Shipan, 2003), but the assumption that the number of words used is an indicator of the extent of authority is decidedly questionable, and indeed in some cases more words may mean less effective authority rather than more. Figures on licences issued and forms to be filled out tend to be fragmented and incomplete in many countries (the United States, where the Paperwork Reduction Act mandates the production of such data in comparable form for all federal agencies, is a notable exception). Hernando de Soto's (2000) famous method of comparing government demands or similar activities across countries by experiments in which subjects do comparable things (set up a high street shop, replace a lost driving licence, enter the country) is probably a more direct and reliable way of getting at the weight and incidence of authority wielded by governments, but the cost, effort and bureaucratic resistance involved in measuring authority that way are anything but trivial.

Similar issues arise for organization. Figures for government employment tend to be even more problematic over time and across countries than data for government spending, because answering even apparently simple questions like numbers of police relative to the general population is plagued by different conventions on who is included in a count of 'police', and the same applies to comparisons of spending on police (see European Committee on Crime Problems, 1999, p. 78, Table 1.B.3). The OECD ceased to publish its comparative figures for general government employment in the late 1990s for this reason. Nevertheless, within any one country, figures for the size of the government estate and some other aspects of organization are available, and the size of each agency's operating budget relative to its overall expenditure gives some indication of the importance of organizational capacity as a resource, albeit with sizeable measurement error.

It is with respect to nodality in particular that the prospects for efficient measurement seem to have significantly improved. Rising use of the internet by government and by society at large means that in countries where internet penetration is high, there are new ways to assess the relative nodality of government. The field of webmetrics is still in its infancy, but even so a research team including one of the authors of this book (Escher *et al*., 2006; Petricek *et al*., 2006) has made a start at measuring the online nodality of government departments along a number of dimensions. Escher *et al*. (2006) looked at the online presence of foreign offices in three countries, the USA, the UK and Australia, using both structural metrics (which map the underlying link structure of websites) and user metrics (which measure the ease with which users find information on sites). They assessed the websites of the three foreign offices across the following dimensions, all of which might shape a governmental organization's ability to disseminate information to citizens:

- *Visibility* – the extent to which the site is easily found using search engines
- *Accessibility* – the extent to which a search return for the site

will take the user 'deep' inside the site, or will deposit them at the top page

- *Navigability* – the extent to which the user can easily find relevant content within the site
- *Competitiveness* – the extent to which the site 'competes' well with other information-providers when users are seeking government-related information.

Table 6.2 below shows estimates of two of these dimensions ('visibility' and 'accessibility') for the three foreign office sites.

The UK Foreign Office site emerged as the site with by far the greatest number of in-links per internet user, thereby making it the site most likely to be found by search engines and therefore scoring most highly on the 'visibility' dimension defined above. Turning to 'accessibility', for Australia only 31 per cent of in-links coming to the site pointed to the home page, suggesting that the other 69 per cent penetrated deeper into the site and may well provide more useful content. In contrast 80 per cent of in-links to the UK site pointed to the home page, suggesting that only 20 per cent provide the user with any more focused information. Thus Australia scored highest for 'accessibility'. For 'navigability', the UK site again emerged as the leader, using a combination of structural and user metrics, while for competitiveness the Australian site scored well, with users turning to this site rather than other online information providers when seeking foreign office-related information in an open search. Table 6.3 below shows a summary comparison of these four 'dimensions' of nodality.

As noted in Chapter 2, nodality is the dominant tool of foreign offices, so such comparisons are particularly important for such agencies. Other ways of putting nodality into numbers include

TABLE 6.2 ***Visibility and accessibility of three foreign office sites***

	Internet population (millions)	*No. of external in-links (normalized for internet population)*	*No. of links to top page*	*Links to top page as % of total links*
Australia	14.2	6,070	26,495	31
UK	37.8	22,730	684,797	80
US	203.8	4,210	386,220	45

Source: adapted from Escher *et al.* (2006), p. 14.

TABLE 6.3 ***Dimensions of nodality compared across three foreign offices***

	Visibility	*Accessibility*	*Navigability*	*Competitiveness*
Australia	Medium	High	Medium/Low	High
UK	High	Low	High	Low
USLow	Low	Low	Low	

Source: adapted from Escher *et al.* (2006), p. 24.

website usage (see OECD, 2005 for such information relating to tax collection agencies, for example) and Google's famous 'page rank' indicator which suggests how high agencies will come in a Google search. Given that there is good evidence that most internet users employ search and few stray beyond the first 10–20 results returned from a query, such figures can give us a handle on government's online nodality and enable us to look at nodality in new ways. They offer ways of quantifying nodality that were not available a generation ago, though the technology-specific nature of such measures precludes their use to assess changes in nodality other than in the short term.

Conclusion

The Irish proverb with which we began this chapter has a point. If a framework for studying what government does is to be put to effective use, policy analysts and practitioners need to be shown some ways in which the framework can be applied in research and practice. We have argued here that the toolkit approach can indeed be applied to the main forms of comparative analysis: to compare 'what government does' across and within governments and over time. Building on our own work and experience, we have also suggested some ways in which such comparisons might be carried out and even moved into the realm of cardinal numbers, like the bicycling child in our analogy who moves from a slow/fast/in-between set of qualitative judgements to quantification of speed – and in the process starts to ask questions of a quite new kind. In the next chapter we explore how the approach might be used to make more normative judgements about public policy interventions.

Chapter 7

Evaluating Government's Toolkit

> It's a poor workman who blames his tools.
>
> (Old saw)

Having looked at its uses for comparison in the previous chapters, this chapter looks at a second way we can use the toolkit approach. We can use it to design and evaluate public policy. After all, everyone from the most abstract philosophers to the most 'practical' policy-makers have to start with whatever is available, and we need to be able to use the toolkit approach in heuristic, investigative and even evaluative ways. For the latter kind of application, the analytic toolkit needs to be combined with some criteria or canons by which we might judge whether the deployment of particular tools is 'good' or 'intelligent' in some sense: for example, whether it is efficient, effective, appropriately matched to the job in hand and morally acceptable. We discuss that issue at the end of the chapter.

Appraising government's use of tools: intelligent policy design

Up until now we have looked at government's tools with a dispassionate eye. We have sought to analyse and understand, not to judge or evaluate. We have drawn dark examples from less than attractive regimes as well as more heart-warming cases. We have noticed the diversity of ways in which government uses its tools in different contexts: the variety of tools used across countries and across governmental units and the ways in which the pattern can change over time as government tries to find the right tools for a job. This section addresses more directly the question of what makes a *good* choice of tools.

We discuss in turn four possible requirements for 'intelligent' policy design:

- Deliberative choice: the instrument or mix of instruments used in any given case should be selected after some examination of alternative possible tools for the job.
- Fitness for purpose: the tool should be matched to the job. Since there is no general-purpose tool that will serve government effectively in all circumstances, government needs to understand the circumstances which favour each of the instruments available.
- Economy: effectiveness is not enough – the desired effect must be achieved as economically as possible, with the minimum 'spending' of governmental resources and the minimum burden, in terms of form-filling, obligations and (except in rare cases, for instance when saturation policing is intended to reassure) highly visible signs of governmental presence, on the general public.
- Moral acceptability: the choice must not be 'barbaric'; it must satisfy certain ethical criteria, notably justice and fairness.

'So what else is new?' readers might think at the sight of such a list. After all, these are very simple, apparently common-sense requirements. But common sense never gets you far in matters of government and each of these canons turns out to be anything but simple when we try to put them into practice, as we will show. Moreover, they belong together. Each requirement depends upon and in some cases limits the others. If government does not have any sense of what alternatives are available for any job, it is unlikely to know what circumstances favour which instruments. If it does not know the latter, it has no basis for choosing tools that will be effective, except on the basis of blind trial and error. And if this condition is not met, government has in turn no basis for achieving economy – a choice of tools that will be effective with minimum deployment of effort. Again, any idea of bringing ethical criteria to bear presupposes that there *is* some choice to be made: in other words, that alternatives can be identified. And if government does not make its choices within certain ethical parameters, there ceases to be any defensible reason for wanting government's tools to be applied effectively or economically. On the contrary, we may positively welcome ineffectiveness and waste of resources in those circumstances.

Reviewing alternatives: a rational choice?

One possible criterion by which we might judge the selection of administrative instruments is the procedure by which the choice is made.

Now we may, by luck or intuition, make a brilliantly successful choice by trusting a hunch, or by any one of a hundred arbitrary methods of making a snap decision. There are plenty of millionaires who owe their success to doing just that. But that is not a *rational* way to choose.

Conventionally, a chooser must adopt a quite different approach if the choice is to qualify as 'rational'. Formally, he or she must: (a) specify the goal(s) to be reached; (b) identify all the possible ways or means by which the goal might be reached; (c) ascertain the likely consequences of each alternative; and (d) choose the alternative that is likely to reach the goal(s) with the greatest certainty, to the greatest extent, or with the minimum of effort.

Having thus baldly stated the orthodox canons of rational choice, we immediately encounter all sorts of theoretical puzzles, familiar in the literature on the subject. At what point, for example, does the chooser decide that the costs of extra search for information about alternatives are likely to outweigh the advantages of making a better choice as a result of further search? How are risk and uncertainty to be accommodated? This is crucial, for to the extent that there is less than perfect certainty in the information available to the chooser, a choice may turn out to be disastrously wrong in practice, even if it faithfully follows the procedure of examining all the feasible alternatives that seem to be available.

In spite of these very familiar problems, the conception of rational choice does at least serve to offer one *procedural* criterion for a good choice. Can this computer-chess formula for decision be applied to the choice of government's administrative tools? Up to a point, yes; but only up to a point.

As was pointed out in the last chapter, looking through a simple inventory of government tools such as that discussed in Chapters 2 to 5 may serve as a guide for noticing the different types of instrument that might be available to tackle any given problem. And, certainly, one might expect any able policy adviser or public manager to be capable of ranging freely and automatically among the contents of the administrative toolbox, either by intuition or from long experience. Traditionally, high public officials have often been said to be the master mechanics of government's machine, though today that expertise may be shared by consultants, think tanks and other players. To be credible, all of those players are expected to be capable of choosing with some show of rationality, presenting and discussing alternatives and choosing the tool for the job after due deliberation, so that the process can at least be defended after the event.

In reality, it is common knowledge that choice normally falls far short of this procedural standard. Perhaps one could say that a choice which at least seriously considers some alternatives is *more* rational than a choice which plumps for one instrument without even considering the possibility that there might be other ways of going about the job. But choosing among government's instruments cannot be a fully rational process, even in theory.

Combinations

As identified throughout the 'NATO' chapters, tools may be and often are combined in some way; looking at government as a basic toolset can serve as a variety-generator as well as a variety-reducer. So a key reason why policy-making cannot be dependent upon rational choice alone is the huge number of possible alternative combinations of government instruments. Even on the very simplified scheme presented in this book, the number of combinations runs into billions or even trillions if one assumes no incompatibilities or mutual exclusivities. The eight basic types of tools – effectors and detectors based on nodality, authority, treasure and organization – can produce over 40,000 combinations, provided there are no mutual incompatibilities in sequence or in space. Divide each of these eight basic types into only two subtypes (say, particular and general, or active and passive) and, on the same assumptions, the number of possible mixes runs to over 21,000,000,000,000. So, however desirable it might seem, any strict application of rational-choice procedure is simply impossible in this case. No matter how clever they were, no one, in any finite time, could possibly consider systematically so large a number of alternatives in any specific context.

It follows, then, that government cannot examine *all* feasible alternatives in most cases. The choice in practice merely lies between examining a greater or smaller number of combinations of instruments, depending on the circumstances. Certainly, one might expect the search to intensify when government perceives itself to have failed in tackling some problem. But, even in that case, the choice of the tool for the job must in practice also rest heavily on intuition, experience, tradition, faith and serendipity.

Instrument choice as (hot?) politics

Given that all feasible alternatives cannot be systematically appraised, it follows that in many cases *politics* will play a large part in the selection of tools for the job. The idea of government coolly and open-mindedly browsing round its tool-shed to select the most effective instrument for the job in hand – the image with which we began in Chapter 1 – is, of course, quite unrealistic. Just as some weapons may be eschewed in war for high strategic or political reasons, so there are typically political or ideological constraints on the use of some of the instruments in government's tool-shed to attack domestic policy problems. Governments will use massive police swoops for fiscal or public-order purposes, but not to enforce such things as safety-at-work laws. As Schaffer and Lamb (1981, p. 7) put it, 'search for alternatives . . . is neither random nor open-minded'.

Indeed, for all the instrumental and means–ends managerial language in which modern policies tend to be wrapped much of the time, very commonly it is the instrument selected for realizing a policy aim that is far more contentious than the aim itself. This point was touched upon in Chapter 1. Karl von Clausewitz said that war is a continuation of politics by other means, and he might say the same of the choice of instruments for any given goal. For example, few would argue that it is completely wrong for government to take measures to prevent diseases. Governments in many countries have been seriously engaged in trying to prevent the spread of cattle disease since the eighteenth century, and extended their concern to human diseases in the nineteenth century (see Baldwin, 1999). But by what instruments should government pursue this laudable goal? Should it systematically exterminate potentially disease-carrying wild animals such as badgers or stray dogs? Should it license experiments with animals to ensure the safety of medicines? Should it conduct intimate medical examinations of everyone entering the country? Should it operate its own brothels (as governments do in some countries) as a means of trying to check sexually transmitted diseases? Should it add chemicals to the water supply?

Questions such as these are 'hot politics', linked to complex and often unstated assumptions about the causes and effects of social phenomena, as with the familiar argument about 'tough' versus 'soft' treatment of criminals. The simplistic but beguiling 'steering not rowing' idea that 'politics' is about 'the big picture', the broad aims or major goals, and that the 'delivery' or implementation of these goals is a relatively non-political task for technocrats or managers (see Osborne and Gaebler, 1992) is often the exact opposite of the truth. Commonly, the real politics only *begins* when it comes to the choice of means and implements.

Matching the tool to the job

Effective choice requires more than a review of alternatives, to the extent that such a review is possible. It also requires some understanding of the policy context, to match instruments to circumstances. There are some contexts where a specific government tool performs well, others where the same tool performs badly. Working assumptions and rules of thumb are constantly used in the workshop of government bureaucracy; each agency has its own store of experience and pragmatic folk wisdom about what works in its own specific area. But the lore is often not written down; and, since it is rarely made explicit, its reliability is hard to test.

Here we might apply the contingency theory which grew up in the 1960s as an attempt to specify what types of organizational structures are likely to be found in what contexts, once it had been recognized that there was no single blueprint for the 'best' organizational structure in any circumstances. Renate Mayntz (1981) made an early attempt to develop an equivalent theory for matching government instruments to policy contexts, given that there is no single policy instrument that is ideal for all. She suggested that where government is dealing with networks of organizations (rather than working in fields where there are few or no large organizations), it will tend to rely on persuasion, treasure and general standard-setting rather than on direct action or on other types of official token. Second, echoing an observation that goes back to David Hume, she suggested that tokens of authority of the ordering or forbidding type will be inadequate where the aim is to achieve some voluntary effort on the part of government's subjects and not just grudging compliance. However – this is Mayntz's third point – where government's aim is to redistribute income, wealth or access to other resources within society, it will require 'hard' regulatory instruments. What 'hard' regulatory instruments are was not precisely set out by Mayntz, but presumably they mean constraints and enablements rather than certificates, direct action rather than money-moving or propaganda, requisitions and ergonomic detectors rather than nodal receivers or rewards. Fourth, where government is already deploying a multiplicity of instruments in some specific context, the addition of others may have diminishing, nil or negative results owing to mutual self-cancellation and/or diminishing returns.

Pressing Mayntz's analogy with contingency theory in organizational analysis a little further, it is worth noticing that the three main predictors of organizational structure that have been established by contingency theories are size of organization, environment and technology. Of these, by far the most powerful is size. The effects of environment and technology are much less clear-cut and universal, partly because they are very difficult to conceptualize and measure in a way that can be applied to all organizations. But all three of these can be useful when we consider the task of matching policy instruments to circumstances and here we consider each in turn.

Size of clientele certainly seemed to be important for each of the four NATO tools in the chapters above. We suggested that, by and large, the larger the population, the more government is likely to want to switch the balance of emphasis from active to passive instruments or from particular to general ones. In the latter case, a common load-shedding device is to concentrate on intermediaries or 'conduits' in matters such as cheque-book operations, information or even official tokens. Most government organizations deal with a subgroup of a country's population, and the size of that group will to some extent shape the viability of certain types of tool. For example, it may be possible for an agency which delivers benefits to only a small group (such as a war pensions agency in a largely peaceful country) to do so in an organizationally intensive way that would just not be feasible with a general social welfare department dealing with a mass clientele.

Environment is also an important factor, if more difficult to measure. As we noted in each of the chapters above, a population with high levels of consensus and trust in government is more likely to lead to a culture of compliance which will make all the tools more viable. In particular, it is more likely to be possible to rely on nodality and authority – generally the less expensive tools to use – which provide no clear incentives for citizens to comply with government's wishes. In a climate of disaffection and low levels of trust, governments are more likely to have to resort to the use of treasure or organization to effect changes in societal behaviour. These differences imply that intelligent use of tools will involve understanding, as far as is possible, the distinctive characteristics of the population relevant to a particular policy. For instance, tax collectors have a range of effecting tools available to them: the dissemination of information about tax liability and filing deadlines, the issuing of tax demands, financial incentives for prompt filing, tax inspections and audits and, in the last resort, a visit from tax collection agency officials or bailiffs. A tax collection agency which has a good understanding of which categories of taxpayers are likely to be compliant and which are not will be able to target the most costly resources – treasure and organization – at the most stubborn cases. Much has been talked of 'proportionality' (echoing Augustine's medieval ideas about 'just war') and 'risk-based' responses in government operations, broadly reflecting this idea. But many of those precepts turn out to be of the empty or hand-waving variety if government cannot obtain the deep contextual intelligence needed to assess its human environment in a robust and discriminating way.

Technological context also shapes the use of tools. As noted in each of the chapters above, the use of digital technologies has become increasingly central within government in most developed countries but perhaps even more so across society at large in those countries. In such a context 'smart' use of government tools in the digital age will depend on an understanding of the extent to which society is also smart. For example, government agencies can only combat rising levels of global 'cyber-crime' and virtually organized criminal units if they keep abreast of technological devices and scams at large, as we noted in Chapter 5. Similarly, an understanding of what individuals in various social groups are willing and able to do online can help government to switch effectively from office-counter or paper-based processing of cases into electronic channels with far lower marginal costs. Similarly, using the internet as a vehicle for new forms of taxation requires effort, understanding and imagination to spot new tax handles and niches as well as internet-based threats to traditional taxes.

In short, intelligent use of government's tools requires effective contextual knowledge. That means a good understanding of the size of the population or relevant segments thereof (a condition dramatically missed in the case of publishing old census data online, noted in Chapter 2), a good understanding of levels of public satisfaction or disposition to compliance (a condition dramatically missed in the case of government reformatories for alcoholics, noted in Chapter 5), and keeping abreast of technological development in society at large (a condition dramatically missed in the 'Individual Learning Accounts' fiasco that we referred to in Chapter 4).

Economizing on bureaucracy

Another possible criterion for judging a 'good' selection of government tools is that of *economy*. The real test of policy engineering is to achieve the effect desired with the very minimum of bureaucratic building materials. Anyone (well, almost anyone) can make a house stand up if, as our ancestors did, they build enormously thick walls. But building that way is grossly wasteful of labour, materials and space. It takes the professional skills of the architect or of the trained builder to construct a strong building with the minimum of materials. Similarly, it is not sufficient for government to find tools that are effective, in the sense that they do the job required of them. Strictly, to do a good job, the tools must also be *efficient*, performing the task in the most economical way.

However, the idea of using the tools sparingly has more than one possible meaning. It could mean:

(a) Economy in governmental effort: minimizing the effort, expense and staff needed by government to perform a certain task; and
(b) Economy in public burden: visiting on the public at large no more 'trouble, vexation and oppression', in Adam Smith's (1910, p. 309) classic phrase, than is absolutely necessary to achieve the aim in view.

These two possible ways of using the tools sparingly by no means always lead in the same direction, as we will see in the following sections. Achieving one often comes at the cost of achieving the other. To meet each of these two criteria, we discuss how the use of the four basic resources of nodality, authority, treasure and organization might be minimized.

Minimizing government's effort, expense and staff

'Saving on tools' in the first sense mentioned above will tend to lead government to prefer general to particular effectors and passive to active detectors. In a wider sense it may lead government to prefer to base its operations on resources that are contingently depletable (nodality and authority) rather than those which are immanently depletable (treasure and organization).

As we have seen, particular effectors are typically expensive weapons, because of the discrimination effort they involve, and for that reason government is often drawn to the use of general types or group 'conduits' as load-shedding devices, applying the ancient principle of tax-farming to ever-new contexts. As noted in each of the four NATO chapters above, digital technologies can help in new forms of group conduiting, at least when dealing with broadly compliant individuals, though when that condition does not hold this weapon can be used against government.

For example, in most countries governments in practice encourage the use of tax agents to act on behalf of individuals or small businesses when filing tax returns. Electronic devices such as business portals and specially designed software have further developed this practice. Where the cost of such a service puts it out of the reach of middle- and low-income taxpayers, some governments (such as that of Chile) provide 'public' tax internet cafés, where individuals are provided with free assistance by trained tax advisers in completing their forms online, while in Italy taxpayers can take their return to a local union cooperative to get help. Working with such intermediaries can reduce the administrative burden on the tax collection agency, more than compensating for the cost of having to plug the gaps in this way.

The same applies to passive as against active detection. We saw in the four NATO chapters that active detection, almost by definition, requires more in the way of bureaucratic effort than passive detection; here again, a government keen to cut its own costs at the expense of others will tend to move from the former to the latter when they are substitutable. An obvious example is the move towards self-assessment of individual tax liability noted in Chapter 3, a practice long in operation in the USA and adopted by the UK government in 1996. We also saw in the NATO chapters that digital technologies can aid the effectiveness of passive detection (via fixed scanners, electronic turnstiles and the like) as well as by the matching of data held by government for different purposes, so in principle reducing government's costs.

Saving on bureaucracy in a rather broader sense may point to using government resources that are 'contingently' rather than 'immanently' depletable. As noted at various places above, two of the tools – organization and treasure – are in most cases immanently depletable, like fossil fuels. That is, these resources by their nature tend to be used *up* as they are used, unless they are replenished. Typically, the more treasure a government uses, the less there is left (exchanging one kind of treasure for another would not count as 'using' treasure in this sense). Similarly with organization: it is the nature of government's armies, bureaucratic as well as military, that they have to be resupplied (if only to counter the effects of fatigue, hunger, wear and tear and enemy action). There may well be political reasons as well why policy-makers will want to go easy on these particular tools – to avoid the impression of an overweening state or to work with contractors rather than government organization if the latter can supply campaign finance – but the depletability issue remains even where such political considerations do not apply.

Nodality and authority are rather different, because it is not in the nature of these resources that they are used up as they are used. Indeed these resources may even be augmented as they are used. Using nodality successfully, for example, may actually increase government's nodality – a successful information campaign on a specific issue such as public health or a terrorist threat will make citizens more aware of the government in general. As we noted in Chapter 2, the terrorist attacks on the USA of 11 September 2001 caused many individuals to turn to government agencies for information and the use of the government portal firstgov.gov rose sharply in subsequent days and weeks. Likewise, the sharp wielding of authority can be regarded as a warning sign to others to be more compliant in the future, as in Voltaire's famous characterization of eighteenth-century British naval administration as based on the principle of executing an admiral from time to time 'pour encourager les autres'. Pictures of handcuffed executives from the failed US corporation Enron in the 2000s – at a time when many had believed that such senior personnel were immune from the type of prison sentences they eventually received – caused some commentators to argue that the trial would be 'the showcase trial for the government in its war on fraud in the corporate boardroom' (Orin Snyder, former federal prosecutor, quoted at www.money.cnn.com, 12 July 2004) and that corporate responsibilities would be more fully complied with in the future.

However, there is also a sense in which these two 'contingent' resources can be weakened by over-use; individuals may eventually rebel against an authoritarian or over-regulated regime just as a child can rebel against an overbearing and strictly controlled upbringing. Alternatively, they may become resistant to government's official tokens or commands, in the same way that a horse's mouth can become hardened (and therefore more difficult to control in the future) by heavy-handed riders. Likewise, too many messages from government can weaken its nodality, as citizens become immune to warnings so that when they really matter, no one even listens and they are ignored. Police agencies have to think carefully before issuing bomb alerts for this reason. Most blanket messages have a tendency to decrease in effectiveness over time, which is why many countries wishing to discourage their populations from smoking have moved from imposing mild 'government health warnings' on cigarette packets, through stronger messages such as 'smoking kills' to lurid pictures of the damaged lungs and arteries of long-term smokers. Thus the depletability of these two resources, while not immanent, is contingent and they can be both self-renewing (like wind and wave power as opposed to fossil fuels) and self-destructing.

Minimizing 'trouble, vexation and oppression' of citizens

What are the implications of economy in the second sense, mentioned earlier, of minimizing the burden of government on individuals? Of course, this canon is not always in practice a dominant consideration for government, particularly when it is dealing with individuals who are not citizens. (Howard Jacobson (1987, p. 170) satirized this approach: 'It was me who hit upon the idea of the Prologue to Piers Plowman (Text B) [a text in obscure medieval English] in response to the . . . government's request for an appropriate language test to be taken by problematical migrants and dubious visitors.') Following the canon of not applying heavier bureaucratic tackle to the population at large than is strictly needed, government will tend to prefer low- to high-constraint instruments and precision instruments to non-precision ones.

Preferring low- to high-constraint instruments means preferring the use of nodality and treasure to the use of authority and organization, wherever these are substitutable. Up to a point, this precept may take government in the same direction as 'using bureaucracy sparingly' in the first sense, as can be seen from Figure 7.1.

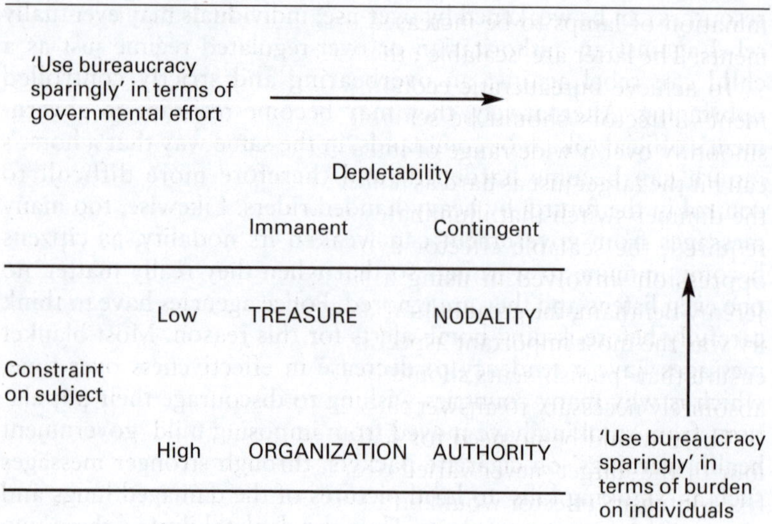

FIGURE 7.1 *'Constraint' and 'depletability'*

'Using bureaucracy sparingly' in both major senses would lead us to prefer nodality as a resource, because it involves low constraint *and* contingent depletability. Organization, which has the reverse characteristics, would likewise be a resource to be avoided wherever possible for both reasons. It is mainly in the choice between treasure and authority that the two senses of economy tend to come into conflict, because they reflect different preferences for depletability as against level of constraint.

If government aims to be economical in the second sense, it will prefer 'precision' to 'non-precision' instruments, and this again is likely to lead to conflict with the implications of economy in the first sense. 'Precision' tools are those which have the properties of 'scalability', 'directness' and 'non-substitutability', and these are likely to mean a preference for 'particular' tools that are bureaucracy-intensive in the first sense. Each of these characteristics of 'precision' will be briefly discussed.

Scalability

This term denotes the degree to which an instrument can be varied in its intensity. Ordinary light switches have only two positions, 'on' and 'off'; but dimmer switches (as in theatres) enable the illumination of lamps to be increased or decreased by smooth increments. The latter are 'scalable'; the former are not.

To achieve bureaucratic economy in the second sense, government's effectors should be scalable, that is, capable of moving smoothly over a wide range of intensities. In this way government can hit the target just as hard as it needs to be hit, and no more. Like the dimmer switch that illuminates a room to the precise intensity required, the scalable effector avoids the 'trouble, vexation and oppression' involved in using a sledgehammer to crack a nut. Jeremy Bentham, the great utilitarian philosopher, thought scalability was the most important aspect of punishment, because it could ensure that 'punishments should have only that degree of severity absolutely necessary to answer their end' (Bentham, 1931, p. 338).

There would be no need for scalability, of course, if the behaviour of the 'target' never varied over time or from case to case. A fixed-intensity effector would be adequate in those circumstances if we could get the initial setting right. But wherever the 'target's' behaviour may vary, a fixed-intensity effector is certain to hit the target too hard at least some of the time, producing bureaucratic 'overkill'. It is also likely to produce 'underkill' at least some of the time; and indeed the more that government tries to avoid 'underkill' without scalability, for example by relying on the execution of offenders as the only penalty, the more serious is the overkill problem likely to be (literally, in that case).

The scalability criterion is easier to state than to realize in many cases. In principle technological development could help to develop scalability, for example in methods of stunning or stupefying suspects rather than shoot-to-kill approaches, but in practice the recurrent promise of technology to deliver such scalability has proved elusive. For example, in 2006, a brown bear released in Italy, as part of a policy of reintroducing traditional wildlife in forest and mountain areas, wandered over the border into Germany and began to kill sheep and pose a public danger. In spite of weeks of effort on the part of the German government, encouraging the use of tracker dogs specially brought from Finland for the purpose, efforts to capture the bear alive failed and it was eventually shot by government marksmen, creating protests from animal lovers and a diplomatic incident with the Italian government. And unless such technological fixes can be developed, the problem is that it is difficult to build scalability into government effectors except by using 'particular' types that tend to be bureaucracy-intensive in the first sense. The same applies to 'directness'.

Directness

In order to avoid visiting more 'bureaucracy' on the population at large than is absolutely necessary, government's instruments must not only be scalable; they must also be direct. 'Directness' refers to the precision with which an instrument can be directed to a specific beneficiary or maleficiary.

Here again, the problem is that government has to sacrifice directness whenever it uses a general instrument to influence the behaviour of an individual or a specific group. If the real target is struck at all in those circumstances – and it may not be – the effect is achieved only at the cost of hitting other targets that are not relevant. Government's effectors cannot be confined to those against whom the action is really directed.

Examples of government effectors that do not hit the target 'cleanly' are not hard to find. Notoriously, blanket fines on business corporations for breaches of the law do not specifically reach the corporation officials who are directly responsible for those breaches (Stone, 1975, p. 50); at worst, they may just be an extra tax on the consumer, as with fines on utility companies. Bans on trade with a country whose government regime is disfavoured do not specifically reach those directly responsible for the character or behaviour of that regime: typically, those are the very last to suffer (Fisher, 1971). Hosepipe bans may affect environmentally conscious gardeners more than profligate water consumers such as golf-players or owners of swimming pools. Threats of general tax increases to counter high pay demands will, if carried out, affect both those 'guilty' and those 'innocent' of such behaviour.

Most of us are familiar with the phenomenon of group punishment from our schooldays, when a whole group is made to suffer for the acts of miscreants who cannot be identified or reached, but such approaches are by no means confined to the classroom, even today. One of the aspects of the eighteenth-century 'Enlightenment' was the move by governments away from group punishments to the hanging, torture or mutilation of specific individuals (Stone, 1975). Indeed, Jeremy Bentham, whom we quoted earlier, made directness central to his philosophy of law and government:

> Punishment ought to bear directly upon the individual who is subject to influence. If you desire to influence Titius, it is upon Titius that the punishment ought to act . . . No torture is so cruel that it ought not to be employed before punishing the wife for the

acts of the husband, or children for the offences of the father. (Bentham, 1931, p. 329)

Indirect applications may sometimes be effective (they may actually reach the real target as well as hitting other targets). But the by-products or externalities (in the language of economists) involved inevitably means involving non-combatants, as it were. It is not so much using a sledgehammer to crack a nut (the scalability problem) as of being obliged to use an instrument that is only capable of cracking packets of nuts – not necessarily the ones we really want and more than we strictly require.

Substitutability or incidence

A third feature of a 'precision' instrument is non-substitutability. Substitutability is closely related to directness. It refers to the extent to which an implement can be blunted or deflected from its target even if it is able to reach the target directly. To the extent that this can happen, there will again be a spillover of bureaucratic impact from the target to others.

Just as in reality taxes are commonly paid by people quite other than those who are legally responsible for paying the relevant money to the government (shifting and incidence of taxes, in the jargon of economists), government's instruments in a wider sense often turn out to be shiftable even if they are direct. For example, government may be able to strike directly at an individual responsible for a motor offence by removing his or her driving licence. But the target individual may be able to deflect the blow in large part, even though in the sense of the last section it has fallen on him or her directly. Such a person may, for instance, be able to take out insurance cover which provides for a chauffeur in the event of loss of licence. The insurance premiums may be underwritten by an employer and in effect 'paid' by the employer's customers in the prices they pay for services. In a case like this, substitutability renders the directness of the instrument nugatory.

The same may apply in many other circumstances. Companies may indemnify directors or other employees from government fines for the illegal actions they may perform (Stone, 1975; Cranston, 1979). Trade unions may be able to parry regulatory measures aimed at them by government, as did British trade unions in the early 1970s before the Thatcherite reforms of the 1980s finally hit their target squarely (Thomson and Engleman, 1975). So simply reaching the target is not enough. Somehow the blow must be aimed so that it does not bounce or ricochet, if the impact is not to spill over from the intended target.

Policy trade-offs: the problems of choice

By developing the implications of the 'economy' principle at somewhat greater length than the other three, some of the complexities of appraising government instruments can be seen. In this case, the problems go through at least four levels.

First, one cannot think of 'economizing' without a basic understanding of the determinants of effectiveness, which is often absent in public policy. Even in building and engineering – activities, one might suppose, that are subject to relatively 'hard' laws of operation – there is a very fine line between maximum economy and ineffectiveness (perhaps disaster) through skimping on materials, meaning that a margin of error or tolerance has to be left. Structures are 'over-engineered' and materials are stronger and heavier than they absolutely need to be, according to theory.

When we come to administrative control, the same applies – only more so. Each context is unique: the content of the 'materials' used varies in several ways. The tolerances are in practice enormous. Often they are entirely unknown so that we cannot reliably talk about over- and under-engineering. Usually we do not know what might be the effect of using lighter or heavier bureaucratic tackle in this or that context; or, to change the metaphor, we can only guess the point at which the dam will break (Hood, 1976, p. 64). In practice, we often *do* end up building the administrative walls three metres thick, without knowing whether that will prevent collapse.

Second, 'economy' as a criterion for policy choice plainly has to be balanced against other criteria. Typically, for example, administrative cheapness has to be set against the unfairness or inconvenience that general or passive instruments may create.

Third, even if economy is preferred over other requirements in cases of conflict, 'using bureaucracy sparingly' turns out to have at least two principal meanings which do not always drive in the same direction, as we showed earlier.

And fourth, even *within* each of those two principal meanings of 'economy' can be found subcomponents which do not necessarily run together and which therefore have to be balanced one against the other. For example, not only is a preference for 'precision' instruments likely to conflict with a preference for 'general' ones:

the components of 'precision' may themselves have to be traded off against one another.

Balancing the components of 'precision': a hypothetical example

Table 7.1 illustrates the last point with an imaginary, and probably exaggerated, case. After much-publicized problems with diseases such as E. coli and BSE, and a general rise in vegetarianism and concern with animal rights, it supposes that a government committed to the cause of vegetarianism has come to power. Fresh from its triumph, this government is considering which instruments in its toolbox may be deployed to promote the dictatorship of the vegetariat. Suppose further – somewhat unrealistically – that the possibilities were narrowed down to the eight set out in Table 7.1.

This is a contrived example, deliberately leaving out several options so that the eight shown conveniently cover the whole range of possible combinations of the three components of precision. This means that all but one of them are less than fully 'precise', and that one – option (7), the custodial treatment of offenders – is, significantly, precisely the instrument that would be likely to encounter the heaviest political opposition. Short of employing that as a front-line measure, government would be forced to trade off the advantages of one option against the advantages of another, or to use the options in 'matching opposite' combinations, such that the weakness of one instrument on some of the components of precision was matched by pairing or combining it with another instrument with the opposite pattern of strength or weakness.

So, as we noted at the outset of this chapter, at first sight 'using bureaucracy sparingly' may appear an entirely common-sense and unexceptionable idea and that is why in one form or another it so often figures in recipes for better government. But most of those recipes tend to be cast as platitudes and they live in a conceptual world that is devoid of dimensionality or trade-offs. As soon as those elements come into the picture, 'using bureaucracy sparingly' *does* start to get into the realm of rocket science.

A moral dimension?

Part of the reason for the 'hot politics' involved in selecting government tools is the *uncertainty* of the link between wish and fulfilment

TABLE 7.1 *Implementing a government drive for vegetarianism: eight possible measures*

	(1)	(2)	(3)	(4)	(5)	(6)	(7)	(8)
Measure	Ban all meat	Fixed fines on firms	Prohibit all meat-eating	Government propaganda	Limit sales of meat	Threaten to raise tax	Treat individuals	Meat rationing
Parallel or analogy	Bans on import, e.g. of pornographic material	Trading standards (fixed fines on firms for food adulteration, etc.)	Prohibition of alcohol, smoking, football	Health education (e.g. against smoking, drinking, glue-sniffing)	Control of drug sales, etc.	Tax amnesties, 'open compacts' in wage controls	Treatment of alcoholics, etc.	General rationing (in wartime, etc.)
Precision								
Scalability	No	No	No	Yes	No	Yes	Yes	Yes
Directness	No	No	Yes	No	Yes	No	Yes	Yes
Substitutability	No	Yes	No	No	Yes	Yes	No	Yes
Comment	Does not directly touch eaters of domestic meat	Miscreants may not be reached directly; costs can be passed on in prices	Blunt instrument; can't be turned up or down	Message goes to vegetarians as well as to meateaters	Registered addicts could resell supplies	Falls on 'guilty' and 'innocent' alike; tax costs could be passed on	Fully precise	Rations could be exchanged

in many areas of government activity. Improving health, reducing crime and increasing economic prosperity: these are only three obvious cases in which the instruments that are appropriate for delivering these apparently unexceptionable goods are highly uncertain and disputed. The 'politicization' of government's selection of tools highlights the moral dimension involved in that choice. Are there ethical criteria which any choice of tools must satisfy?

Such a requirement is in fact just as problematic as all the others. It is easy enough to argue, as does Christopher Hodgkinson (1978, p. 65), that administrators should be unusually sensitive to ethical questions: who would seriously argue the opposite? But to *what* values exactly should government be sensitive? Modern writers on ethics have to face up to the fact that many societies contain a variety of different and competing moral codes, not a single overarching one. In those circumstances, many such writers are forced into advancing canons for moral choice that are purely procedural (van Gunsteren, 1981, p. 6) – and that includes Hodgkinson, too (1978, p. 220). What that means in practice is the adoption of 'responsible' procedures and attitudes when making a choice. That comes close to the rational-choice canon that we explored earlier and leads to exactly the same difficulties.

Nor is that the only difficulty. Are moral judgements to be applied to instruments themselves or only to the *applications* of such instruments? This book began by making a simple comparison between government's administrative instruments and a set of garden tools, or a carpentry set. Plainly, it would be absurd to seek to apply moral judgements to the latter, separating 'evil' instruments from 'good' ones, as the epigraph to this chapter suggests. But does the same apply to the former? Are government's tools 'mere' instruments?

In one sense one may confidently say that there is no such thing as good or bad tools, only good or bad purposes. The axe that one person might use to cut down a dangerous tree or to rescue victims trapped in a fire might be used by another to hack some innocent person to pieces. Good or evil lies in the purpose or application, not the instrument.

But does this apply equally to *government's* tools? Some would argue the tough-minded case that government's tools *are* exactly like garden tools in this sense. They are evil only when they are used by the other side (so to speak) or for the wrong political purposes. By implication this is the position of every group of revolutionaries which, on coming to power, employs the very instruments of coercion that, in the hands of the old regime, attracted the group's moral condemnation.

Against that is a widespread feeling, regularly expressed in political argument and behaviour, that some government instruments *are* intrinsically more acceptable than others. Some weapons of warfare, for example, have been singled out as especially 'immoral' by critics, from the longbow in the Middle Ages to the machine-gun in 1914 and the nuclear or chemical weapons of mass destruction of our own times. Indeed, all the instruments we looked at in Chapters 2 to 4 raise keen moral questions. Direct action tools and propaganda are obvious cases; and detection similarly raises questions, particularly when accompanied by biometric identifiers and sophisticated data-matching across government agencies, raising the image of hydra-headed government snooping into our affairs, even our bodies. Denunciations of such government tools are a commonplace of modern political argument.

There are two well-known difficulties with this kind of approach. One is that there is no such thing as an intrinsically 'innocent' instrument of government. It might seem plausible to suggest that a 'civilized' government would, wherever possible, prefer tools that involve low constraint on individuals to those involving high constraint (preferring, for example, propaganda to treatment, certification to constraint, money-moving to direct action, nodal receivers and rewards to requisitions and ergonomic detectors). But this does not really solve the problem. We have to face up to the possibility of unpleasant applications even of low-constraint instruments, for example propagandizing young children or using 'ear trumpet' methods to encourage busybodies to tell government's secret police about ideological deviations on the part of their relatives or neighbours. And scientific advances – such as genetic modification, stem-cell research and nanotechnology – threaten to present government with equally tricky moral dilemmas if those developments shape its instruments. No government instruments are inherently 'clean'. Deny government those instruments that might be applied barbarically, and you deny it almost the whole toolbox.

The other difficulty is the age-old argument that government may sometimes, even frequently, be obliged to use 'the instruments of evil to do good', as Ostrom (1982) puts it, invoking a familiar religious phrase (see also Ignatiaff, 2005); and this can apply even if we do not see government's toolbox as ethically neutral, like garden tools. This is the 'dirty hands', teleological–deontological dilemma that has been discussed by political theorists since Augustine and Machiavelli (Kagan, 1978, p. 9; van Gunsteren, 1981, p. 6): what if unpleasant instruments produce beneficial results? Or the reverse, as with the standard argument that outlawing the most powerful weapons of warfare only serves to make wars more frequent, less controllable and more prolonged? No one would deny that the use of government's tools, even for everyday purposes, is shot through with moral problems and choices, and that any appraisal of the use of these tools must include this dimension (Hodgkinson, 1978). But there is no rule of thumb that can be applied here. Each case has to be argued on its merits.

Conclusion

The four possible requirements for 'good' or 'intelligent' application of government's instruments that have been discussed in this chapter indicate some of the practical difficulties involved in judging those instruments as good or bad, except on a highly pragmatic and individualistic trial-and-error basis. Each of the requirements discussed here quickly becomes faltering and ambiguous when it is examined carefully.

Moreover, the criteria may conflict with one another at the margin. For example, effectiveness and economy might point to the use of government instruments that would attract moral censure as unduly coercive. This was the case in our imaginary example of a government drive for vegetarianism. As we shall see in Chapter 9, some see this conflict as lying at the heart of the 'government effectiveness problem' in modern democracies. Indeed, if you spin the wheel again, you can find conflicting canons *within* each canon, as we have just seen with 'economy'.

It is perhaps futile to look for purely intellectual ways of 'resolving' such conflicts. The political process does that. Governments in different circumstances will give primacy to different criteria; and indeed the relative emphasis given to each criterion is likely to alter continuously with every shift of the political wind. For example, a long period of evident failure in some endeavour is likely to put the emphasis on the first and second canons, accentuating and extending government's search for alternative tools for the job. On the other hand, the advent of a highly 'ideological' regime after a political upheaval may give more importance to the fourth canon, requiring each act to be justified in terms of the high-flown principles to which the new regime adheres. Again, a government in 'fiscal crisis' – a problem which overtook many Western governments in the 1970s and which some see as a problem likely to return in the twenty-first century – may well give more emphasis to the canon of economy, taking an urgent interest in ways of making government cheaper, perhaps at the expense of putting more costs on to individuals as they spend hours navigating a maze of websites or telephone-routing systems. But when it is government's very existence, rather than its 'store of treasure', that is in question, effectiveness is likely to elbow out the other canons: defeat the enemy, by fair means or foul, and damn the expense.

Chapter 8

Alternative Approaches to the Tools of Government

> It is a curious circumstance, that nearly all the English books upon war, including the only one intended as an *aide memoire* for field service, are from the pens of men who have never seen a shot fired in anger.
>
> (Wolseley, 1869, p. 5)

The general account of government's tools that we have set out in this book is not the only approach of this type to have developed over the past few decades. So what makes it special and how does it compare with the alternatives? In this chapter, building on a few remarks in Chapter 1, we look briefly at how this approach fits into the broader study of government and public policy, how it compares with other approaches, and what challenges the digital age presents for each type of approach.

As we have already noted, government generally does not produce analytic accounts of its own toolkit of the kind detailed in this book. Of course it distinguishes different methods of operation in the way it sets out the public accounts, in the typologies of organization it works with, and in the positions it takes in debates over how to provide public services, for instance through contracting out or direct provision, or about what approach is deemed to count as 'best practice' in different fields of public policy. But, as with those military texts that frustrated Sir Garnet Wolseley in the nineteenth century, it has mostly been left to the civilian equivalents of armchair soldiers to produce general and systematic accounts of government tools.

Among the works of that kind that have been produced over the past twenty years, we can distinguish at least three main approaches. All of them have earlier antecedents but most are concerned with questions different from those dealt with in this book. One, contrasting with our broadly institution-free approach focusing on interactions between individuals and government, looks at government tools or instruments in terms of the different forms of organization available to government – such as ministerial departments, state-owned enterprises, independent public authorities, contractors and public–private partnerships. A second well-established approach, also contrasting with the approach taken in this book, focuses centrally on the politics of instrument selection, in the sense of the interests or ideas that shape the choice of tools. A third set of approaches – the category in which this book belongs – aims to be institution-free and to focus more on cataloguing the toolkit in a generic way than on the politics of instrument choice.

Against that background, this chapter aims to do three things. First, it aims to show that the first two approaches, albeit sometimes portrayed as rival ways of understanding 'tools', are in fact answers to questions different from those dealt with in this book, not different ways of approaching the same question. So no real issue of gladiatorial combat arises, since those approaches are complementary rather than conflicting. Second, the chapter aims to bring out the advantages of the toolkit approach set out here relative to other approaches that share its broad characteristics of being institution-free and generic. Third, picking up a theme that has been developed in all of the previous chapters, we conclude by exploring what kinds of challenges each of the three broad approaches considered here faces in an age of digital technology.

The institutions-as-tools approach: the tools of government as forms of organization

As was mentioned in the first chapter, one way of thinking about the tools of government is to identify different specific forms of organization through which public policy is conducted. That is the traditional approach of academic public administration, with its heavy focus on the accountability issues associated with different ways of organizing government and public services. And it is certainly an issue on which debates tend to run hot in politics. After all, over the past twenty years, the question of how far public services or public utilities should be delivered by core government, private or third-sector organizations has been a litmus test of ideology or cultural bias in most countries. Similarly, in the affluent Western states of today, issues such as the way that regulators are constituted, the extent to which issues such as monetary policy or national statistics should be handled directly by public bodies distanced from the core of government, and the extent and type of services to be delivered by various forms of public–private partnerships are often in the foreground of party politics and public debate.

So conceiving instruments in the sense of alternative organizational types clearly links to issues of enduring salience.

One of the well-known contemporary accounts of government's tools, namely Lester Salamon's (2002) edited book that is also titled *The Tools of Government* (a development of an original written more than a decade before whose main title was *Beyond Privatization* (Salamon and Lund, 1989)), partially tracks into the institutions-as-tools approach, in so far as it pays considerable attention to various forms of public–private partnerships. The general framing argument is that new types of institutional forms for public policy are central to a 'new governance' paradigm that is linked up with the rise of 'New Public Management' and related better-government doctrines of the past few decades.

How far those public–private institutional forms are as truly distinctive to the modern era as Salamon asserts (Salamon, 2002, p. 2) can be contested. After all, governments have for a long time used apparently commercial and independent forms of organization in the world of espionage, black propaganda and other forms of unconventional warfare (see Mackenzie, 2002). 'Private organizations', often closely bound to governments in practice, have been central to armaments production and supply, and thus to one of the most fundamental functions of government, for at least two centuries. Such organizations have provided numerous public services in earlier eras, including prisons and lighthouses in some times and places. We would need some quantitative analysis over time for the claimed distinctiveness of the modern era to be demonstrated. And whether a focus on tools and instruments must necessarily be linked to any particular doctrine of good government, be that the so-called 'new governance' or any other, is debatable as well. But that is not really the point here. Rather, the point is that a minute categorization of the specific forms of organization that government can call on (still the main stock-in-trade of academic public administration all over the world) is not really a different answer to the 'what does government do?' question posed at the outset of the book. It is an answer to a different question.

The politics-of-instrument-choice approach

If the institutions-as-tools approach to thinking about the tools of government links to all those debates about what detailed forms of organization should be used to provide what kinds of public services or government functions, a second approach is concerned with the politics that lies behind the selection of whatever tools governments use, whether conceived as generic instruments or as forms of organization.

From this perspective, the important thing is to understand the political struggles, ideological mindsets and cognitive frames of politicians and policy-makers that lead to the pursuit of public policy through one kind of instrument rather than another. As with the institutions-as-tools approach, this approach is far from new, though it has traditionally been as much the province of historians as of political scientists. For example, in the middle of the last century, Erwin Ackerknecht (1948) explored the different ways in which nineteenth-century European states approached the control of contagious diseases such as cholera, TB and syphilis, the mass killers of those days. Ackerknecht's argument was that aetiology and prophylaxis were inextricably mixed up with politics, and that authoritarian states approached the control of contagious diseases by measures quite distinct from those used by liberal states. The first, Ackerknecht claimed, tended to favour 'quarantinist' measures designed to break the chain of disease transmission, while the latter tended to apply 'sanitarian' measures that tackled the disease at source, for instance by public health infrastructure such as sewerage and drainage. More recently, Peter Baldwin (1999) has argued that the historical picture was rather more complex than that painted by Ackerknecht, but even in the 1980s new diseases such as AIDS were handled in different ways in different state traditions, reproducing in part those nineteenth-century differences.

In recent decades, Stephen Linder and Guy Peters (1989, 1992, 1998) have been particularly associated with the politics-of-instrument-choice approach in the public policy literature. They distinguish four approaches to the understanding of public policy instruments, contrasting what they call 'instrumentalists' (those who concentrate on and often seek to champion some particular tool, such as those economists who see price mechanisms as the answer to every policy problem), 'proceduralists' (those who see tool selection as a product of political processes that are so complex and unique to every case that it is impossible to make any general assessment of 'appropriateness'), 'contingentists' (a rather awkward label for those who see the appropriateness of tool use as depending on types of task, for instance as between 'compliance cultures' and cultures of resistance to government policy), and 'constitutivists' (those who see the appropriateness of tool use as turning on subjective and contested meanings). They say their own thinking about policy instruments has developed over time away from approaches such as contingency or instrumentalism towards what they call 'constitutivism', arguing in postmodern vein that there is 'a growing understanding that instrument selection is not a simple mechanical exercise of matching well-defined problems and equally well-defined solutions. Rather, it is fundamentally an intellectual process of constituting a reality and then attempting to work within it' (Linder and Peters, 1998, p. 45).

Some of these claims seem puzzling. Whether there was ever a time when the choice of policy instruments was really seen as an ideology-free zone seems unlikely, as the example of Ackerknecht's 1940s work given earlier (but not referred to by Linder and Peters) suggests. Where exactly the line is to be drawn between 'constitutivism' and 'proceduralism' is hard to see as well. Constitutivism seems to differ from proceduralism in that some generalization is possible and therefore appears to imply some cultural quasi-contingent theory of instrument selection (in the sense that particular beliefs and world views will predictably cohere with a preference for particular tools and instruments of policy), but we are not told how or whether the four approaches fit into some underlying theory of different world views. More to the point here, to compare the tools favoured or perceived by policy participants with others that could have been chosen or perceived by others with different ideological or cognitive baggage cannot be done without some overall categorization of the tools available in principle, to play against those actor perceptions. So the politics-of-instrument-choice approach of the type represented by Linder and Peters' work is not really an alternative to the sort of analysis developed in this book either, but rather assumes the existence of such analysis as a point of departure for exploring why political actors choose the policy instruments they do.

Generic institution-free typologies of tools

In contrast to the institutions-as-tools approach and the politics-of-instrument-choice approach, a third approach focuses on cataloguing the toolkit in a relatively institution-free way, and that is the approach taken in this book, as already explained. To some extent this general approach can also be traced back to an age before modern policy analysis. In the late eighteenth and early nineteenth century, for instance, the great utilitarian philosopher Jeremy Bentham was much preoccupied with cataloguing some of the different ways of controlling crime (for example, by incarcerating prisoners or transporting them to Australia) and of providing public services. (He even coined the handy term 'aneunomothetico-scopic' to denote this branch of knowledge (see Bentham, 1983, pp. 205–6), but for some mysterious reason the label failed to catch on.) And economists have long been concerned with identifying different generic instruments for the conduct of economic policy, for instance in distinguishing price mechanisms and rationing systems. In the early 1950s two famous American public policy scholars, Robert Dahl and Charles Lindblom (1953), followed a variant of this approach in attempting to catalogue a range of socio-economic instruments available to government, though their approach was a mixture of the institutions-as-tools approach and the generic institution-free approach.

Over the past few decades the generic institution-free approach has developed in several variants in the public policy literature. Some are applicable in principle to the instrumental choices made by any kind of organization, while others focus more specifically on the instruments available to government specifically. In the former category can be found approaches such as the broad policy intervention strategies identified by Richard Elmore (1987). Elmore conceived government instruments as variants on a four-fold division of basic intervention strategies, comprising mandates, inducements, capacity-building and system-changing. Anne Schneider and Helen Ingram (1990) elaborated and modified this approach with a closely similar but fivefold categorization, comprising authority tools, incentive tools, capacity tools, symbolic or hortatory tools and learning tools. And a further, perhaps more well-known, generic account of policy instruments is the distinction between 'carrots, sticks and sermons' as alternative methods of intervention and control. That approach originates in a 1960s analysis of types of organizational control by the famous sociologist Amitai Etzioni (1961), but was developed and introduced into the public policy literature by Evert Vedung (Bertelmans-Videc *et al.*, 1998).

In contrast to such generic approaches, applicable in principle to control and intervention strategies available to any organization, is the analysis offered in this book, which is more specific to the resources available to government or the state. It was originally developed by one of us (Hood, 1983) as a way of identifying the range of instruments available to government for gathering information and affecting behaviour at the point where government comes into contact with individuals and organizations. Later in this chapter we will explore further the similarities and differences between this approach and other 'generic' approaches to understanding the tools of government. But before doing that we will discuss how far the three broad approaches we have distinguished are complementary or conflictual, and what each is good for.

The three approaches compared: a phoney war?

This three-part classification of approaches does not cover all the possible ways of conceiving the instrumentalities of the state, just some of the commonest ones. And as we have already noted, there are numerous analyses that straddle the categories, such as the Dahl and Lindblom approach we referred to earlier and the Salamon approach, which cuts across the institutions-as-tools and generic types of analysis. But this trichotomy perhaps captures enough of the conventional forms of 'instruments' analysis to allow us to explore how far such approaches are really in conflict.

Academics naturally like to play up the novelty of their own analytic schemes, to juxtapose different analytic approaches and stress the conflicts between them. As the late John Austin observed for a rather different kind of academic behaviour, that would be their occupational disease were it not their occupation (Austin, 1962, p. 38). But the three broad approaches identified earlier are in conflict mainly in what are considered to be the most interesting questions rather than as truly rival ways of answering the same question. In that sense, pitting them against one another is something of a phoney war.

That is, no one could deny the value of cataloguing the different organizational forms available to government, even though this book for the purposes of analytic simplicity mostly takes government as a single analytic entity. Nor could anyone deny the fascination of delving into the politics and cognitive processes that lie behind the choice of different policy tools, as we ourselves have done from time to time in the earlier chapters. But these approaches are not truly different ways of answering the question posed by this book. They are answers to different questions, changing the subject rather than a different way of tackling the same subject. Moreover, a generic institution-free analysis of policy instruments is not a substitute for those other forms of analysis, but rather a complement or even a prerequisite for developing them.

For instance, categorizing different organizational forms available to government only makes sense as an account of policy intervention if it can be supplemented by an analysis of the intervention instruments that those organizations can use. It is often said that organizations at the core of government tend to be used when it comes to the most authority-intensive instruments of policy, while the use of nodality and treasure is often entrusted to a range of other organizational forms, such as special-purpose authorities or contract organizations. But there are some important exceptions to that rule and, even more importantly, 'organization' in the generic sense used in this book – the direct use of people and equipment for physical processing of one kind or another – does not obviously match with any single administrative form. It is used both by bodies at the 'core' of government, such as armies and the police, and by bodies nominally independent from government, as in the spy-thriller world of 'unacknowledgeable means' and disavowable institutions in war and foreign policy, such as all those 'front organizations' that nominally take the form of private firms or independent movements. Indeed, the advantage of keeping generic accounts of government tools and categories of forms of government institution analytically separate is precisely that institutional type and method of intervention may not always be tightly connected.

Similarly, as has already been noted, a true understanding of the politics of instrument selection presupposes and requires an analytic categorization of instruments available – whether in the form of institutional types or broader methods of intervention. That is because such an understanding necessitates a comparison between the tools that a given set of decision-makers chose to tackle the problems they faced (as with Ackerknecht's authoritarian states facing the nineteenth-century equivalents of AIDS today) with those that they could have chosen, but either did not see or did not use. The one kind of analysis in fact requires the other, and in that sense is not truly an alternative.

How the tools analysis of this book relates to other generic institution-free analyses of public policy instruments

However, when it comes to the third approach to understanding government tools – of the generic institution-free variety that we sketched out earlier – there are alternatives, as we indicated earlier, and the approach taken in this book needs to be assessed against those alternatives.

Clearly there is a lot of common ground among the various generic approaches mentioned earlier, though they vary in the nature of what they take as generic. For instance, the Elmore categorization, and the Schneider/Ingram modification of it, incorporates some of the purposes that governments and their managers aim for, such as system-changing, capacity-building and symbolism, while our analysis (and the Vedung 'carrots, sticks and sermons' approach) separates the tools available to government from the purposes, good or bad, to which they might be put. Again, which approach is most useful depends on the question to be answered.

However, the approach taken here differs from all of the other 'generic' approaches mentioned earlier in at least one of three ways that we think are important. First, the approach taken here is concerned with the instruments specifically available to *government*, arising out of its particular legal and other qualities, at the point where it meets its subjects or citizens – or, and perhaps increasingly in the modern world, other countries' citizens. All the other approaches mentioned above are concerned with tools that are in principle available to any organization and at any level of intervention, including reform of government's own organization. They can equally be applied to private sector management. The approach taken here is intended to be government-specific, even if it might be stretched to other organizations in some ways.

Second, as will be familiar to the reader by now, the approach to analysing government's tools that is taken here is concerned both with 'effecting' and 'detecting' tools – that is, tools for gathering information as well as for modifying or shaping behaviour in other ways. That gives it a dimension that is not explicit in any other approach – and, we would argue, a critical one, given that the gathering of effective information is foundational to any control system and is often the main rock on which ambitious state projects for social transformation have historically tended to founder (see, for instance, Scott, 1998).

Third, the approach we offer here rests on theoretical and conceptual foundations that are rather different from the other types of generic institution-free accounts of government tools that were mentioned above. Those accounts tend to be based on heuristic lists of strategies for control or managerial intervention, the foundations of which are left largely implicit in most cases. For instance, Salamon's (2002) *Tools of Government* takes a broad, eclectic view and argues that 'tools' can be understood in many different dimensions (singling out for particular attention the aspects of 'directness', visibility, coerciveness and automaticity), but what foundational set of categories underpins the four dimensions of instrumentality that Salamon picks out is far from clear. The account given in the preceding six chapters is explicitly rooted in the theory of cybernetics, the foundational science of control, and in the basic and distinctive properties of government rather than of organizations in general.

Further, apart from distinguishing detecting and effecting instruments, the schema offered here draws attention to some instruments that are not easily classified under the headings of 'carrots, sticks and sermons', which in principle has the strong attraction of simplicity. (If all else is equal, scientists conventionally prefer simpler explanations, representations and analytic approaches to more complex ones (following the 'Occam's razor' principle of *entia non sunt multiplicanda praeter necessitatem*) – and students certainly do.) One notable example of a type of instrument that does not fit very readily into the 'carrots, sticks and sermons' (CSS) typology is the case where environments are physically structured so as to shape behaviour, for example by making violation impossible, or very costly, such as fencing to shape crowd behaviour, for instance at sporting events or near pedestrian crossings on the roads. This set of activities – sometimes called 'architecture', particularly in the literature on digital codes (Lessig, 1999), but 'organization' in the schema offered in this book – cannot really be forced into the 'CSS' trichotomy. But it has historically been one of the most important ways by which governments have gathered information and shaped behaviour, has been taken as a central aspect of government activity by philosophers from Bentham to Foucault, and is likely to remain so, particularly with digital-age technology.

Of course the value of any map or categorization for understanding government activity depends on the analytic purposes to which it is to be put, and no doubt on other factors as well, including our own individual tastes and cognitive 'wiring'. But precisely for that reason it is important to understand just what is similar and different in the various approaches that are on offer, the niche that each approach is designed to fill, and what is distinctive about the approach being offered here.

The challenge of digital-age technology for the analysis of public policy instruments

Each of the three broad 'tools' approaches discussed in this chapter can help us to explore what difference if any digital-age technology makes to the array of policy instruments. But as yet that exploration has not gone very far, mainly because the 'tools' scholars and the 'information technology' scholars have hitherto tended to live in different worlds (if not exactly on different planets). Joining up those worlds is a key challenge for contemporary study of government. In the next chapter we shall return to issues about how digital-age technology may shape government's instruments in the future, but we will close this one by exploring the challenges such technology offers to each of the 'instruments' approaches that we set out at the beginning of the chapter.

For the institutions-as-tools approach, the central issue is how far and in what ways digital-age technology changes the set of institutional arrangements available to government. After all, technological change has often been argued by historians to herald major institutional change. One of the best-known claims of that type is Lynn White's (1962) controversial argument that the invention of the stirrup in eighth-century Europe (and the consequent possibility of creating for the first time a corps of mounted warriors who could strike deadly blows without being unseated) was a decisive element in the creation of the institutional arrangements associated with the age of feudalism. Later historians (such as Bachrach and Baratz, 1970) have heavily and increasingly challenged White's argument as problematic and oversimplified. But could the advent of digital-age technology today produce as decisive a shift in government organization as White thought the stirrup had brought to medieval Europe?

There are at least three possible routes by which that might happen. First, much of the thrust of digital-age technology is in functions that were once distinctive (if not unique) to public bureaucracies. New ways of fitting cases into categories, filing and recalling information (the traditional casework of bureaucracy) are after all central to the filing and memory functions that were once distinctive to public bureaucracies, paving the way for forms of privatization and outsourcing to global corporations that were not available in the pre-digital age (see Dunleavy, 1994; Dunleavy *et al.*, 2006).

Another way that information-age technology could reshape the institutional forms available to government is through the new forms of communication it involves. Much has been written about the way such developments reshape organizations in a geographical sense, for instance in having 'back office' functions once co-located with strategy units or front-line delivery conducted in different regions, countries or even continents (see, for instance, Bellamy and Taylor, 1998). Some scholars, like Paul Frissen (1996, 1999), have claimed that such developments work against traditional hierarchies within government, though such claims have been countered by scholars like Ian Holliday (2001), who argues that traditional central agencies in government are more than capable of using developments in information and communications technology (ICT) to maintain and consolidate their power. Moreover, as we have suggested in earlier chapters, there may be a broader sense in which all organizations providing modern forms of communications may become tools of government, in its battles against terrorism, subversion or tax evasion. For example, a report on the capture of a Chinese journalist working for the *New York Times* (Zhao Han) in 2004 indicated that the unlucky Mr Zhao was detected by police in a Pizza Hut restaurant in Shanghai as soon as he switched on his mobile phone to complain about a cockroach in his food (see *Daily Telegraph*, 24 December 2005, p. 12). In the digital age, for some states all of the time and all states some of the time, mobile phone networks can work as a tool of government detection (through the medium of authority) whoever formally owns them.

Third, digital-age technology may provide computational power that makes new forms of organization possible by dramatic reduction of transaction costs for certain kinds of activity. For instance, electric power is a good that cannot readily be stored once it has been generated, meaning that a spot market was not really practicable in the early twentieth century when electric power generation developed, and in effect the only organizational alternatives were direct state organization or regulated private monopoly. But by the late twentieth century, a virtual spot market in electric power became possible through digital-age technology, creating the possibility of a different (commercial market) kind of provider structure (see Foster, 1992, p. 73). And the same sort of technology opened up new possibilities for users of utilities such as gas and telephones to choose among alternative providers in a way that would have been either impossible or very costly in the pre-digital age.

The advent of digital-age technology also raises important questions for the second, politics-of-instruments approach to the tools of government. On the face of it, such technology seems to be a dramatic case of what Linder and Peters (1992) call 'instrumentalism' in the politics of policy instruments, though they do not discuss ICT in detail, or really at all, in their analysis. Digital-age technology tends to be treated by, or presented to, governments as a panacea for many of the problems associated with traditional bureaucratic functioning – such as high cost, inflexibility, overload, difficulties in tracking down elusive lawbreakers – and thus to figure large in upbeat trade-off-free political visions of new ways to deliver public service, at least since the 1993 US National Performance Review presented information-age technology as a pathway to several kinds of bureaucratic salvation.

Explaining such 'instrumentalism' over ICT raises a familiar but difficult issue about the relative place of ideas and interests in tool selection. Is it just a product of ideas or beliefs? If so, the idea that new technology can bring about a new and better form of society and politics is a long-standing one, going back at least to Marx and Saint-Simon more than a hundred and fifty years ago. Charles Dunlop and Rob Kling (1991, pp. 16–17) point out that such visions typically focus on the possibilities that can be reached from the use of the chosen technology in a world of high trust and social cooperation where sabotage, conflict, politics and adversarial legalism are unknown or at least unimportant. Many of the bright visions of 'information-age' government do indeed have precisely those qualities (see also Margetts, 1999).

But interests may be equally important in driving this policy 'instrumentalism' and indeed it is notable that enthusiasm for re-engineering government through digital-age technology has dramatically increased as the internet and many kinds of software have moved from domains dominated by egalitarian 'hippy' technophiles (or indeed state bureaucrats) to a world of multinational private corporate oligopoly. The obvious historical parallel is with the way that nineteenth-century Europe saw many kinds of arms manufacture move from a domain dominated by state arsenals to one dominated by private arms companies, albeit closely linked with governments. If the nineteenth and early twentieth centuries saw the rise of the military–industrial complex, the late twentieth century saw the rise of an information–industrial complex with large corporate interests in treating digital-age technology as a universal solution looking for problems – though of course the solution often turned into the problem, as the endless roll call of government IT fiascos shows.

Indeed, what is interesting today are the rare cases where government continues to use 'organization' for managing how individuals relate to the digital world, as in the contemporary case of Saudi Arabia where (following a 2001 Council of Ministers Resolution prohibiting users within that kingdom from publishing or accessing certain content on the internet) government's own Internet Services Unit (ISU) directly operates the high-speed data links that connect the country to the international internet. Jonathan Zittrain (Zittrain and Edelman, 2004b) commented of this unusual use of 'organization':

> while Saudi internet users may subscribe to any of a number of local internet service providers, all Web traffic is apparently forwarded through a central array of proxy servers at the ISU, which implements Internet content filtering roughly in line with parts of the Resolution . . . The ISU administrative web site explains the implementation of the government's content filtering regime, presents the reasoning behind it, and lets Saudi internet users request that a particular site or URL be blocked or unblocked. Citing the Qur'an as a basis, the government describes its task with filtering as 'preserv[ing] our Islamic values, filtering the Internet content to prevent the materials that contradict with our beliefs or may influence our culture.'

However, such internet filtering techniques also vary in the strength with which they are enforced: Zittrain (China's Digital Future Conference, 30 April 2004, Berkeley, California, webcast at journalism.berkeley.edu/events/) has also observed that in Saudi Arabia, the government's 'bark is worse than its bite', whereas in China, an extremely sophisticated internet filtering regime (see Chapter 2) gives the government a 'bite' worse than its 'bark'.

Such issues have been remarkably little explored, though they are central to the politics of digital-age tool selection. Moreover, a key present-day equivalent to the question explored by Ackerknecht in the last century, as explored earlier, is how the use of digital-age tools is shaped by differences in political regime. Just as with Ackerknecht's case of the various ways that different types of states handled a common set of contagious diseases in the nineteenth century, we might expect the politics of digital-age tool selection to work out differently in different kinds of state, and indeed Kraemer and King (1986) long ago argued that technologies in government tend to mirror and reproduce the different cultures they develop within (see also Hood, 2000).

In the sort of regime or policy domains where concentrated business groups dominate the state, digital-age tool selection will be just as dominated by 'rent-seeking' strategies to extract the highest possible profits from the taxpayer as in any other age – and cases in point are not exactly far to seek. Where the state has more autonomy, the politics of digital-age tool selection may be more coloured by its efforts to use digital-age technology to maximize its own power – as in the examples given earlier of the Saudi government operating internet servers and of the Chinese government using mobile phone companies as a means of tracking its enemies, radically extending government's traditional capacity to detect and punish (see Rule, 1973; Bunyan, 1976; Ackroyd *et al.*, 1977; Brin, 1998).

In types of state or policy domains dominated by strong egalitarian or individualist world views, digital-age technology will be seen respectively as a way to join everyone up and level social differences, or to introduce more markets and choice into social affairs. And, as we suggested in several earlier chapters, in states or policy domains where government is weak and bankrupt, digital-age technology may be a sideshow confined to a small wealthy elite of 'digital liberals' or well-resourced criminals and closed to everyone else, as in the case of a developing country known to one of us where a major hospital has had no computer-based records since the antiquated IT system fell prey to the 'Y2K' bug in 2000. Surprisingly, given the massive amount of research funding that has gone into digital technology and government, we still do not have even basic comparative studies that focus sharply and squarely on such differences.

For the third set of approaches to analysing the tools of government – the classification of generic forms of action for the purpose of exploring alternatives and combinations – the question posed by the digital age is how far and in what ways the new technology has changed that repertoire of instruments. And as we have seen in previous chapters, at some level the basic resources available to government do not change with changes in technology. Carrots, sermons and sticks or nodality–authority–treasure–organization remain the fundamentals in a digital age as in any other. In that sense, it is not clear that the advent of information-age technology brings fundamentally new instruments to government of the same order as nodality, authority, treasure and organization, any more than the railway age of the nineteenth century brought fundamentally new principles to the law (see Holmes, 1920, p. 196). Moreover, as we saw in the NATO chapters, there are sharp limits to 'virtualizing' government, particularly for those situations that most call for government action, where normal facilities or civilities have broken down, the chips are down and the stakes are high. *Pace* some of the more exaggerated prophets of virtual government, even in a world where much is digitized and 'virtual', many of those virtual processes ultimately depend for their efficacy on processes that are unavoidably physical rather than virtual. For example, all forms of digital technology depend on electric power, so if the power supply fails or is deliberately destroyed, computers become junk. Indeed, the limits of virtuality show up sharply with those types of government operations that involve unavoidably physical operations, especially for disaster-relief activity or operations at the coercive end of government's relationship with individuals when government faces principled or opportunistic recalcitrance.

Nevertheless, as with the advent of railways 150 years or so ago, government has to adapt those basic resources to the new technological context and produce the digital-age equivalents of its traditional instruments. For instance, as already noted in Chapter 3, digital-age government may involve using internet providers or mobile phone companies as information conduits in the same way as some European governments treated innkeepers in the eighteenth century. It may involve producing the digital-age equivalent of stamps, the great fiscal invention of the seventeenth century, for taxing email and internet traffic.

Moreover, as we have suggested in the previous six chapters and will summarize in the next, the digital age may dramatically change the costs and practicality of different modes of action. As we have shown, the cyber age has produced some particularly striking changes in the information-gathering tools available to government, for instance with the near-universal ownership of mobile phones. And we have argued that in many of government's traditional policy domains, it is the 'detector' or information-gathering part of those operations that has changed more as a result of information-age technology than the 'effector' part of the operation. It is the effecting end of the process – such as 'boots on the ground' to tackle rioters, the physical tracking down of tax non-payers to haul them off to justice, the burning or burying of infected animals or the enforcement of quarantine systems – that seems to have been less transformed by the information age, or at least transformation has been slower to arrive.

Conclusion

This chapter has explored some of the different ways of understanding government's tools that have developed over the past few decades, though all of them have earlier antecedents. It has aimed to show how the analysis of government's tools developed in this book compares with some of the other approaches available today. The argument has been that at least two of those other approaches, namely the institutions-as-tools approach and the politics-of-instrument-choice approach, are not really alternatives to the way that government tools are analysed in this book, but ways of answering different questions. Our approach complements rather than competes with such approaches. However, there are also a few generic institution-free approaches to the analysis of government tools that are genuine alternatives to the approach taken here. There are some strong overlaps, but our approach is distinctive in distinguishing information-gathering tools from those for shaping behaviour, and in rooting the analysis in basic properties of government rather than organizations or management generally.

All of the three main approaches discussed above were developed before the advent of the modern digital age, and digital-age developments present an important challenge for all of them – a challenge which has been surprisingly little taken up as yet. This is the challenge which we have tackled in the earlier chapters and return to in the next. Contrary to the tone taken by some of the cyber-prophets, we argue that technology-free analyses of government's tools do not need to be abandoned in the digital age. Indeed, it is only by applying technology-neutral analytic frameworks such as this one that we can see precisely what alters when technology changes.

Chapter 9

Looking Ahead: The Tools of Government in the Digital Age

> If all the intellectuals in the plays of Chekhov who spent all their time guessing what would happen in twenty, thirty or forty years had been told that in forty years interrogation by torture would be practised in Russia . . . not one of Chekhov's plays would have gotten to its end.
>
> (Solzhenitsyn, 1973, p. 733)

With Solzhenitsyn's sobering comment in mind, this short concluding chapter aims to summarize this book's argument and to look cautiously ahead, in three ways. First, building on the previous chapter and our earlier analysis, it aims to project forward the trends we have identified in the tools of government. If the future turned out to be like the recent past, what would happen to the tools of government? Second, moving away from the simplifying generic account of government tools given in this book to the real world of huge differences between states and regimes across the world, we explore what kind of variety we see now and how that might develop. Third, we discuss the potential that the digital age may offer for a 'sharpening' of government tools, both to economize on governmental effort and to make government's interactions with individuals less obtrusive.

The future as an extrapolation of the past: a new world of cyber-detection, group-targeting and variable nodality

Everyone knows the perils of predicting the future by extrapolating from the past, even on matters far more mundane than those that engaged those high-minded Chekhovian intellectuals. In the nineteenth century, people thought the growth of cities would mean an ever-growing problem of horse dung as traffic increased, or that economic growth would stop when all the coal mines had been worked out; and in the twentieth century, some saw airships and flying boats as the wave of the future. Nevertheless, past trends can *sometimes* be a guide to future developments, and if the future *does* turn out to be an extended version of the past, we can expect to see further developments in the digitally enabled changes to the tools noted in the four NATO chapters above. Two of these we observed across all the tools (advances in cyber-detection and group-targeting), and the third, variable nodality, reflects the ways in which the digital age presents a new environment for government's use of nodality.

Cyber-detection

First, we might expect to see advances in the instruments available to government for detection, building on more developed forms of the technological changes we noted in Chapters 2 to 5 above. For example, the camera technology that has transformed the way government detects speeding drivers can in principle be extended to form the basis of comprehensive, variable and finely discriminatory road-pricing schemes that would have required the roads to be covered by a host of expensively staffed physical toll gates forty years ago (*provided* the technology is robust enough, or the population law-abiding enough, for the cameras to avoid being disabled). Such a development could form the twenty-first-century equivalent to the way computers allowed the development of spot markets in electricity in the 1980s, as mentioned earlier. The same digital technologies that allow gas and electricity users to switch from one supplier to another without physical reconnection to different pipes (as used to happen in an earlier age of competition between water companies in London) could in principle be used to ration supplies more discriminatingly in times of shortage, cutting off the young and fit while leaving the elderly and vulnerable connected. And data-matching technology in the financial sphere could also develop to a point where government starts to be more like the more sophisticated private sector corporations of today in its detailed knowledge of our financial affairs (and consequent ability to tax and monitor us), drawn from all the various ways we use cards and electronic accounts.

Likewise, intelligent turnstile systems, touched on in Chapter 5 but still in their infancy at the time of writing, could in principle allow government to track who goes where in physical space. Indeed, in the 'land of the free' itself (the USA) there has been discussion of implanting microchips in babies at birth so that not only was the identity of each individual known, but their precise location could be tracked at any time (Kilde, 1999). (Government already requires such chips to be implanted in dogs of 'dangerous' breeds in several countries, horse-racing authorities require them for racehorses, and some years ago the chief medical officer of Finland claimed that in Sweden, permission had been given to implant prisoners and nursing-home patients as far back as the 1970s (Kilde, 1999).) In fact, in the USA it is already possible to buy Global Positioning System (GPS) locators which can be locked on to a child's wrist and transmit the wearer's location to a central receiver, such that concerned parents can log on to a website or use a phone to check their child's location to within a metre or so. But of course such use of technology is a classic case of the 'worried well' seeking reassurance, because these devices only work as long as the children concerned, or whoever might abduct them, fail to disable it, and so will tend to fail just at the point where they are really needed.

We have also observed various ways in which cyber-detectors double up as effectors, as in the classic case of drivers slamming on their brakes whenever they think they are on camera. The presence of CCTV cameras is also often advertised, on the assumption that such knowledge will deter anti-social or criminal behaviour. There are, of course, circumstances in which they might have the opposite effect, as is said to have happened in an experiment some years ago when the registration numbers and speeds of speeding drivers were flashed on to roadside gantries in the UK, which only encouraged some gung-ho drivers to try to beat everyone else's speed record and caused the experiment to be abandoned.

Indeed, in some of the most extreme sci-fi happy-robot visions of the cyber-future, government might be able to link effectors and detectors by implanting tracking devices such as microchips and RFID (radio frequency identification) tags in every individual it wished to control, with the beguiling prospect of government thereby acquiring the power to do everything from calming down road-rage drivers to managing paedophiles. Kilde (1999) has claimed that:

> when a 5-micromillimeter microchip . . . is placed into the optical nerve of the eye, it draws neuro-impulses from the brain that embody the experiences, smells, sights, and voice of the implanted person. Once transferred and stored in a computer, these neuro-impulses can be projected back to the person's brain via the microchip to be re-experienced. Using a RMS, a land-

based computer operator can send electromagnetic messages (encoded as signals) to the nervous system, affecting the target's performance.

Group-targeting

Similarly and relatedly, we might expect to see further development towards the digitally enabled group-targeted use of government's tools, which was a theme that came out of each of the four NATO chapters earlier in the book. We argued there that technological developments had tended to make applications of effecting tools in the middle of the spectrum from general to particular easier for government, but at the same time made both highly particular and widely generalized applications proportionately more difficult and expensive. If such trends continue in the future, we might expect a development of ever more sophisticated group-targeted messages from government, in what is called narrowcasting, in the jargon of communications theory. So if we belong to some group that government has in its sights for some reason – for instance, if we are smokers or obese, put the wrong kinds of garbage in our recycling bins, or have homes or cars with a heavy carbon footprint – government can in principle send direct messages to our inbox or mobile phone relatively easily, and not just generalized posters and the like for us to ignore.

When it comes to government's tokens of authority, we might similarly expect digital technology to produce ever more sophisticated ways of electronically discriminating between those favoured groups which are to be fast-tracked or given the highest levels of access and those of us at the other end of the spectrum who are to be blocked or slow-tracked. Some authors have labelled the trend towards such discrimination the 'social sorting' of citizens (see Bowker and Star, 1999; Lyon, 2003). And when those digital-age authority tokens are linked up with organization, we can expect even inanimate objects like walls and barriers to behave differently according to the group we belong to. Similarly, in the use of treasure we might expect the 'zero touch' approach that we have discussed at several points in previous chapters to mean that our benefits or tax credits are paid electronically if we fit into some social or demographic category that triggers government's cash-dispensers – and our e-bank accounts automatically depleted when the boot is on the other foot. If that is indeed to be the wave of the future for government, it will be following in the footsteps of those US supermarkets and burger restaurants which at the time of writing were testing new biometric systems that allowed shoppers to pay for their food by scanning their fingerprints into a computer and having money withdrawn automatically from a credit or debit account.

However, we have also argued in the earlier analysis that government's use of its effecting tools either for individuals who do not fit conveniently into group categories or for the population at large does not seem to have been correspondingly enhanced by digital-age developments so far, and has arguably become relatively more expensive. If that continues to be the case, as we argued in the last chapter, we can expect the weak point of digital-age government increasingly to lie at the point where government has to deal with individuals who do not conveniently fit into digitally identifiable groups, have plastic digital identities or choose not to play the digital game at all.

That lack of fit sometimes comes about for innocent reasons, and projections of an ageing population across the developed countries seems certain to make it an increasing problem for government's digital dealings with individuals in the future (since as we become elderly we are less likely to be able to remember complicated passwords and PINs, and biometric identifiers like iris patterns and fingerprints alter too). The lack of fit may also come about if social developments such as increasing migration mean that a rising proportion of the individuals governments deal with fall outside the 'full citizenship' category as discussed in Chapter 1. Further, as we have noted earlier, the lack of fit is also produced when those whom government is trying to target choose to make themselves digitally invisible, and when recalcitrant individuals or groups use digital weapons against government, for instance in increasingly sophisticated forms of identity theft that drain government's coffers in fraudulent benefit claims. Indeed, if we project that development forward, we might expect an increasingly sharp cultural and political divide between those individuals who choose to live in the sort of orderly digital world that governments want them to inhabit, and those who choose individually or collectively to live in a different form of digital world that works against government's version, or to step outside 'digi-world' altogether.

Variable nodality

When it comes to nodality, it could be argued that up to now, this is the government instrument that has been most strongly affected by digital-age technology, in both collecting and distributing information, and we might expect that to develop further if the future were to be an extrapolation of the past. But these digital developments seem to cut two ways. On the one hand, for much of the ordinary – or extraordinary – business of life, the diversification of media channels and the quantity of data of every kind available on the internet mean that government may be relatively less visible as an information source to the public at large than in an earlier era, as we suggested in Chapter 2. For example, since 2001, the US Federal Bureau of Investigation (FBI) has advertised on the 'Most Wanted' section of its website a reward of $25 million offered by the US Department of State for information leading to the apprehension and conviction of Osama bin Laden (noted in Chapter 4). But a Google search for 'bin Laden' in 2006 did not return that FBI site– nor, indeed, that of any other US federal government department – in the top twenty returns, beyond which, research suggests, most users do not access. (Rather, the top twenty listings included various media reports, an entry on bin Laden's life in the free online encyclopaedia Wikipedia, the full transcript of videotapes sent to the Arab TV station al-Jazeera in 2004 and 2001, the text of bin Laden's Fatwa against the American people issued in 1996 and 1998 (http://www.mideastweb.org) and a collection of 'Anti-Osama' flash games and movies to either download or play online from a private sector media company.)

Competition can come from many sources, including other governments (as in the example of the 2004 Asian tsunami in Chapter 2). In some cases, private sites put together publicly available government information in a form more accessible than government's own websites, meaning that government becomes nodal at one remove as it were (as in the case of the UK www.upmystreet.com site, originally created to illustrate the lack of visibility of government on the Web). Competition can also come from organizations with malign intent, as with the case of a scam run in the UK by an organization offering to handle applications for a European Health Insurance Card for UK citizens travelling in the EU, at the cost of £15, when in fact the service was available online for free from a government site. By obtaining good rankings in the search engine listings, the site (ehic-card.com) was able to 'beat' the official site (buried in the Department of Health site at dh.gov.uk/travellers) and many UK citizens ended up paying for a service they could easily have had for free (*Guardian*, 15 July 2006). Indeed, in an online world where at the time of writing the auction site eBay had 168 million users, the social networking site www.myspace.com had 100 million users, the online bookshop www.amazon.com had 35 million customers in over 250 countries and the community site www.craigslist.org linking urban communities all over the world had four billion page views a month (*Observer*, 13 August, 2006), governments may find themselves struggling for online nodality.

This competition puts governments under continual pressure to keep up with societal trends in internet use. In countries with higher levels of internet penetration, the mid-2000s brought widespread use of technologies and applications loosely described as 'Web 2.0', such as 'blogs' (online diaries), 'wikis' (information sources written and edited by users) and the social networking, entertainment and community-based websites noted above. Such sites allow users to generate content which is then shared by other users, either by posting comments, writing and editing content, putting up photographs or video clips, creating 'networks' of friends for distribution of messages, information and photographs, or by creating a bespoke website (a 'mashup') just by typing in a key word such as a postcode. These applications can lead to large-scale data generation, such as the popular www.ratemyteacher.com, with 9 million users ranking 1.3 million teachers in 54,000 schools in the US and 500,000 users in the UK, where pupils and parents score their teachers along a number of dimensions. In general such applications were little used by government at the time of writing, and the reluctance of government departments even to link to them was perhaps understandable given the informal and unofficial nature of the type of content they generate. But their clear popularity and rapidly growing use, with the potential for users to assist in raising an organization's nodality, suggested that the lag between government and other sectors in the race for public attention, noted above and in Chapter 2, could widen.

If those developments continue in the future, we might expect to find government to be decreasingly nodal in the Google-search sense, in a world in which the route to visibility and access to virtual information lie through the most heavily used search engines (Google, Yahoo and MSN at the time of writing) rather than through traditional government-controlled physical nodes such as the local post office or town hall. The algorithms that these powerful multinational corporations use are more tightly guarded than any state secret against the strategizing of those who want to reach the top of search engine listings and thus maximize *their* nodality. If that position is projected into the future, governments must not only join that (expensive) competition to try to move their websites up the search engine listings, but also to be lighter on their feet than governments usually are when the algorithms change. For instance, if a leading search engine company failed, government might find its entire online presence effectively disappearing from view unless it moved fast. So if such trends continue, government nodality in the digital age may be increasingly hard-won, fragile and volatile across much of its activity.

Against that scenario, it might be argued that the development of such corporations is actually God's gift to government, because it gives government new opportunities for giving itself nodality without all that expensive organization, of the post-office and town-hall type. Indeed, the mere use of its formal authority may suffice to put all those impressive private sector facilities to work for government. Just as it is often said that most governments no longer need to own and operate telephone companies or post offices to monitor their suspects or enemies, instead using their authority to compel whoever does operate such facilities to provide the information required, exactly the same principle could apply to the cyber-world. We noticed in the last chapter that governments can use mobile phone companies to enhance their detection power in this way, for good or ill. And indeed numerous US corporations, including Google, have been berated by human rights groups who claim they have been releasing personal records that have led to the incarceration of cyber-activists, for example in Burma, Egypt and China. In Russia, regulation introduced in 2000 required all Internet Service Providers (ISPs) to reroute, in real time, all electronic transmissions to the Federal Security Service, with ISPs required to pay for the technology and train agents to use it, facing the revoking of their licences should they fail to comply (*St Petersburg Times*, 15 June 1999). Just as private banks have historically been an instrumentality of government as much as an alternative to government, so the intermediaries of the digital world could develop in the same way. For instance, they could be used as conduits for taxation and a means for government to watch particular classes of individuals in which it might be interested (such as users of pornographic websites).

Admittedly, that does not seem to be the main direction of travel at the moment. Indeed in 2005 when the US Department of Justice requested one million anonymized records of the users of pornographic websites in 2005 from the search engine Google, in an attempt to explore the pervasiveness of pornography on the internet and the usage patterns of such sites, they were refused (*The Boston Globe*, 21 January 2006 at boston.com). However, it can still be argued that the competition for nodality, and indeed cybernodality itself, operates only in a limited range. As we suggested in the last chapter, in extreme situations when power supplies fail, natural disasters strike and other civilities break down, the digital world may go into the background and more traditional, inescapably physical and inescapably governmental forms of nodality come into the foreground. Messages may have to be dropped out of the sky, from planes or helicopters, rather than sent along virtual channels. Warnings may have to be conveyed house to house or information dispensed on physical noticeboards at central points. Government in *those* circumstances rarely finds itself competing with private companies, though it may well be competing with resistance groups or non-government organizations facing the same kinds of constraints. We can of course (in Chekhovian–intellectual style) imagine that such situations might occur less in the future, but that would be a triumph of hope over experience, in a world where disasters and major breakdowns of civil order show no signs of disappearing. If the future is indeed to be an extrapolation of the past, nodality is not likely to disappear from government's toolbox.

Same tools, different governments

In the previous chapters, we have deliberately used the term 'government' in a mostly generic and undifferentiated sense. To show the range of applications of the tools we have described, we have drawn examples both from historical and contemporary cases and from authoritarian and democratic states. For the most part we have argued that the available tools are generic, but that applications and effects vary with politics and culture. Indeed, we argued in Chapter 6 that one of the advantages of the toolkit framework presented in this book is that it lends itself to comparison, across time and across and within governments.

In Chapter 6 we suggested that different kinds of regimes could be expected to use the set of tools in different ways and to different extents in their dealings with individuals, depending on how readily they can marshall nodality, authority, treasure and organization, with predatory and failed states likely to rely heavily on organization and the latter on 'group treatment'. And in the last chapter, discussing the politics-of-instrument-choice approach, we pointed out some of the different types of digital-age application we might expect in different political circumstances, dependent on conditions such as the power of rent-seeking private business corporations in shaping the state's choices and the relative power of different world views in the political culture. The extent and ways in which government in the future uses the heightened ability that the digital age theoretically gives it to message members of particular groups it wants to influence (as mentioned earlier) will depend heavily on the way political culture develops in different societies.

Beyond that, the opportunity for government to incorporate digital applications of its tools will vary according to the extent to which society itself is 'digital', but governments can also vary in whether they are ahead of, in step with or behind the level of digital 'savvy' in the population they deal with. To draw a crude motoring analogy, some governments are in effect using horses and carts in an environment where some or all of the population has a state-of-the-art modern vehicle; some are using horses when everyone else is too; some are driving state-of-the-art modern vehicles when everyone else is using horses; and a few (mainly but not only the wealthy Western democracies) are in effect driving relatively modern vehicles when much of the population also has the same kind of vehicle.

Clearly those differences are important for what government can do (and if you don't believe us, try driving a horse and cart in modern city traffic), and Table 9.1 summarizes the array of possibilities, with some examples.

For states in cell (1), which we can expect to become steadily more populated over time, the problem for government is to keep up with digital developments in society to develop or at least maintain the efficacy of its tools. That requires the ability to manage or procure skills and expertise likely to be in high demand in market economies and increasingly the ability to manage large-scale technologically complex contracts with multinational corporations – a major challenge for the digital age. Dunleavy *et al.* (2006), in a cross-national study, discovered large variations in the capacity of seven governments in some of the wealthiest democracies to run large-scale government information systems and work successfully with IT contractors, and that challenge is arguably equally or more severe for less developed countries.

At the time of writing, a few small states seemed to be in cell (2) in Table 9.1 – the equivalent of the horse and cart surrounded by at

TABLE 9.1 ***Digital government and digital society: four types***

		Government	
		Significantly digital	*Largely non-digital*
Population	*Significantly digital*	(1) *Analogy*: driving modern car among modern traffic *Example*: Wealthy liberal democracies, China, Arab states	(2) *Analogy*: driving horse and cart in modern traffic *Example*: Special small states such as Grenada and Oman
	Largely non-digital	(3) *Analogy*: driving modern car surrounded by horse-drawn traffic *Example*: LDC states such as Yemen and Mozambique, some Central and Eastern European as Lithuania	(4) *Analogy*: Driving horse and cart among other horse-drawn traffic *Example*: LDC states such as much of sub-Saharan Africa, Turkmenistan, North Korea

least some modern vehicles. They included the sultanate of Oman, with no governmental websites at all but in a society where internet penetration was beginning to be significant (at just below 5 per cent), and the tiny state of Grenada, where internet penetration was over 6 per cent, yet UNPAN rankings put the government's online presence below that of Yemen (UNPAN, 2005, p. 220). Of course we have to be careful about taking government websites as a proxy for the general level of digital applications of a government's tools (it would not include satellite tracking systems, for example), and in general this category seems 'exotic' in the sense that, just as only a few eccentrics would regularly drive a horse and cart in modern traffic, governments in practice are likely to have to move out of this box, particularly if they find themselves challenged by societal movements crossing national boundaries and organized online.

Cell (3), where government is significantly digital but the population at large is not, also seems likely to be a temporary or transitional category. At the time of writing, it included states such as Yemen and Mozambique, which had some web presence and were moving towards some interactive services, but in societies where internet penetration was less than 0.1 per cent. In such cases, either government's online presence is really aimed at audiences overseas, rather than the domestic population, or the government is aiming to 'lead' digital developments in the society at large. Where it is the latter, government may need to expend large amounts of scarce treasure and organization in encouraging the home population to interact with it digitally, as in the example of the government-organized tax internet cafés in Chile that we gave in Chapter 7.

Cell (4), where neither government nor society is digital, is little discussed in the 'digital-age' literature but is far from insignificant even today. At the time of writing this category included the governments of Somalia, Zambia, Liberia and Haiti (for example) which had no internet presence at all (UNPAN, 2005, p. 239) and operated in societies with negligible levels of internet penetration (zero for Somalia, 0.1 per cent for Liberia and below 0.5 per cent for Haiti and Zambia). This category also included a number of decidedly non-liberal states such as Zimbabwe, Turkmenistan (no governmental internet presence and internet penetration of 0.04 per cent) and North Korea (zero in both cases). If cell (3) states were trying to reach people outside their borders or move their societies into the digital age, cell (4) governments seemed to want to keep the world outside at bay and to keep their home populations outside the digital age.

Looking forward, it is obvious that, as the digital age develops, more and more states will move from the other cells into cell (1) of Table 9.1, as the informational equivalents of horses and carts are consigned to oblivion. But whether such a move will necessarily go together with democratization and debureaucratization is harder to say, though modern-day equivalents of those late-nineteenth-century Chekhovian intellectuals might hope so. At one time it was often an unspoken assumption among observers of computer and digital-age applications in government that such developments would almost automatically tend to foster 'citizen empowerment', a move away from rigid state bureaucracy and even a new kind of democracy. But this assumption is challenged by regimes like the

People's Republic of China, adapting to the digital age by using authority to gain nodality otherwise lost since the heyday of the Maoist party state (by inserting governmental nodes at strategic points in citizens' online communications using internet-filtering techniques), and the even more sophisticated and centralized government management of individuals' access to the Web in Saudi Arabia. These examples suggest that liberal democracy is not necessarily the only game in town for government in the digital age, particularly in the quasi-market but non-liberal states. Even for these states, however, it is probably possible to predict a net loss of nodality for the future, because of the inevitability of expert internet users reaching the outside world through search engines based in other jurisdictions (such as google.com as opposed to the local Chinese version, discussed in Chapter 2).

Sharpening government's tools

In the digital age as in every other, the challenge for governments is to find new ways of using a limited basic array of tools effectively and creatively, as technology and social patterns change.

In Chapter 7, we discussed some of the general criteria for 'smart usage', showing some of the complexities that arise in attempts to achieve the apparently unexceptionable aims of economizing on bureaucracy and of limiting the obtrusive impact of government's detectors and effectors on the individuals with whom it deals. We argued that a government wishing to save on bureaucracy will tend to prefer instruments that are general rather than particular, that are passive rather than active and that draw on its contingently rather than immanently depletable resources – normally nodality and authority rather than treasure or organization. We also argued that a government wishing to limit obtrusive impact on those with whom it deals will prefer 'low constraint' to 'high constraint' tools, meaning that it is nodality and treasure that will be chosen over authority or organization, wherever they are substitutable (and will generally aim to maximize the precision and scalability of its detecting and effecting tools, so that it hits only its intended targets and hits them only as hard as they need to be hit to achieve the desired effect).

Although, as we noted earlier, recipes for better government and policy-making often seem to live in a trade-off-free 'win–win' parallel universe far removed from the planet most of the rest of us inhabit, those two simple criteria evidently lead in rather different directions. But nodality as an instrument does seem to have 'win–win' qualities, since it is the only basic form of government instrument that can simultaneously achieve economy in both of the senses that we explored in Chapter 7. So governments preferring nodality as a resource wherever it can viably be used can stay in the comfort of that trade-off-free nirvana desperately sought by politicians, because nodality is usually *both* cheaper *and* less obtrusive than the other resources available to government.

One of the key challenges of the digital age is therefore for government to use its nodality in a sharper and smarter way than before, in a world where government may face more competition for nodality in some of its operations and also faces new threats to its nodality from pranksters, hackers and other challengers operating in digital mode. In an earlier age, government's road signs or information posters could be physically switched, removed or replaced by practical jokers, vandals or political activists (from minority-language groups, for example), but their electronic equivalents (such as the 'No podemos conducir para ti' (We can't drive for you) beamed over Spanish motorways on electronic gantries in the 2000s) are also vulnerable to such treatment. Hackers in the United States have already succeeded in using wireless networks to change electronic transport and airport signs to display their own messages – a way of undermining government's nodality that obviously requires government to be technologically smarter than before in tracking down or combating the perpetrators.

Similarly, where it faces greater competition for nodality in an internet age, government may need to be more active in its efforts to obtain information or put its messages across. For instance, as government complements or replaces pre-digital-age methods of conveying information on matters such as vaccination of children (leaflets in doctors' surgeries, posters on walls, newspaper advertisements, TV and radio messages) into information conveyed on websites, it faces the challenge of ensuring that internet users access its messages, rather than those on the websites of other interested parties, such as pressure groups or medical researchers with opposing points of view. The extent to which that happens will depend on several factors, all demanding greater 'smartness' on government's part. One of them is the extent to which government is able to ensure that its own websites figure in the top ten or twenty sites listed when a search query is made through a search engine, as noted in the first section. A second is the extent to which a user can find the information they need quickly on the website, given that most users only stay on a site for a few clicks before leaving if they do not find the information they need (Huberman *et al.*, 1998; Escher *et al.*, 2006). Government may need to follow successful private corporations' efforts at 'usability testing' and clustering related information together, given that those users who arrive at its websites through search engines (as most do) are unlikely to start at the home page.

A third is the extent to which government can marshall the kind of technological expertise needed to use its web nodality not just for unprompted and prompted query responses (in the language of Chapter 2), but also for direct notification. That means emulating those successful internet outlets which use direct-notification methods such as email alerts and the proactive provision of streams of associated information (known as 'RSS feeds' in internet jargon) – developments which may make internet users as a group more likely to expect information to be delivered rather than going out to seek it.

Finally, the extent to which enquirers come to government's nodes may depend on the success with which government can insert itself into other informational networks. Of course, governments in the pre-digital age often faced much the same kind of challenge, both in conveying messages to hard-to-reach groups, such as those with counter-culture lifestyles, and in gathering intelligence from them, as in the case of undercover police agents inserting themselves into subversive and revolutionary groups. It is now commonplace for government to try to insert its message into radio talk shows and the like. But in the internet age government's ability to insert itself into other networks takes the specific form of participating in or linking with chat rooms and other networked groups, and the technology offers new opportunities for doing so. 'Web 2.0' applications, discussed above, could even allow governments to create alternative networks for social care agencies or small businesses which would then share information among themselves as well as government. That too involves more active and 'smart' behaviour on the part of government than the passive waiting-to-be-asked mode.

Accordingly, we have argued earlier that the digital age in principle provides new opportunities to make government's nodality even cheaper and less obtrusive than before, but that, at least in some middle range of application, new forms of competition may also make it less effective and that the tools based on authority, treasure and organization must continue to be central to the working of government. However, digital-age developments also in principle offer possibilities for smarter or sharper use of those tools – as well as an increasing need for governments to get smarter as individuals and groups use the very same digital-age developments to work against government.

In the 1990s it was fashionable to argue, especially in the United States and Britain, that trends such as outsourcing, privatization, globalization and the increasing involvement of private interests in public policy were bringing 'hollow' government, weakening the state's autonomous power and policy-making capacity (see, for example, Foster, 1992; Goldstein, 1992; Weller *et al.*, 1997). But an alternative interpretation might be that such developments, far from weakening the state's central capacity to direct and control, rather allowed government organization to be pinpointed for maximum purchase, instead of being dissipated in large-scale employment for a set of miscellaneous and diffuse activities. And digital-age developments of the type we discussed in Chapter 5 in principle allow that pinpointing of organization to be taken to another stage, allowing government to be much leaner organizationally without necessarily weakening its capacity to detect and effect. Such effects are most likely to apply within developed countries and in conditions where government authority has sufficient purchase to obtain nodality without organization, as in the Chinese mobile phone example given in the previous chapter. Moreover, government in some conditions can compel and not merely allow individuals or firms to deal with it electronically, by providing information only online, insisting that applications (for instance for university places) be made online or compelling firms to file their tax returns online. In that way, government can use authority to cut back on its own bureaucracy, like those airlines or banks that only allow us to deal with them by phone or on the internet, rather than by mail or over the counter, to relieve themselves of the need to hire clerks and tellers to listen to our complaints, excuses and special pleading.

When it comes to the other desideratum that we discussed in Chapter 7 – that of minimizing 'trouble, vexation, and oppression' on those with whom government deals – those digital-age developments also in principle allow government to increase the precision with which it directs its array of instruments, but also offer new escape routes or methods of deflection. In Chapter 7 we argued that that such precision could be broken down into three properties: scalability, directness and non-substitutability. In principle, digital-age developments could allow governments to extend scalability, but are likely to cut both ways when it comes to directness and may be equally if not more problematic for non-substitutability.

Scalability, the ability to apply effectors at a variable range of intensity rather than in on/off mode, is in principle something that digital-age technology could help government to enhance. We have already noticed the potential of digital technology to produce more finely discriminated rationing of power supplies and road pricing (for instance by emptying drivers' wallets only when they are driving the car and polluting the environment, and relating charges to road congestion and potentially other factors too, such as speed and vehicle emissions). But, as we have also argued, when levels of recalcitrance are high, a scalable response may be easier for sellers of technological gizmos to promise than to deliver on the ground, and the development of 'stun' technology, for example to enable government to stop suspects in serious crimes without use of lethal force, has up to now been surprisingly slow and ineffective.

Directness, the ability to apply effectors at the specific beneficiaries or maleficiaries government wants to target, without spillover effects, is also something that digital-age developments could help government to extend. We have already noted the way that such technology can be used to provide information tailored to a particular postcode or zip code rather than to the world at large, and to restrict the eligibility to pass through a country's border controls or drive into a city centre, using electronic forms of authorization, such as biometric passports, or barriers that open in response to a transponder on authorized vehicles. We have also noted the development of 'zero touch' technologies that allow government agencies to automatically identify and communicate with certain categories of firms or individuals, reducing compliance burdens by only sending out official forms to those who need them and 'prepopulating' those forms rather than requiring them to be filled out from a blank page – in principle substantially reducing the burden on potential form-fillers. As the digital age develops, there would seem to be much scope for government to emulate those private firms who base their marketing strategies on special discounts linked to loyalty card data and 'click through' advertising geared around search terms used on search engines.

However, as we also noted in Chapter 7, when levels of recalcitrance or hostility to government are high, anti-directionality strategies on the part of those who government is aiming at may work against government's efforts at targeting, often by using precisely the same technology against those efforts. For example, to parry government's ability to pinpoint its enforcement activity more precisely within its own jurisdiction by using digital data more discriminatingly, cyber-criminals and internet hackers can locate themselves in jurisdictions other than those in which they commit their crimes, even while in some cases maximizing their own nodality by advertising their skills on websites. At the time of writing, the site http://www.ug100.com/ ranks an astonishing range of underground sites on a points scale, including those which offer hacking devices, password breakers, credit card generators and numerous illegal products and services (and there are an ever-increasing variety of such sites). In 2006 the head of the cyber-crime unit of the US Federal Bureau of Intelligence (FBI) stated that 80 per cent of the cases dealt with by his unit were carried out in countries over which the FBI had no law enforcement powers or powers of extradition (WWW Conference, Edinburgh, 26 May 2006).

Digital technology also seems to cut both ways when it comes to the third and closely related component of precision, namely non-substitutionality, the extent to which a target can be reached without the detector or effector concerned being blunted or deflected (as with a ricochet). The cyber-crime example given above is in fact a problem both for directness and non-substitutionality. Of course, as we noted in Chapter 5, when digital-age technology is linked to weaponry, it offers the possibility of military strikes that hit only very precisely defined targets without being deflected – levelling the enemy leader's palace while leaving the nearby hospitals and orphanages intact, for instance – and thus improve both directness and non-substitutionality. There have certainly been some notable instances where precisely such an effect has been achieved but, as we noted in Chapter 5, the obvious counter-strategy is for leaders and combatants to embed themselves in 'soft' civilian areas in such a way that would-be precision strikes are likely to fall far short of their theoretical promise.

Moreover, when it comes to civilian applications, the digital age offers no obvious ways to limit shifting and incidence of taxes and creates new opportunities for concealing identity – notably by identity theft, perhaps the classic 'substitutionality' problem – in strides proportionate to the advancement of high-integrity identification systems. Many of the group-targeted applications discussed above rely for their effect on governments being able to use digital techniques to collect, store and use new forms of electronic identity, but those new forms of identity lead to new forms of identify theft, now a familiar and growing problem in the banking and business world as well as that of government. At the time of writing a case had come to light in the UK of an individual assuming the identity of some 200 others to take a driving theory test *Evening Standard*, 29 September 2006), and the digital age makes it increasingly possible for individuals to assume multiple identities. The FBI official quoted above claimed that the internet was the perfect environment to market fake passports, licences and credit cards and that it took only five minutes to learn to steal fully functional credit card information online, from easily available websites giving access to unsecured databases of thousands of credit card numbers.

Databases of electronic information are also vulnerable to hackers and pranksters, as noted above, who can carry out their activities from remote locations and can do huge damage to government's operations if they are smart or lucky enough. For example, suppose that such individuals managed to mount a cyberattack on one of government's biometric databases, in such a way that proper names were randomly reassigned around the biometric identifiers. Even if we make the bold assumption that the system was securely backed up, before recovery could take place there would be an interesting intervening period when everyone's biometric identity was wrong.

To the extent that there are technological ways to overcome such problems, they can present challenges to orthodox liberal democratic values. Back-up procedures themselves necessarily involve more copies of highly sensitive information, security risks in their own right. Two hundred years ago, Jeremy Bentham's authoritarian–rationalist solution to the identity problem was to tattoo all individuals from the moment of their birth with a unique identifier (see Bentham, 1931, p. 418), and, as we noted above, the digital-age equivalent of that proposal allows the movements of individuals to be tracked in real time as well (if they cannot disable the microchips implanted at birth). Only in a world society prepared to adopt such solutions on a universal scale could the substitutionality problem in identity control be removed, and maybe not even then.

At the time of writing, the digital age is still at a relatively early stage. Although governments of many developed countries have long been using digital technologies, the real potential for a step change in the way governments interact with society arguably came only with the advent of the internet and associated technologies. For most developed countries, therefore, the digital age only really arrived at the end of the 1990s as internet penetration approached some kind of critical mass. In many other countries it has not even started, as we pointed out in the last section. We can therefore only point at the possibilities and challenges facing the tools of government today, rather than making any definitive historical assessment. And of course, the impact of digital tools, like that of any other instruments, will depend on the social, cultural and environmental context. Predicting changes in that is no easier today than it was for those intellectuals in Chekhov's plays as they looked to the future – and there may be as many unpleasant surprises ahead too. We have been careful to point out that the digital age offers new instruments for authoritarian governments as well as democratic ones, and have also argued that the basic trade-offs involved in the use of government's tools in the pre-digital age are very unlikely to disappear. But a new potential for the 'digital sharpening' of government's tools for bureaucracy-saving and greater precision, combined with greater competition for nodality and new ways that individuals and groups can use the very same technology to counteract government control, all suggest that governments will have to run even to stay still in the digital future.

References

Ackerknecht, E. H. (1948) 'Anticontagionism Between 1821 and 1867', *Bulletin of the History of Medicine*, 22(5) pp. 562–593.

Ackroyd, C., Margolis, K., Rosenhead, J. and Shallice, T. (1977) *The Technology of Political Control* (London: Pluto Press).

Alderman, G. (1982) 'Jews and Sunday Trading: The Use and Abuse of Delegated Legislation', *Public Administration*, 60, pp. 99–104.

Amnesty International (2003) *Annual Report*, at http://web.amnesty.org/report2003/index-eng

Arendt, H. (1961) *Between Past and Future* (New York: Viking Press).

Ashby, W. R. (1956) *An Introduction to Cybernetics* (New York: Barnes & Noble).

Austin, J. (1962) *How to Do Things with Words* (Oxford: Clarendon).

Bachrach, P. and Baratz, M. (1970) *Power and Poverty* (Oxford University Press).

Baden-Powell, B. H. (1990) (orig. 1907). *The Land Systems of British India: Being a Manual of the Land Tenures and of the Systems of Land Revenue Administration Prevalent in the Everal Provinces* (Delhi: Low Price Publications).

Baechler, J. (1979) *Suicides* (Oxford: Blackwell).

Baldwin, P. (1999) *Contagion and the State in Europe 1830–1930* (Cambridge University Press).

Bankruptcy: A Consultative Document, Cmnd 7967 (HMSO, 1980).

Bardach, E. (1977) *The Implementation Game: What Happens After a Bill Becomes a Law* (Cambridge, MA: MIT Press).

Barnes, D. and Reid, E. (1980) *Government and Trade Unions: The British Experience 1964–79* (London: Heinemann).

Beer, S. (1972) *Brain of the Firm* (London: Allen Lane).

Bellamy, C. and Taylor, J. (1998) *Governing in the Information Age* (Buckingham: Open University Press).

Bentham, J. (1931) *The Theory of Legislation*, edited by C. K. Ogden, trans. by R. Hildreth from the French of E. Dumont (London: Routledge & Kegan Paul).

Bentham, J. (1983) (orig. 1817) *Chrestomathia* (ed. M.J. Smith and W.H. Burston) (Oxford: Clarendon).

Bertelmans-Videc, M.-L., Rist, R. C. and Vedung, E. (1998) *Carrots, Sticks and Sermons: Policy Instruments and Their Evaluation* (New Brunswick, NJ: Transaction).

Binney, J. E. D. (1958) *British Public Finance and Administration 1774–92* (Oxford University Press).

Black, J., Lodge, M. and Thatcher, M. (eds) (2005) *Regulatory Innovation* (Cheltenham: Edward Elgar).
Bowker, G. C. and Star, S. L. (1999) *Sorting Things Out: Classification and Its Consequences* (Cambridge, MA: MIT Press).
Bradshaw, J. (1980) *The Family Fund: An Initiative in Social Policy* (London: Routledge & Kegan Paul).
Breyer, S. G. (1982) *Regulation and Its Reform* (Cambridge, MA: Harvard University Press).
Brin, D. (1998) *The Transparent Society: Will Technology Force Us to Choose Between Privacy and Freedom?* (Reading, MA: Perseus Books).
Brown, D. (2003) *The Da Vinci Code* (London: Corgi).
Brown, J. A. C. (1963) *Techniques of Persuasion: From Propaganda to Brainwashing* (Middlesex: Penguin).
Bunyan, T. (1976) *The History and Practice of the Political Police in Britain* (London: Friedmann).
Cabinet Office (2003) *Innovation in the Public Sector* (HMSO).
Clark, Sir F. (1971) *Central Office of Information* (London: Allen & Unwin).
Colby, W. and Forbath, P. (1978) *Honorable Men: My Life in the CIA* (New York: Simon & Schuster).
Committee of Privy Councillors (1957) *Report of the Committee of Privy Councillors Appointed to Inquire into the Interception of Communications*, Cmnd 283 (HMSO).
Conquest, R. (1978) *Kolyma: The Arctic Death Camps* (London: Macmillan).
Cranston, R. (1979) *Regulating Business* (London: Macmillan).
Crombie, Sir J. (1962) *HM Customs and Excise* (London: Allen & Unwin).
Dahl, R. and Lindblom, C. (1953) *Politics, Economics and Welfare* (New York: Harper & Row).
Dalziel, D. (2004) *Government Online: A Multi-Country Study of e-Government Usage* (World Association of Research Professionals).
de Soto, H. (2000) *The Mystery of Capital: Why Capitalism Triumphs in the West and Fails Everywhere Else* (New York: Basic Books).
de Tocqueville, A. (1945) *Democracy in America*, Vol 2 (New York: Vintage Books) (first pub. 1835)
Delamare, N. (1913) *Traité de la Police* (Paris: Michel Brunet).
Dixon, M. and Margo, J. (2006) *Population Politics* (IPPR).
Dunne, F. P. (1899) *Mr Dooley in Peace and War* (London: Richards).
Dunleavy, P. J. (1994) 'The Globalization of Public Service Production: Can Government be "Best in World"?', *Public Policy and Administration*, 9(2) pp. 36–64 (Oxford: Blackwell)
Dunleavy, P. and Margetts, H. (1999) *Government on the Web*, National Audit Office Value for Money Report (London: The Stationery Office, HC 87).

Dunleavy, P. and Margetts, H. (2002) *Government on the Web II*, National Audit Office Value for Money Report (London: The Stationery Office, HC 764).
Dunleavy, P., Margetts, H., Bastow, S. and Tinkler, J. (2006) *Digital-era Governance: IT Corporations, the State and e-Government* (Oxford University Press).
Dunlop, Charles and Rob Kling (Ed, 1991). *Computerization and Controversy: Value Conflicts and Social Choices* (Boston: Academic Press).
Dunsire, A. (1978) *The Execution Process*, 2 vols (Oxford: Robertson).
Dutton, W. H., di Gennaro, C. and Millwood Hargrave, A. (2005) *The Internet in Britain: The Oxford Internet Survey (OxIS), May 2005* (Oxford: Oxford Internet Institute).
Edelman, M. (1971) *Politics as Symbolic Action: Mass Arousal and Quiescence* (Chicago, IL: Markham).
Edelman, M. (1977) *Political Language: Words That Succeed and Policies That Fail* (New York: Academic Press).
Elmore, R. F. (1987) 'Instruments and Strategy in Public Policy', *Policy Studies Review*, 7(1), pp. 174–86.
Enzensberger, H. M. (1970) 'Constituents of a Theory of the Media', *New Left Review*, 64 (November–December), pp. 13–36.
Escher, T., Margetts, H., Petricek, V. and Cox, I. (2006) 'Governing from the Centre? Comparing the Nodality of Digital Governments', paper delivered at the 2006 Annual Meeting of the American Political Science Association, 31 August–4 September 2006.
Etzioni, A. (1961) *A Comparative Analysis of Complex Organizations* (New York: Free Press).
Etzioni-Halevy, E. (1979) *Political Manipulation and Administrative Power: A Comparative Study* (London: Routledge & Kegan Paul).
European Committee on Crime Problems, Council of Europe Directorate of Legal Affairs (1999) *European Sourcebook of Crime and Criminal Justice Statistics* (Strasbourg: Council of Europe Press).
Fagen, R. R. (1966) *Politics and Communication: An Analysis* (Boston, MA: Little, Brown).
Fainstein, S. S. and Fainstein, N. I. (1980) 'The Political Economy of American Bureaucracy', in C. H. Weiss and A. H. Barton (eds), *Making Bureaucracies Work* (Beverly Hills, CA: Sage), pp. 279–97.
Fisher, R. (1971) *Basic Negotiating Strategy: International Conflict for Beginners* (London: Allen Lane).
Foster, C. D. (1992) *Privatization, Public Ownership and the Regulation of Natural Monopoly* (Oxford: Blackwell).
Friedman, M. (1977) *From Galbraith to Economic Freedom*, Occasional Paper 49 (London: Institute of Economic Affairs).

Frissen, P. H. A. (1996) *De Virtuele Staat: politiek, bestuur, technologie* (Schoonhoven, Netherlands: Academic Service).
Frissen, P. H. A. (1999) *Politics, Governance and Technology: A Postmodern Narrative on the Virtual State* (Cheltenham: Edward Elgar).
Froman, L. A., Jr (1968) 'The Categorization of Policy Contents', in A. Ranney (ed.), *Political Science and Public Policy* (Chicago: Markham), pp. 41–52.
Fry, G. K. (1979) *The Growth of Government* (London: Cass).
Galbraith, J. K. (1971) *The New Industrial State*, 2nd edn (New York: Houghton Mifflin).
Gandy, O. (1993) *The Panoptic Sort: A Political Economy of Personal Information* (Boulder, CO: Westview Press).
Gatti, J. F. (1981) *The Limits of Government Regulation* (New York: Academic Press).
Giddings, P. J. (1974) *Marketing Boards and Ministers* (Westmead, UK: Saxon House).
Goldstein, M. (1992) *America's Hollow Government: How Washington Has Failed the People* (Boston, MA: McGraw-Hill).
Gore, A. (1994) *From Red Tape to Results: Creating a Government that Works Better and Costs Less*, Report of the National Performance Review (US Government Printing Office).
Grunow, D. and Hegner, F. (eds) (1980) *Welfare or Bureaucracy? Problems of Matching Social Services to Clients' Needs* (Bonn: Oelgeschlager, Gunn & Hain).
Gunsteren, H. R. van (1981) 'The Ethical Context of Bureaucracy and Performance Analysis' (ZiF, Universität Bielefeld), ZiF Forschungsgruppe 1981–2, Preprint Series, 7.
Hain, P. (eds) (1980) *Policing the Police*, Vol. II (London: Calder).
Haldane, A. R. B. (1962) *New Ways Through the Glens* (Edinburgh: Nelson).
Hall, J. and Eggers, W. (1995) *Health and Social Services in the Post-Welfare State: Are Vouchers the Answer?*, Policy Study No. 192, Reason Public Policy Institute, http://www.rppi.org/es192.html
Hartley, J. (2005) 'Innovation in Governance and Public Services: Past and Present', *Public Money and Management*, 25(1), pp. 27–34.
Heald, D. A. (1983) *Public Expenditure* (Oxford: Robertson).
Heclo, H. (1978) 'Issue Networks and the Executive Establishment', in A. King (ed.), *The New American Political System* (American Enterprise Institute), pp. 87–124.
Heller, J. (1969) *Catch-22* (London: Corgi) (first pub. 1962).
Herman, R. D. (ed.) (1967) *Gambling New York:* (Harper & Row).
Hodgkinson, C. (1978) *Towards a Philosophy of Administration* (Oxford: Blackwell).

Hodgson, G. (1980) *All Things to All Men: The False Promise of the Modern American Presidency* (London: Weidenfeld & Nicolson).
Hogwood, B. W. (1979) 'Analyzing Industrial Policy: A Multi-Perspective Approach', *Public Administration Bulletin*, 29 (April), pp. 18–42.
Holliday, I. (2001) 'Steering the British State in the Information Age', *Government and Opposition*, 36(3), pp. 314–29.
Holmes, O. W. (1920) 'The Path of the Law' in *Collected Papers* (London, Constable) pp. 167–202.
Hood, C. (1976) *The Limits of Administration* (London: Wiley).
Hood, C. (1983) *The Tools of Government* (London: Macmillan).
Hood, C. (2000) 'Where the State of the Art Meets the Art of the State', *International Review of Public Administration*, 5(1), pp. 1–12.
Huber, J.D. and Shipan, C.R. (2002) *Deliberate Discretion? The Institutional Foundations of Bureaucratic Autonomy* (Cambridge University Press).
Huberman, B., Pirollie, P., Pitkow, J. and Lukose, R. (1998) 'Strong Regularities in World Wide Web Surfing', *Science*, 280(5360), pp. 95–7.
Ignatieff, M. (2005) *The Lesser Evil: Political Ethics in an Age of Terror* (Edinburgh University Press).
Jacobson, H. (1987) *Redback* (London: Black Swan).
Jarvie, I. C. (1970) *Towards a Sociology of the Cinema: A Comparative Essay on the Structure and Functioning of a Major Entertainment Industry* (London: Routledge & Kegan Paul).
Jerome, J. K. (1998) *Three Men on the Bummel* (Oxford University Press) (first pub. 1900).
Jones, N. (1999) *Sultans of Spin* (London: Orion).
Kagan, R. A. (1978) *Regulatory Justice: Implementing a Wage-Price Freeze* (New York: Russell Sage Foundation).
Kilde, R. L. (1999) 'Microchip Implants, Mindcontrol, and Cybernetics', *Spekula*, 3rd Quarter, 23 October pp. 1–7.
Kings College London (2005) *World Prison Population List* (Kings College London).
Klaus, G. (1973) *Kybernetik und Gesellschaft*, 3rd edn (Deutscher Verlag der Wissenschaften).
Knightley, P. (1975) *First Casualty: From the Crimea to Vietnam: War Correspondent as Hero, Propagandist and Mythmaker* (London: André Deutsch).
Knoepfel, P. and Wiedner, H. (1980) 'Normbildung and Implementation: Interessenberücksichtigungsmuster in Programmstrukturen von Luftreinhaltepolitiken', in R. Mayntz (ed.), *Implementation Politischer Programme* (Konigstein: Hain), pp. 82–104.
Kogan, M. (1971) *The Politics of Education: E. Boyle and A. Crosland in Conversation with M. Kogan* (London: Penguin).

Kohlmeier, L. M. (1969) *The Regulators: Watchdog Agencies and the Public Interest* (New York: Harper & Row).

Koslowski, R. (2002) 'Information Technology, Migration and Border Control', paper presented to the Institute of Government Studies conference, University of California, Berkeley, April.

Koslowski, R. (2005) *Real Challenges for Virtual Borders: The Implementation of US-VISIT*, Migration Policy Institute Report, June.

Kraemer, K. L. and King, J. L. (1986) 'Computing and Public Organizations', *Public Administration Review*, 46, pp. 488–96.

Kramer, N. J. T. A. and de Smit, J. (1977) *Systems Thinking: Concepts and Notions* (Leiden, Netherlands: Martinus Nijhoff).

Kurtz, H. (1998) *Spin Cycle: Inside the Clinton Propaganda Machine* (New York: Free Press).

Larsen, E. (1980) *Wit as a Weapon: The Political Joke in History* (London: Muller).

Lasswell, H. D. and Fox, M. B. (1979) *The Signature of Power: Buildings, Communication and Policy* (New Brunswick, NJ: Transaction).

Lasswell, H. D. and Kaplan, A. (1950) *Power and Society: A Framework for Political Inquiry* (New Haven: Yale University Press).

Lasswell, H. D., Lerner, D. and Speier, H. (eds) (1980) *Propaganda and Communication in World History* (Honolulu: University of Hawaii Press).

Lessig, L. (1999) *Code and Other Laws of Cyberspace* (New York: Basic Books).

Levi, M. (1988) *Of Rule and Revenue* (Berkeley, CA: University of California Press).

Lijphart, A. (1968) *The Politics of Accommodation: Pluralism and Democracy in the Netherlands* (Berkeley, CA: University of California Press).

Lijphart, A. (1977) *Democracy in Plural Societies: A Comparative Exploration* (New Haven: Yale University Press).

Linder, S. H. and Peters, B. G. (1989) 'Instruments of Government: Perceptions and Contexts', *Journal of Public Policy*, 9(1), pp. 35–58.

Linder, S. H. and Peters, B. G. (1992) 'The Study of Policy Instruments', *Policy Currents*, 2, pp. 1–7.

Linder, S. H. and Peters, B. G. (1998) 'The Study of Policy Instruments: Four Schools of Thought', in B. G. Peters and F. K. M. van Nispen (eds), *Public Policy Instruments: Evaluating the Tools of Public Administration* (Cheltenham: Edward Elgar), pp. 33–45.

Llewellyn Smith, Sir H. (1928) *The Board of Trade* (New York: G.P. Putnam's Sons).

Lowi, T. J. (1964) 'American Business, Public Policy, Case Studies and Political Theory', *World Politics*, 16(2), pp. 677–715.

Lowi, T. J. (1969) *The End of Liberalism* (New York: Norton).
Lowi, T. J. and Stone, A. (eds) (1978) *Nationalizing Government: Public Policies in America* (Beverly Hills, CA: Sage).
Lyman, S. M. and Scott, M. B. (1975) *The Drama of Social Reality* (Oxford University Press).
Lynn, J. and Jay, A. (eds) (1981) *Yes Minister: The Diaries of a Cabinet Minister*, Vol. I (London: British Broadcasting Corporation).
Lyon, D. (ed.) (2003) *Surveillance as Social Sorting: Privacy, Risk and Automated Discrimination* (New York: Routledge).
Machin, H. (1977) *The Prefect in French Public Administration* (London: Croom Helm).
Mackenzie, W. J. M. (1958) *Free Elections: An Elementary Textbook* (London: George Allen & Unwin).
Mackenzie, W. J. M. (2002) *The Secret History of SOE: The Special Operations Executive 1940–1945* (London: St Ermin's Press).
Madgwick, D. and Smythe, T. (1974) *The Invasion of Privacy* (Oxford: Pitman).
Margetts, H. (1995) 'The Automated State', *Public Policy and Administration*, 10(2), pp. 88–103.
Margetts, H. (1997) 'The National Performance Review: A New Humanist Public Management', in A. Massey (ed.), *Globalization and Marketization of Government Services* (Basingstoke: Macmillan), pp. 47–70.
Margetts, H. (1999) *Information Technology in Government: Britain and America* (New York: Routledge).
Martin, R. M. (1980) *Trades Union Congress: The Growth of a Pressure Group 1868–1976* (Oxford University Press).
Marx, K. and Engels, F. (1968) *L'Idéologie allemande*, ed. G. Badia (Paris: Editions Sociales) (first pub. 1932).
Mayntz, R. (1977) 'Die Implementation politischer Programme: Theoretische Uberlegungen zu einem neuen Forschungsgebiel', *Die Verwaltung*, 10, pp. 51–66.
Mayntz, R. (ed.) (1980) *Implementation politischer Programme* (Athenäum: Hain).
Mayntz, R. (1981) 'The Changing Conditions of Effective Public Policy: A New Challenge for Policy Analysis' (ZiF, Universität Bielefeld), ZiF Forschungsgruppe 1981–2, Preprint Series, 9.
Mitchell, J. (1971) *Reminiscences of My Life in the Highlands*, Vol. I (Newton Abbot: David & Charles) (first pub. 1883).
Mitchison, R. (1970) *History of Scotland* (London: Methuen).
National Audit Office (2007) *Government on the Web 3* (London: The Stationery Office).
National Commission on Terrorist Attacks (2004) *The 9/11 Commission Report: Final Report of the National Commission on Terrorist Attacks Upon the United States (Authorized Edition)* (New York: W. W. Norton & Company), p. 256.

Nelson, R. and Winter, S. (1982) *An Evolutionary Theory of Economic Change* (Cambridge, MA: Harvard University Press).
Newman, O. (1972) *Defensible Space: Crime Prevention Through Urban Design* (New York: Macmillan).
O'Connor, J. (1973) *The Fiscal Crisis of the State* (New York: St Martin's Press).
OECD (2005) *Survey of Trends in Taxpayer Service Delivery using New Technologies*, February (Paris: Centre for Tax Policy and Administration).
Offe, C. (1975) *Berufsbildungsreform: Eine Fallstudie über Reformpolitik* (Frankfurt: Suhrkamp).
Offer, A. (2002) *Why has the Public Sector Grown so Large in Market Societies? The Political Economy of Prudence in the UK, c.1870–2000*, University of Oxford Discussion Papers in Economics and Social History, no. 44, March.
Ogilvy-Webb, M. (1965) *The Government Explains: A Study of the Information Services* (London: Allen & Unwin).
Olennu, L A A, Owusu, G K and Thresh, J M (1989) 'The Control of Cocoa Swollen Shoot Disease in Ghana', *Cocoa Growers Bulletin* 42: 25–35
Olmstead, C. (1967) 'Analyzing a Pack of Cards', in R. D. Herman (ed.), *Gambling* (New York: Harper & Row), pp. 136–52.
Orwell, G. (1954) *Nineteen Eight-Four* (Harmondsworth: Penguin) (first pub. 1948).
Osborne, D. and Gaebler, T. (1992) *Reinventing Government: How the Entrepreneurial Spirit is Transforming the Public Sector* (Reading, MA: Addison-Wesley).
Ostrom, V. (1982) 'Who Guides, Controls and Evaluates Whose Performance: An Inquiry into Some Basic Constitutional Considerations', paper presented to conference on 'Analyzing Interactions among Multiple Actors in the Public Sector', ZiF, Universität Bielefeld, 1–6 July 1982.
Peters, B. G. and Hogwood, B. W. (1980) 'Policy Succession: The Dynamics of Policy Change', *Studies in Public Policy*, 69 (University of Strathclyde Centre for the Study of Public Policy).
Petricek, V., Escher, T., Cox, I. and Margetts, H. (2006) 'The Web Structure of E-Government – Developing a Methodology for Quantitative Evaluation', paper presented to the World Wide Web Conference, Edinburgh, 23–26 May 2006. (See www.governmentontheweb.org for paper and presentation.)
Prescott, E. S. and Tatar, D. D. (1999) 'Means of Payment, the Unbanked, and EFT '99', *Economic Quarterly*, Federal Reserve Bank of Richmond, Fall, pp. 49–70.

Prisons in Scotland: Report for 1978, Cmnd 7749 (HMSO, 1979).
Pryor, F. (1968) *Public Expenditures in Communist and Capitalist Nations* (Homewood IL:, Richard D. Irwin Inc).
Report of the Committee of Inquiry into the UK Prison Services, Cmnd 7673 (HMSO, 1979).
Rose, R. (1976) 'On the Priorities of Government: A Developmental Analysis of Public Policies', *European Journal of Political Research*, 4(3), pp. 247–89.
Rose, R. and Peters, B. G. (1978) *Can Government Go Bankrupt?* (New York: Basic Books).
Rosenberg, W. G. and Young, M. B. (1982) *Transforming Russia and China: Revolutionary Struggle in the Twentieth Century* (Oxford University Press).
Rule, J. B. (1973) *Private Lives and Public Surveillance* (London: Allen Lane).
Salamon, L. M. with Elliott, O. V. (2002) *The Tools of Government: A Guide to the New Governance* (Oxford University Press).
Salamon, L. M. and Lund, M. S. (1989) *Beyond Privatization: The Tools of Government Action* (Washington, DC: Urban Institute Press).
Savage, J. D. (2005) *Making the EMU: The Politics of Budgetary Surveillance and the Enforcement of Maastricht* (Oxford University Press).
Schaffer, B. and Lamb, G. (1981) *Can Equity Be Organized?* (Farnborough: Gower).
Schneider, A. and Ingram, H. (1990) 'Behavioral Assumptions of Policy Tools', *Journal of Politics*, 52(2), pp. 510–29.
Scott, J. (1998) *Seeing Like a State: How Certain Schemes to Improve the Human Condition Have Failed* (New Haven: Yale University Press).
Security of the Census of Population, Cmnd 5365 (HMSO, 1973).
Self, P. and Storing, H. J. (1962) *The State and the Farmer* (London: Allen & Unwin).
Sennett, R. (1977) *The Fall of Public Man* (Cambridge University Press).
Simon, H. A., Smithburg, D. W. and Thompson, V. A. (1950) *Public Administration* (New York: Knopf).
Smith, A. (1910) *The Wealth of Nations*, 2 vols (London: Dent) (first pub. 1776).
Solzhenitsyn, A. (1973) *The Gulag Archipelago 1918–1956* (London: Fontana).
Steel, T. (1975) *The Life and Death of St Kilda* (London: Fontana).
Stirton, L. (2005) 'Regulatory Governance in the National Health

Service 1985–2005: Analysing Selected Reform Initiatives', PhD thesis, London School of Economics, Department of Government.
Stockwell, J. (1978) *In Search of Enemies: A CIA Story* (New York: Norton).
Stone, C. D. (1975) *Where The Law Ends: The Social Control of Corporate Behavior* (New York: Harper & Row).
Taxation (1964) 74(1935) (7 November).
Taylor Nelson Sofres (2003) *Government Online: An International Perspective* (New Zealand: Taylor Nelson Sofres).
Thomson, A. W. J. and Engleman, S. R. (1975) *The Industrial Relations Act* (London: Robertson).
Tocqueville, A de (1949) *L'Ancien Regime* (Oxford, Clarendon).
Troup, Sir E. (1925) *The Home Office* (New York: G.P. Putnam's Sons).
UNPAN (United Nations Public Administration Network) (2005) *Global E-government Readiness Report 2005: From E-government to E-inclusion* (United Nations Department of Economics and Social Affairs).
US Census Bureau (2006) *Statistical Abstract of the United States: 2006* (US Census Bureau).
Weidenbaum, M. L. (1969) *The Modern Public Sector: New Ways of Doing the Government's Business* (New York: Basic Books).
Weller, P., Bakvis, H. and Rhodes, R. A. W (eds) (1997) *The Hollow Crown: Countervailing Trends in Core Executives* (Basingstoke: Macmillan).
White, L. (1962) *Medieval Technology and Social Change* (Oxford University Press).
Wildavsky, A. (1980) *The Art and Craft of Policy Analysis: Speaking Truth to Power* (London: Macmillan).
Wilson, T. and Skinner, A. S. (eds) (1976) *The Market and the State: Essays in Honour of Adam Smith* (Oxford University Press).
Winnifrith, Sir J. (1962) *Ministry of Agriculture, Fisheries and Food* (London: Allen & Unwin).
Wittfogel, K. A. (1959) *Oriental Despotism: A Comparative Study of Total Power* (Yale University Press).
Wolseley, G. J. (1869) *The Soldier's Pocket Book* (London: Macmillan).
Wrong, D. H. (1979) *Power: Its Forms, Bases and Uses* (Oxford: Blackwell).
Zijderveld, A. C. (1979) *On Clichés: The Supersedure of Meaning by Function in Modernity* (London: Routledge & Kegan Paul).
Zittrain, J. and Edelman, B. (2004a) *Documentation of Internet Filtering in China*, website of Berkman Center for Internet & Society, Harvard Law School, at http://cyber.law.harvard.edu/filtering/china/

Zittrain, J. and Edelman, B. (2004b) *Documentation of Internet Filtering in Saudi Arabia*, website of Berkman Center for Internet & Society, Harvard Law School, at http://cyber.law.harvard.edu/filtering/saudiarabia/

Index

3G mobile phone licences 51

Accenture 27
accessibility, websites 141–3
accidents 53
active proposition 83–4
advertised rewards 81–2
agriculture 33, 38, 63, 130–3
  subsidies 107
AIDS 136, 170, 174
al-Qaida 23, 42, 48
Albania 130
alcoholism 109, 152
Amin, Idi 29
amnesty 65–6
Amnesty International 87, 112
'aneunomothetiscopic' 172
Anglo-American Venture Fund 90
anti-social drinking 13
applications 82
arbitrament 63–4, 70
Argentina 76, 127
at-large treatment 114–16
attention 47–8
Australia 64, 73, 83, 110, 141–3
authority 5–6, 50–77

Bahrain 30
bankruptcy 55
banks 43, 54, 87, 199
  France 107
  accounts 97, 121, 124, 187
bear, brown 157
bearer-directed payments 92–3, 99
Bell, Henry 22–3
Bentham, Jeremy 22, 157, 158–9, 172, 202
bespoke messages 31–3
bicycles 80, 91, 97, 138–9
Big Conversation 84
Bin Laden, Osama 23, 84, 189
biometrics 59, 73, 188, 202
bird flu 111, 135
blanketed tokens 65, 70, 72
Bluewater Shopping Centre 71
bounty 91–2
breathalyser test 56
broadcast messages 35–8
broadcasting authorities 63, 137
BSE *see* cattle plague
bullying (school) 14
business regulation 53, 62, 73

Canada 27
capacity 6
Catalonia 129
cattle plague 39, 53, 148
  BSE 134. 136
CCTV 71, 104, 116, 119–20, 137, 186
census 42, 56, 151
certificates 57–9, 70
Chechen rebels 81–2
child handicap (UK) 82, 90
Child Support Agency (UK) 97
Chile 153, 195
China 29–31, 41, 50, 61, 94, 109, 111, 112, 135, 178, 180, 195–6
Chrysler loan (US) 60
CIA 80, 87, 88, 90
cigarette packs 30, 68, 155
citizens 18, 188
City academies (UK) 87
Civil Aeronautics Act 1938 (US) 137
cocoa swollen shoot virus 63, 76–7
compliance costs 68
computer privacy 12
conditional tokens 59–60
conduits 89–91, 99
congestion charge 23
Congregatio de Propaganda Fidei 37
Congress of Cultural Freedom 88
consensus 45–7, 75–7, 99–101, 123–5, 150–1, 200–1
constitutivism 171
constraints 62–4
context 137
contingency theory 150
contracts 86–8
Cooper's Snoopers 27
counselling 33
credibility 6
customized payments 85–6
customs duties 56, 133
cyber-activists 191
cyber-bullying 14
cyber-crime 14, 18, 72, 121–2, 151, 197, 201
cyber-detection 185–7
cybernetics 3, 176
Cyprus 63

Dalai Lama 31
data 139–141
dating agency 79, 83
dead person's estate 69–70
Debt Collection Improvement Act 1996 (US) 96
defence ministry 130
defensible space 115–6
deliberative choice 145–9
Department of Justice (US) 53, 191–2
deportation 111

detectors 3–5, 8–11
digital technology 13, 33, 42–3, 119–22, 131, 137–8, 151
direct action *see* treatment
direct information propagation 30–1
direct inquiry 27
direct notification 31–2
directed tokens 57–9, 70, 72
directness 158–9, 176, 200–1
Disability and Carers Service (UK) 34
diseases, contagious 170, 180
disinfection 114, 123, 170
disinformation 29
dob-a-job 25
dogs, dangerous 107, 186
driver licences (UK) 74
drug addicts 109
drug prescribing 34–5

'E' award (US) 57
e-government 27, 96
ear trumpet 24–6
economic sanctions (Iran) 75
economy (policy designs) 145, 152–61
effectors 3–5, 7–8, 9
electoral administration 58, 107, 110
electoral register (France) 29
electric power 178, 185
Elf Acquitaine 91
emissions quotas 62, 66
employment, government 141
enablements 60–2, 70
Enron (US) 154
epidemic 39
ergonomic control 114
ergonomic detectors 8, 103–6
EURES 83
euro 39
European Commission 128
European Growth and Stability Pact 140
European Health Insurance Card 189
European Journal 47
European Union 140
  Savings Directive 2005 54, 71
extraordinary rendition 87, 128

Falkland Islands 127
Falun Gong 31
family history 33, 42
'FAQ' approach 37
Federal Bureau of Investigation (US) 105, 121–2, 189, 201
Federal Government (US) 79–80, 102
Federal Office of Pipeline Safety (US) 42
Federal Security Service (Russia) 191
Federal Trade Commission (US) 62
fishing 93
  quotas (NZ) 66
fitness for purpose 145, 149–52
fluoride 114, 118, 148
food labelling 30
foreign office 130, 141–3
France 53, 79, 91, 92, 107, 111, 134, 135
freedom of information 24, 33
fuel efficiency 58

gambling 14
garbage collection 109–10
General Accounting Office (US) 25
General Strike 1926 (UK) 110
Geneva Convention (1949) 56
Germany 51, 53, 67, 73, 157
  East 135
  West 74
Ghana 63, 76–7
Glasgow 135
goat hair (UK) 123
Gold Coast *see* Ghana
Google 43, 143, 190–1, 196
  Earth 41
government 1–2, 15–6
government contracts (US) 79–80
government time 65, 67
Great Seal (US) 50
Grenada 194
group-targeting 187–8
  messages 33–5
  tokens 64–5, 70
group treatment 113–14
Guantanamo Bay 108, 112

health data 24
herring subsidies (UK) 92
HIV tests 55, 82
  Aids 136, 170, 174
hollow government 199
Hong Kong 23, 110, 135
hop quotas 66
housing 135

identity cards 73, 74
identity theft 188, 201–2
Illinois (US) 62
Immigration and Naturalization Service (US) 73
income tax liability 74–5
India 41, 134
  British 113
Individual Learning Accounts (UK) 94, 152
individual treatment 106–13
information exchange 82–3
inspection 55–6
institutions-as-tools 168–9
international aid payments 94
International Red Cross 44
internet 14, 30, 37, 136, 151, 202
  service providers (Russia) 191
  Services Unit (Saudi Arabia) 180–1
internment camps 108
interrogation 55–6
interventionist 17
Iraq War 2003 121
IT systems 95, 178, 180, 193
Italy 90–1, 153, 157

Japan 79

Jewish Board of Deputies (UK) 64

Korea (North) 195
Kosovo War 1999 121
Kursk 95
Kyoto Protocol 62

labour exchanges 83
  UK 53
laissez-faire 17
Land Acquisition Act (Zimbabwe) 62–3
leakage 30
Lenin 38
letters of marque 60
lighthouses 36, 127, 169
limited liability companies 67–8
Lockheed loan (US) 60
London Fishmongers' Company 60
Lonely Planet 44
lottery 39–40, 92

Maradona, Diego 26
marking 106–7
Mayntz, Renate 149–50
Mexico 66
microchips 185–7, 202
military draft 52, 71
military supply 95
milk quotas (EU) 66
Minimum Use of Force Tactical Intervention Squads (UK) 124
mobile phone networks 40, 178, 181
moral acceptability 145, 161–5
motor vehicles 52, 58
Mozambique 195

National Archives of Canada 42
National Performance Review 1993 (US) 179
National Student Association 88
Nepal 76
New Labour (UK) 46, 84
New Orleans 113–14, 115, 124
New Public Management 169
New South Wales 25
Nicaraguan Contras 88, 89
Nigeria 110
Niyazov, Saparmurat 67
nodal receivers 8, 21–7
nodality 5, 21–49
nuclear installations 41, 53, 134

obligation to display 51–2
obligation to notify 52–4
Occam's razor 176
Octopus card (Hong Kong) 23
Oman 194
ombudsman 25–6
open compacts 65–6
open payments 91
open permits 66
organic status 58
organization 6, 102–25
Orwell, George 29, 119

Oyster card (London) 23

packaged self-serve messages 36–7
Pakistan 134
Paperwork Reduction Act (US) 140
passports 68, 69, 200
  biometric (US) 59, 73
patent applications 36, 59, 82
Pensions Service (UK) 34
People's Panel 84
pests 111
petrol pumps 58
playing cards (UK) 116
police 141
policy diffusion 137
policy succession 136
politics-of-instrument-choice 169–71, 193
pollution 137, 138
population policies 79, 89, 94
population size 44–5, 73–5, 98–9, 122–3, 150
pornography 191–2
post office (UK) 105–6, 137
precision 161–2
press conference 34
prisoners of war 56
prisons 73, 108–9, 117, 127, 169
  UK 124
  US 118–19
privatization 177
privished messages 35–6
processing 111–13
production quotas 62, 66, 94
prompted query response 33
propaganda 28, 37–8, 69, 94, 128
  black 38, 169
  Director of (UK) 48
proportionality 151
psychological warfare 27, 38
public opinion surveys 27, 41
  US 38
Public Record Office (UK) 42
public registration 53
Public Trustee Office (UK) 107

quarantine
  animals 108, 182
  humans 109, 170

racehorses 186
railways 137, 182
  timetables 45
rational choice 146–7, 163
rations 73
  fuel 134
  fuel (US) 52
reproductive technology 12
requisitions 8, 51–6
returns 54–5
rewards 8, 80–5, 97
road-building (Scotland) 88, 115
road pricing 23, 24, 185, 200
  Singapore 71, 98

royal warrant (UK) 58
'RSS feeds' 198
Russia 95, 191

St Kilda 47,113
Saqq 95
SARS (Severe Acute Respiratory Syndrome) 29
Saudi Arabia 30, 112, 180, 196
savings bank 38
scalability 156–7, 199–200
scanner
  fixed 104, 120, 131
  mobile 104–5, 120, 131
  hidden 105–6, 120, 131
Schein 50
scrutiny of free media 26–7
Second World War 27, 29, 38, 52, 53, 57, 63
sex offenders 29
  Australia 64
sex tourism 64
sheltered housing 104
Singapore 41, 64, 79, 83, 96, 109–10, 115
smallpox 53
smart munitions 120–1
soap opera 38
social security 24, 62, 82, 92–3, 129, 150
  UK 79
  US 93
social sorting 187–8
social transformation 175
Socialist Workers Party 105
solvency 6
Solzhenitsyn, Alexander 112, 184
Soviet Union 29, 68, 84, 108, 112, 115
Spain 110, 129
Special Operations Executive (UK) 38
speed bumps 118, 120, 121
speed cameras 69, 72, 185, 186
spies 81–2, 84, 105, 130, 169
spin 29, 38
standard approval 65, 70
standard constraints 67–8, 70
standing 6
state inquisitors 25, 40
State Research Bureau (Uganda) 29
sting operation 27
stirrup 177
storage and custody 107–9
strikes 64, 110, 117
  coal miners (US) 70
stud farms 111
substitutability 159–60, 201–2
suicide 13, 29
suppression of information 28–30
Sweden 39, 109, 111, 129, 186

Taiwanese independence 31
tax 89, 151
  expenditures 94, 100
  payment 107, 124, 159
  returns 24, 26, 54–5, 153, 199
teleological–deontological dilemma 164–5
terrorist attack 23, 43, 154
thalassaemia 63
Tiananmen Square 31
Tibetan independence 31
tobacco 68, 107
  UK 56
tokens of authority 50–1, 56–68, 70, 149, 187
trade unions 58, 65, 127
  Poland 48
  UK 159
transfers 88–9
transponders 52, 72, 120, 200
  UK 98
transportation and distribution 109–11
treasure 6, 78–101
treatment 106–16
tsunami (SE Asia) 44, 189
  Indonesia 90
Turkmenistan 67, 195
turnstile 104, 119, 131, 185

unemployed 93–4
United Arab Emirates 30
UNPAN 194–5
unprompted query response 32
unsolicited propositions 80–1
unsolicited tenders 22–3

vegetarianism 161–2, 165
vehicle licences (Singapore) 61
Venice 25, 40, 95
Venezuela 103, 110
vermilion pen 50
Victoria, Queen 47
visibility, websites 141–3, 189

walls, government 115, 120
war 148
water 67, 134, 158
  London 185
weapons 86, 164–5, 179, 201
weapons of mass destruction (Iraq) 27
weather forecasts 36
Web 2.0 190, 198
webmetrics 141–3
websites 27, 36–7, 40, 41, 141–3, 166, 201

Yemen 194–5
Y2K bug 181

zero touch 31, 72, 97, 187, 200
Zhao Han 178
Zimbabwe 62–3, 130, 195